The Battle of
Fontenoy
1745

'We have had a most bloody battle with the French; yesterday we began at five in the morning and left off at two in the afternoon, all which time the French kept cannonading us; I was forced to be very civil and make a great many bows to the balls for they were very near me. The foot were very sadly cut to pieces, for the French put grapeshot into their cannon and cut them down just as if they were shearing corn.'

Wilson, A., *The Story of the Guns*, 1944, p. 29.

The Battle of Fontenoy 1745

Saxe against Cumberland in the War of the Austrian Succession

James Falkner

Pen & Sword
MILITARY

AN IMPRINT OF PEN & SWORD BOOKS LTD
YORKSHIRE – PHILADELPHIA

First published in Great Britain in 2019 by
PEN & SWORD MILITARY
An imprint of Pen & Sword Books Ltd
Yorkshire – Philadelphia

Copyright © James Falkner, 2019

ISBN 978-1-52671-841-9

The right of James Falkner to be identified as the author of this work has been asserted by him in accordance with the Copyright, Designs and Patents Act 1988.

A CIP catalogue record for this book is available from the British Library.

All rights reserved. No part of this book may be reproduced or transmitted in any form or by any means, electronic or mechanical including photocopying, recording or by any information storage and retrieval system, without permission from the Publisher in writing.

Typeset by Concept, Huddersfield, West Yorkshire.
Printed and bound in England by TJ International Ltd, Padstow, Cornwall

Pen & Sword Books Ltd incorporates the Imprints of Aviation, Atlas, Family History, Fiction, Maritime, Military, Discovery, Politics, History, Archaeology, Select, Wharncliffe Local History, Wharncliffe True Crime, Military Classics, Wharncliffe Transport, Leo Cooper, The Praetorian Press, Remember When, White Owl, Seaforth Publishing and Frontline Publishing.

For a complete list of Pen & Sword titles please contact
PEN & SWORD BOOKS LTD
47 Church Street, Barnsley, South Yorkshire, S70 2AS, England
E-mail: enquiries@pen-and-sword.co.uk
Website: www.pen-and-sword.co.uk
or
PEN & SWORD BOOKS
1950 Lawrence Rd, Havertown, PA 19083, USA
E-mail: uspen-and-sword@casematepublishers.com
Website: www.penandswordbooks.com

Contents

List of Maps and Plates vii
Introduction ix
Chronology xv

PART ONE: THE COMING OF WAR

1. Problems with the *Pragmatica Sanctio* 3
2. The Art of War in the Eighteenth Century 21
3. The German Marshal – Maurice Saxe 47
4. Billy the Martial Boy – Cumberland, the last Captain General 57
5. Gallant Lieutenants – Löwendhal, Waldeck, Königsegg and Ligonier 69

PART TWO: A MOST BLOODY BATTLE

6. Tournai – the Great Fortress on the Scheldt 77
7. A Breaking-in Battle 101
8. The Infernal Column 123
9. Luscious Sweets of Success, Bitter Fruits of Failure 143

PART THREE: HARD ROADS TOWARDS PEACE

10. The Jacobite Distraction 153
11. The Treaty of Aix-la-Chapelle 165

Appendix 1. Orders of Battle of the Armies at Fontenoy 175
Appendix 2. The Deposition of Brigadier General Richard Ingoldsby 181
Appendix 3. British Casualties at Fontenoy 185

Notes 191
Bibliography 199
Index 203

List of Maps and Plates

Maps

The fortresses of northern France and the southern Netherlands, 1745 22

The battle of Fontenoy, 11 May 1745 102

Plates

Maria-Theresa, Empress of Austria, Queen of Hungary and Bohemia.

Maurice de Saxe, Marshal of France.

William Augustus, Duke of Cumberland.

King Louis XV of France.

Lieutenant General Sir John Ligonier.

British infantry advancing, *c.*1745. A still from the excellent Stanley Kubrick film *Barry Lyndon* (1975).

French artillery in action, *c.*1745.

A French contemporary map of the battle of Fontenoy. Although some details are indistinct, the three-sided column of Cumberland's infantry can be seen breaking into the French position.

The siege of Tournai, 1745 (previously thought to represent the 1709 siege by Marlborough).

Tournai, rebuilt by Vauban, besieged by Saxe, 1745.

Introduction

In the grounds of the Hofburg Palace in Vienna, close to where the old, now long vanished, defensive walls once held back the army of the Ottoman Turks, stands a remarkably fine statue of Maria-Theresa, Empress of Austria and Queen of Hungary and Bohemia. She is suitably depicted as a grand and matronly figure, clad in her robes of state, her right hand stretched out as if dispensing justice, bounty and order, while in her left hand is the imperial sceptre, symbol of her power, and looking not unlike a field marshal's baton. The apparent analogy is apt, as she was to prove herself a good war leader. Her left arm rests on a rolled parchment, and that innocent-looking paper is the Pragmatic Sanction, a document of complex technical legality, enacted in 1713 long before her birth, at the instigation of her father Emperor Charles VI. It was the symbol of the legitimacy of her power, although this was only in fact brought about by the eventual election of her husband as the emperor, so that Maria-Theresa, after much aggravation, conflict and delay, could style herself as empress. Even that event had to await the demise of the Wittelsbach claimant, the Elector of Bavaria, who had with French support assumed the disputed title, on grounds that were not without merit. The tale of the struggle to achieve this goal, to secure the imperial throne and make it good, runs like a tangled thread through this book, centred as it is on one of the most significant days, 11 May 1745, of what had become a Europe-wide conflict.

A teeming day of battle, Fontenoy was brutal and bloody, fought in a long-ago war in pursuit of an arcane dispute that had set great nations at each other's throats. Long remembered, but much misunderstood and often mis-represented, the hard-fought battle at Fontenoy sprawled across the fields and copses around that small village beside the river Scheldt, just a few miles from the great Vauban-designed fortress of Tournai (Doornick) in present-day Belgium. The contest was notable for the ferocity of the fighting, and the remarkable selfless gallantry of the soldiers in both the contending armies. The renowned German–born veteran Marshal of France, Maurice Saxe, pitched his French army against the British, Dutch, Hanoverian and Austrian coalition forces which comprised the allied army, led by William Augustus, Duke of Cumberland, young second son of King George II of Great Britain and Elector of Hanover. By curious coincidence there would be three sons of kings active on the field that day: Saxe (although illegitimate), Cumberland of course, and the French Dauphin (King Louis XV, although present at the battle, cannot be counted as such, as his own father, the Duke of Burgundy, died of measles before coming to the throne of France).

Saxe needed to deal Cumberland and his Austrian and Dutch colleagues a telling blow and throw his army back, if his newly begun siege of Tournai, with its Dutch and Swiss recruited garrison, were to proceed. Under the watchful eyes of the king and his son, in this challenging endeavour the marshal was entirely successful, despite being in such a poor state of health as would have flattened a lesser man. Both armies lost heavily, and the casualties suffered were almost eerily distributed evenly between the two – each army ended the day intact though battered and all but exhausted. That being so, as there was clearly a crude arithmetical parity about the whole bloody occasion – who then had won? Well, at the close of the action Cumberland had no choice but to withdraw from the field and regroup, and in so doing leave the governor of the garrison in Tournai to make what defence he could against daunting odds. As a result, the duke would prove unable that summer to maintain the concentration of his army in the field, to infuse any fresh purpose into what became a languishing campaign, or to counter a vigorous and very well conducted French offensive over much of the southern (Austrian) Netherlands. This inability to deal with the dismally unravelling allied campaign was made worse as his attention, and that of many of his British troops, would be diverted elsewhere by demands from London for their recall. Above all else, of course, it was clear that Marshal Saxe achieved his aim at Fontenoy and so had won the day – with that as a springboard for fresh action, he went on to further notable successes while Cumberland did not, at least in the Low Countries.

Saxe's achievement on the day was undoubtedly a solid one, and was rightly celebrated as such, but it must be seen to be truly qualified – not all successes count as outright victories, after all. In a less than charitable frame of mind, the now widely held notion of a French victory at Fontenoy might seem to not suit the facts at all. Despite firmly repulsing Cumberland's hard-pressed attack, the marshal did not follow the withdrawal of his adversaries from the field with anything other than a very modest, almost negligible, effort, when a well pressed pursuit might have reaped substantial rewards. That Saxe was both ill and physically exhausted was well known, but he had reliable subordinates, men who had driven opponents to ruin in the past – that a fine chance to secure a marked victory was missed, with the destruction rather than just a mauling of the allied army, is an inescapable conclusion. It was also quite true that the French army by mid-afternoon on 11 May was standing all but exhausted by the ferocity of the fighting endured, but men who have achieved much can often be brought to achieve more with the right leadership.

However, Saxe's principal aim at this point in the campaign had been to proceed against the garrison in Tournai without molestation, and this he was able to do, and subsequently went on to take many of the most important fortified places held by the allies in the Low Countries. However, these subsequent successes owed a great deal to the distraction posed by the Jacobite rebellion in northern England and Scotland, with Cumberland and much of his army necessarily taken away, and rather more than to any particularly brilliant military merit for French arms in the region. Still, it is best not to cavil when a clear success has been had – such events do not brook of argument – and French grand strategy, Saxe's strategy, in truth, worked very well for a while. That the 1745 summer and autumn campaign was one of accomplishment for the marshal, and of lamentable failure for his opponents, is evident; for those brief few months while the efforts of the allies were necessarily diluted, divided and distracted, the ailing veteran took good advantage of the fact, and was duly commended for doing so by his king.

The battle of Fontenoy was without doubt a notable occasion, and unusual in that a French army achieved a clear, if somewhat limited, success over an army largely composed of British, Hanoverian and Dutch troops. Such an event was understandably celebrated, the events of the day told and retold with relish, and the story had a tendency to grow in that telling. Only two years earlier a French army had been dismally led, beaten in close combat and driven off the field in disarray at Dettingen on the river Main in northern Germany. That the same army which Saxe now commanded in May 1745 was noticeably unsteady, and felt by him not to be trusted with complex manoeuvres or able to endure sudden shocks, can be seen in his cautious use of his troops on the day of Fontenoy – the failure to properly follow up his success must surely be partly attributable to this concern, leaving to one side entirely the severe battering they had received at Cumberland's hands. In fact, the marshal's soldiers, when put to the test, had in the end proved their worth, but this does not detract from the simple fact that he did not feel able to push them to turn a welcome but narrowly achieved success into a resounding victory.

There was certainly a very particular nature to that success, not only because Cumberland came close to breaking the French army in position, but also because of the fierce nature of the fighting itself, with chances for success and failure for either of the protagonists finely balanced at times. At one point the young royal duke could even be said to have won the day, with his victory just waiting to be grasped. But it was not so: his command and control arrangements were lacking, as was his feel for the battle in progress, and he had no way to deploy his powerful cavalry reserve to good effect; in this can be seen his lack of experience as a commander in the field. While displaying conspicuous courage (for which his men greatly admired him), Cumberland was actually too close to the hand-to-hand fighting, and accordingly could not see clearly the opportunity presented, and thus was unable to push home to real effect his desperately hard-won advantage at the right moment. Such things are rarely simple, and while perhaps clear to the later observer, are less so to those striving on a battlefield, throbbing with noise and breathless excitement and wreathed in drifting smoke. Given the circumstances in which the duke found himself that afternoon, perhaps the chance that was apparently presented was after all not to be had. Cumberland's veteran opponent, in a curiously parallel lack of understanding, while desperately shoring up his sagging and tattered line of battle, did not see at that same crucial point that he was beaten – it might follow therefore that Saxe was not beaten, in large measure because he did not see that it was so. The duke's chance to seize a hard-won victory, on the other hand, passed by unnoticed, or perhaps just out of reach in the hurly-burly of a tumultuous general action, and as is always the way of these things it never came again.

Attention must of course be fully paid to the character and nature of the principal characters in this drama: the two army commanders on the day at Fontenoy. They were such different men: the one may be described as amongst the most gifted and notable field commanders in western European military history, although by 1745 well past his prime both mentally and physically, while the other was simply a good, but certainly not outstanding, soldier with few pretensions to be anything more, and who as yet had little practical experience in command of an army. In fact, the Duke of Cumberland was far too conventional a commander to match so subtle and experienced an opponent as Marshal Saxe, whose ability to read the battle as it made its tortuous progress that May morning he could not begin to match. Much, however, was expected of the royal duke, too optimistically of course, although interestingly both men would enjoy, if that is the right term, remarkable reputations which over the years and on careful examination neither fully deserved.

Aside from the complex causes and progress of the war for the imperial throne in Vienna, the nature and background to the Jacobite ''45 Rising' of quixotic romantic memory, although almost a sideshow, must be considered – a chapter is devoted to the sad tale, which is not as peripheral to the story of Fontenoy as it might at first seem. An event that lies on the fringes of history, the '45' remains one of the great tantalising 'what-ifs': militarily of little relevance but of such significance both for the subsequent reputation and character of the Duke of Cumberland as a field commander and a man, and for the conduct of the subsequent campaign fought in the Low Countries after Fontenoy. What Saxe would have achieved if this distraction had not taken place, and the duke and his veterans had been able to remain on campaign in Flanders, can only be a matter for conjecture and yet more 'what-ifs'.

Today, the fields over which the battle of Fontenoy took place are greatly changed from the sylvan charms to be enjoyed in the mid-eighteenth century, and they are now in places untidily built over with modern road junctions and commercial and residential development. A sugar beet factory stands ingloriously on the slight ridge-line carried in such formidable fashion by Cumberland's infantry, and there has been quarrying in the vicinity. The course of the great river Scheldt has changed to permit better navigation, but the small villages around which much of the fighting took place are still readily identifiable, if understandably somewhat enlarged. There are also a number of attractive memorials to the fallen in the battle, and the copses of the Bois de Barri on the French left flank, so balefully important to the tactical dispositions of both army commanders, are still there and in easily recognisable form, so the battlefield visitor will still find much to explore and enjoy. There is unfortunately little if anything to be seen of Vauban's fine massive citadel in Tournai – Saxe had it slighted late in 1745 – but just down the road is the field of Leuze-en-Hainault, a cavalry affair once remembered as 'the battle of the Golden Mountain', fought early in the 1690s, and a true gem to visit while you are in the locality.

A Note on Dating

The Julian Calendar (Old System – OS) was used Great Britain until 1752, when the Gregorian Calendar (New System – NS) hitherto in general use in continental Europe was also adopted. The difference between the two calendars was eleven days by the 1740s, with the Julian version behind the Gregorian by that amount. Thus, 11 May 1745 would be given as 30 April in London, but as the most part of the action described in this book took part on the continent, the Gregorian Calendar (NS) has been used, unless otherwise indicated as taking place on British soil. The proceedings of the Jacobite adventure naturally fall into this (OS) category. Some accounts of the battle published in London at the time certainly use the Old System, so care has to be taken when consulting them.

Grammar and Phraseology

Many of the contemporary accounts of the campaign are phrased in what appears today to be an odd and erratic grammatical form. For clarity, these have been amended, sensitively it is hoped, to reflect modern usage ('march't' is changed to 'marched', and 'ye' to 'the', for instance). Any additional explanatory comments by the author within quotations are contained within square brackets [ ].

The Numbering of British Regiments in the War of the Austrian Succession

By the 1740s the regiments in the British army were numbered, with the older and more senior regiments having the lower numbers of course (the 18th, the Royal Irish, always felt hard done by on this score). The use of the regimental colonel's name was still widespread, so the regiments described here are usually given both titles, as with the 11th (Sowle's) and 13th (Pulteney's) Regiments of Foot. The 31st Foot is often referred to in accounts of the campaign, both contemporary and later, as Handsyde's, but was in fact Beauclerk's, as Lord Henry Beauclerk became the colonel in April 1745. Murray's Highlanders, however, were not yet numbered (this only took place two years after the battle), and were simply known as the Black Watch. For simplicity I have tended to use the plainer form of 12th Foot, 24th Foot and so on, while references to French regiments other than in the Orders of Battle have been anglicised, as with the Touraine and Normandie regiments.

Chronology

War of the Austrian Succession in Northern Europe

Like most large conflicts, the War of the Austrian Succession was complex, although the central point at issue – whether a female could ever ascend the imperial throne in Vienna, or should she give way to a male candidate with a similar claim – was quite simple. The main events in the war fall into three distinct parts: those in northern Europe, those in southern Europe (mostly in Italy), and those in North America and Canada and the West and East Indies, where France and Great Britain were struggling together to establish and maintain overseas empires. As the events in northern Europe, specifically the Low Countries, Germany and Austria, have most relevance to the battle at Fontenoy in May 1745, only passing reference is made here to the other 'theatres of war'.

1711 Archduke Charles of Austria becomes Emperor Charles VI on the death of his older brother Joseph I

1713 The Treaty of Utrecht contains the provisions of the Pragmatic Sanction to ensure that in the absence of a male heir, a daughter of Emperor Charles should inherit the title (thereby incidentally excluding the daughters of his deceased older brother).

1717 Birth of Arch-Duchess Maria-Theresa, oldest daughter of Charles VI.

1740 (October) Death of Emperor Charles VI. The Pragmatic Sanction invoked on behalf of Maria-Theresa. Simultaneous claim to the imperial title by the Elector of Bavaria.

1741 Active hostilities commence, and Prussia invades Silesia (1st Silesian War).

1742 Capture of Prague by French and Saxon troops. Elector Charles-Albert of Bavaria becomes Emperor Charles VII. The French evacuate Prague.

1743 French defeat at the battle of Dettingen by Anglo-Hanoverian army under King George II.

1745 Emperor Charles VII dies. Treaty agreed between Austria and Bavaria. Maria-Theresa's husband, Archduke Francis-Stephen, elected as Emperor.

(April) Saxe concentrates his army to invade the Austrian Netherlands. Siege of Tournai begins. Cumberland moves to lift the siege.
(May) Battle of Fontenoy. Subsequent loss of many allied-held fortresses in the Austrian Netherlands.
(July) Jacobite Rising in Scotland and northern England.
2nd Silesian War begins. Cumberland recalled to Great Britain.
1746 Battle of Rocoux.
1747 Battle of Lauffeldt.
1748 October. Capture of Maastricht by Marshal Saxe. Treaty of Aix-la-Chapelle signed by belligerent parties to achieve an end to hostilities.

PART ONE
THE COMING OF WAR

Chapter 1

Problems with the *Pragmatica Sanctio*

A term employed during the Byzantine Empire to connote a solemn and public Act of State.[1]

The 1713 Treaty of Utrecht, with the subsequent treaties negotiated over the next two years, at last brought to a tired end the War of the Spanish Succession, a conflict that had been fought to decide whether a French prince or an Austrian archduke should inherit the vacant throne in Madrid. In reality, this had been a power play between Louis XIV of France and Emperor Leopold I of Austria – tellingly, both Bourbon and Habsburg interests were adequately served in the end although no one seemed content. The treaty contained amongst its many provisions a most particular one, that the imperial throne in Vienna – the throne of the Holy Roman Empire no less – should pass directly to the eldest son, or failing a son to the eldest daughter, of the Austrian Emperor Charles VI when he died. If only the war had progressed differently that same Charles would have become the king in Madrid, ruling as Carlos III, but instead the young French prince, Philippe, Duc d'Anjou, made good his claim with considerable help from his grandfather, and at last become King Philip V – and unexpectedly proved to be a rather good choice. The young Austrian aspirant to the Spanish throne had, in any case, become Emperor Charles VI on the death in 1711 of his older brother Joseph I, and he could hardly have been expected, or probably even wanted, to occupy both thrones – one in Vienna and the other in Madrid.

The provisions in the treaty pertaining to the throne in Vienna became known as The Pragmatic Sanction (*Pragmatica Sanctio*): 'a public manifesto proclaiming that the German, Bohemian and Hungarian lands of the Habsburgs had become a single state … *the Habsburg domains were indivisible*'[2] (author's italics). Although the emperor had to be elected by the imperial Diet in Frankfurt, this elective process was something of a formality as the imperial throne had by long custom become a kind of hereditary office occupied by members of a branch of the extensive Habsburg family, a dynasty surely seen to be lying weighted under the spell of their own illustrious past by the time of the Treaty of Utrecht.

Leaving to one side the multitude of principalities large and small, electorates, duchies, bishoprics and other lands of the Holy Roman Empire (an entity neither holy, roman nor an empire, as it was once wittily described), the Habsburg Austrian domains were of considerable extent and importance to Europe, at least in part as they served as a bulwark against Ottoman aspirations and incursions from the east. The empire comprised, in addition to Austria itself, much of southern Germany and parts of Poland (mostly Silesia), Hungary (larger than today), Bohemia, Moravia, the southern Netherlands, and wide swathes of the Tyrol and Italy. Austrian interests and influence, therefore, extended across most of Europe, and to a significant degree the well-being of the empire was the well-being of all.

Such apparent all-encompassing power and influence was, however, an illusion, for Vienna lacked a system of strong central government and struggled to exercise real control over such a vast empire, the constituent parts of which each had their own strong opinions, arrangements, liberties and traditions on matters financial, administrative and judicial. Of particular concern, Austria's once formidable military capability had been allowed to fade, with repeated unfortunate and unsuccessful campaigns in eastern and south-eastern Europe, mediocre field commanders and an army that was kept short of both money and innovation by an emperor who chased shadows in attempting to secure for his daughter Maria-Theresa the succession to the imperial throne.

Aware of this lack, and the in-built frailty in Vienna, other European monarchs and rulers cast envious and predatory eyes over the imperial lands, and waited for the right opportunity to strike and take their share of whatever spoils might be available. France, in addition, had a long-held policy of keeping Germany divided and accordingly weak – paradoxically something that the arcane rules of the Holy Roman Empire fostered. 'In the early decades of the eighteenth century, the most important single theme in European politics was the rivalry between the two hegemonal powers of Austria and France.'[3] There was, also, the distraction of an ever-present threat, if temporarily dormant, of Turkish Ottoman invasion from the east – as recently as the 1680s a great battle had been fought to bring to an end a Turkish siege of Vienna. The victory at Zenta in 1697 had bought respite, but that did not last and the possibility of a fresh threat from the Balkans lay like a shadow over everything the Habsburgs tried to do, while there was also the added complication of simmering unrest and occasional rebellion, and a degree of lingering ill-will and mutual mistrust, in Hungary.

Maria-Theresa Walburga Amalia Christina, the first-born child of Emperor Charles VI, arrived healthy and bonny in the morning of 13 May 1717, and this otherwise happy event would in time bring considerable trouble to western Europe. In time the emperor would have no surviving son, despite energetic efforts enjoyed with his wife, Empress Elizabeth-Christina, in the marital bedchamber. The lady was fortified with liberal potations of both alcohol and rich food to encourage her fecundity; despite all this, the next child was once more a girl. The problem that Charles VI chose to avert was that for centuries – in fact since 1438 – the elective office of Emperor of the Holy Roman Empire had been held by the Habsburgs. Imperial law, however, forbade a woman from becoming emperor, so the failure of Charles VI to have sons meant that, with his death, the most distinguished secular title in Europe would pass by the elective process to a non-Habsburg, in all likelihood a member of the House of Wittelsbach.

True enough, there were no surviving boys born, and so the emperor devoted much thought and effort to ensuring that when he vacated the throne his eldest daughter should be accepted as his appropriate heir, most particularly by the imperial Diet in Frankfurt. As far as possible, and yet acknowledging the predatory nature of the politics of the time, he did ensure that all interested parties subscribed to the Pragmatic Sanction terms contained in the Treaty of Utrecht – in effect that when he died, should he still have no surviving son, then his daughter would be accepted by the Diet as his rightful heir. Such an inheritance was of course fraught with potential difficulties but Maria-Theresa would prove to be a formidable and obstinate woman: 'Controlled by self-discipline, in decisive moments she acted with hard determination and always carried out her will.'[4] Emperor Charles had, it might be thought, a worthy successor in his daughter, as time would show.

It should be mentioned that the Pragmatic Sanction excluded from consideration to the succession to the throne in Vienna the two daughters of Charles' deceased older brother, the late Joseph I, who had died of smallpox in 1711. These two women, Maria-Josepha (married to Augustus II, King of Poland) and Maria-Amalia (married to Charles-Albert, Elector of Bavaria), might well have been considered – and perhaps even considered themselves – to have at least as good a claim as their younger cousin. Still the Pragmatic Sanction had excluded them, and helped to store up a deep well of troubled water in the process. The emperor's ruthless intention was clear: his nieces were to be excluded. 'Who could blame him if, as the head of the dynasty, he was to change the order of succession, and give preference to his own children over his brother's daughters?'[5]

The older girls had, in fact, reconciled themselves, by renunciations of any claim at the time of their respective marriages, to what for them was at best an illusion, because at the time of their exclusion by their uncle, he was young and had every expectation of having at least one son. In fact, Emperor Leopold, who died in 1705, had intended that the eldest of his grandchildren, female if there was no boy, should succeed to the throne, but Charles VI changed all that with the Pragmatic Sanction and this was proclaimed on 14 September 1713. A longed-for son would at last be born to Charles and Elizabeth-Christina, but unfortunately he did not live for more than a few weeks, and so was unable to save everyone concerned a great deal of trouble.

Appreciating that the chances of a male heir were diminishing as each year went by, between 1720 and 1730 Charles VI sought to further secure the widest agreement that his oldest daughter was to be regarded as his rightful heir. The various Estates of the empire did agree to uphold the Pragmatic Sanction, but the acceptance of neighbouring states and other interested parties was more costly and qualified. Russia only agreed in return for support in fighting the Ottomans, a course which risked stirring up again long-held animosity which had been thought to be settled, and leading eventually to the catastrophic loss to Austria of Belgrade. The Elector of Saxony required support in his claim to the throne in Warsaw, leading to damaging involvement in the War of the Polish Succession, a conflict in which Vienna had little to gain. In an odd aside, the war was only resolved by Maria-Theresa's husband, Duke Francis-Stephen of Lorraine (a great-grandson of Louis XIII of France), giving up the title and territory to France in return for the Austrian-held Duchy of Tuscany and gaining the title of an Austrian archduke in the process. Great Britain was at war with Spain, largely in a dispute over commerce, and so London's support was only obtained at the expense of Austrian trading concessions with Madrid being given up. Holland's only real concern was for the security of her borders with Austrian territory in the southern Netherlands, while France's support for the Pragmatic Sanction was heavily qualified as Versailles was also treaty-bound to uphold any claim made by the Elector of Bavaria on behalf of his wife Maria-Amalia, the second daughter of the late Emperor Joseph I.

All in all this was a complex and dangerously tangled situation, fraught with the possibility of renewed war if miscalculation, avarice or impatience took hold. All three factors, in the event, would play their part.

Prince Eugene of Savoy, the most accomplished of all the Habsburg's military commanders and also one of the finest diplomats they ever had at their service, had once drily commented to Charles VI that a strong army and a full treasury were better than any such agreement, tentative or explicit, with other states. In this he may have been right, but the emperor had neither of these assets to bequeath to his almost entirely inexperienced daughter, untutored as she was in diplomacy or the affairs of government.

When Charles VI at last went to his grave on 20 October 1740, at the respectable age for the period of 57, storm clouds quickly gathered over the whole matter of the succession. 'Hardly had the last of the Habsburgs been laid in the vault than the princes of Europe began quarrelling over the spoils.'[6] Understandably, 23-year-old Maria Theresa and her husband, Archduke Francis-Stephen – 'a perfect gentleman, an excellent horseman and huntsman, who carried his liquor superbly', it was recalled – felt that her claim to the imperial throne had the most validity.[7] The Elector of Bavaria, Charles-Albert, however, was keen to press his own claim, ostensibly on his wife's behalf, regardless of what had been agreed or thought to have been agreed twenty-five or more years before at the close of the war for the throne in Madrid. Significantly, Charles-Albert had the powerful backing of France in the endeavour, and this despite a clause in the Treaty of Utrecht explicitly binding the French crown to uphold the terms of the Pragmatic Sanction:

> His Most Christian Majesty [the French king, Louis XIV] declares that he considers this heritage, according to the will of His Majesty the Emperor, the eternal and indivisible fee-entail of the Emperor's first-born descendant of either sex.[8]

In actual fact, as early as 1715 the French had expressed a lack of commitment to the precise terms of the Pragmatic Sanction. The intention of Louis XIV was, in fact, to use all the means at his power to elevate the Elector of Bavaria to the imperial title. Maximilien-Emmanuel Wittelsbach, the then elector, had of course been a staunch ally of the French king in the war for Spain, and his ambition to become emperor went back to 1702 when as Governor-General of the Spanish Netherlands he had favoured the French claimant to the throne in Madrid and allied himself to Versailles. In this way he attached the power and influence of France to his claim, disastrously as it turned out in 1704 at the battle of Blenheim, but he regained his position and lands with the Treaty of Utrecht. His son, when the issue became live in 1740, benefited from that same thread of French support, which as a matter of policy was intended at least in part to weaken Austria and its ties with the German states of the empire. Despite all this, French diplomacy had managed to weave a rather tangled web over the whole matter, and one of Louis XV's chief ministers, Cardinal Fleury, wrote in January 1738 to Emperor Charles VI in Vienna:

> The king will observe with the most exact and inviolable fidelity the engagements which he has made with you, and if I may speak of myself after a name so worthy, I venture to flatter myself that my pacific intentions are well enough known for it to be supposed that I am very far from thinking of setting Europe on fire.[9]

Fleury was strongly in favour of diplomatic solutions, but his influence was noticeably waning, and less cautious men waited to be heard.

Maria-Theresa, as a woman, could hardly style herself Holy Roman Emperor, but she was pregnant at the time of her father's death and of course hoped for a son. In the meantime she sought that the imperial title be bestowed on her husband, and that the required election be made by the nine Electors of the imperial Diet (three archbishoprics and six temporal). The outlook was not promising, however, with what was undoubtedly an unprecedented situation – Maria-Theresa recalled that at the unsteady start of her reign she had found herself without money, an army, experience or knowledge of state affairs. She was tough (more so than her easy-going and affable husband) and resilient, and that was just as well, but her father had perversely excluded her from all council meetings and she had to learn things quickly. Also, just to complicate matters, two members of the electoral college were close relations of the Bavarian claimant, which did not bode too well for her husband's chances for easy success.

To add spice to this dynastic mix, Frederick II, the 28-year-old Prussian king (yet to be accorded the rather spurious title 'the Great'), had succeeded his late father Frederick William I on 1 May 1740, and quickly took advantage of apparent Austrian weakness at this time of transition and uncertainty. 'All was foreseen,' the new king wrote, 'all was thought out in advance. So, it is only a question of carrying out the designs that I have long had in mind.'[10] On 16 December 1740 Prussian troops crossed the border and invaded the rich Austrian province of Silesia. The Austrian commander in the region, Lieutenant General Maximilien Browne, withdrew with understandable caution, although leaving garrisons in important places, as he could not hope to match the Prussian numbers until reinforced by troops called for from Vienna.

Frederick's threadbare excuse for this clear act of uncalled-for aggression was set out in a letter sent to King George II in London in January

1741: 'Far from desiring to disturb Europe I demand only that heed be paid to the justice of my incontestable rights ... The tyranny under which the Silesians have groaned is frightful, and the barbarity of the Catholics towards them.'[11] He went on in increasingly avid but still improbable terms:

> If your majesty desires to attach to yourself a faithful ally of inviolable constancy, this is the time; our interests, our religion, our blood is the same, and it would be sad to see ourselves acting against each other. It would be still more grievous to oblige me to concert in the great plans of France, which I intend to do only if I am impelled.

Just how constant an ally Frederick would prove to be would soon be seen, and George II would need to use a long spoon when supping with the Prussian, who had famously declared that, 'If there is anything to be gained from being honest, let us be honest; if it is necessary to deceive, let us deceive.'[12]

Frederick's lame reasoning, quite apart from the implied threat to George II as the Elector of Hanover if he did not take heed to what was being proposed, was an old and certainly rather doubtful Brandenburg claim to certain Austrian lands. These included the disputed succession to the Duchy of Berg, but all was cloaked in a pretended desire to protect his co-religionists in Silesia. It was, in fact, just simple opportunism, and also a fine example of misplaced confidence and presumption on the part of the inexperienced Prussian ruler, thinking that his support for Maria-Theresa's claim to the imperial throne could be bought with Silesia as the price to be paid. 'I am bringing the key to Austria's prosperity and the imperial crown,' the Prussian envoy in Vienna told Maria-Theresa's outraged husband Francis-Stephen; 'my sovereign is ready to support the queen with his treasury and his army. As a reward for his service and compensation for the risk he takes, he claims Silesia. Nothing less is acceptable.' A figure of 1 million florins in hard cash was mentioned as a clumsy inducement for Vienna to accept the Prussian aggression and say no more on the matter. The response given to such arrogant presumption was cool and crushing: 'The queen's position is by no means so perilous that she should have to strike a bargain at all costs ... as long as there are Prussian troops on Silesian soil there can be no negotiations.'[13]

Such a stance was coloured, in part, because of the thriving industry and commerce in Silesia, which was more active than in much of the Austrian territories and provided a major part of the vital tax revenue enjoyed by, and depended on, by Vienna. An added and perhaps overriding complication in all this was the strict proviso in the Pragmatic Sanction that the Habsburg lands as constituted in 1713 should remain undivided. If then Silesia, as a key part of that inheritance, should be meekly let go, then it could be argued that the Sanction and Maria-Theresa's claim to the imperial title really meant very little at all. The invasion of Silesia had broken the explicit terms of the Pragmatic Sanction, as the then King in Prussia (Frederick Wilhelm I) had been a party to the treaty that set the requirement so precisely that the Austrian possessions should not be divided. As it was, with such a flagrant breach now made by his son, other parties felt free to take a hand and see what pickings could be obtained, and open war on a wide scale soon came to Europe once more.

Spain, influential and powerful again under the French-born King Philip V, would become involved in the dynastic argument, largely in an attempt to gain Austrian-held territory in Italy. The Duchy of Piedmont-Sardinia ranged itself against both Spain and France, with the same kind of aspirations in mind concerning lands held by them both. Despite this, recognition of the validity of the claim of Maria-Theresa to the imperial throne was sent by the Duke of Savoy to Vienna, but this seemed mostly to be a case of playing for time while seeing what other opportunities arose. In the meantime, Prussian troops occupied Breslau without difficulty, and inflicted a serious defeat on the reinforced Austrians commanded by Field Marshal Niepperg at the battle of Mollwitz on 10 April 1741. The Prussian cavalry and their king were routed and forced into inglorious flight from the field – Frederick ended the day hiding from his pursuers in a windmill, convinced that he had been beaten. In the interim, the staunch Prussian infantry under command of Marshal Schwerin saved the day, although wasting a great deal of ammunition fired off at long range, and he rightly claimed the victory. Frederick was eventually persuaded that it was safe to return to the battlefield.[14] The loss in casualties to both armies was about the same, but the Austrians had to withdraw. In the wider strategic context, the Austrians laboured under any number of disadvantages, for they had no navigable waterways, apart from a very few miles of the upper river Elbe, so all their supplies and heavy ordnance had to be hauled overland. Worse still, the impending loss of Silesia and its fortresses left the rearward Austrian provinces of Moravia and Bohemia devoid of significant protection.

The long-standing policy of Louis XV's key advisers had been to further French interests by avoiding war and instead to rely on skilful diplomacy. Fleury's calm influence had faded, and so this wise approach was abandoned in 1741 with the adoption of a tacit policy of actively interfering in the disputed succession in Vienna. French support for the Bavarian claimant had quietly been agreed some years earlier, and was made formal at the Treaty of Nymphenberg, together with the provision of large cash subsidies to increase the strength of the Bavarian army. When Maria-Theresa, who had no intention of allowing her inheritance to be lightly set aside, was crowned Queen of Hungary in June of that year, a French army under command of the Duc de Broglie was made ready to invade Austrian territory. It was apparently clear to Versailles that, for all his declared intentions, the Elector of Bavaria was not going to be able to enforce his claim, other than in the electoral college. Therefore, a show of force would have real value to drive home the point, and there was also concern that the Prussians might be just too successful in their campaigns in Silesia, which a powerful French presence in Lower Austria and Bohemia would counter-balance. However, the French commander allowed himself to be distracted, and marched on Prague instead of concentrating on Vienna, with unforeseen and dire consequences.

Great Britain had inclined to support Maria-Theresa, in part at least to try to hamper French involvement and interests, particularly in Italy and the Mediterranean. This stance had already been made formal in 1731 at the Second Treaty of Vienna, but only as long as Maria-Theresa did not marry a Bourbon (French or Spanish) prince. When, as a result, a threat appeared to grow against the security of Hanover from both French and Prussian troops, this British support was rather hastily withdrawn. A Convention of Neutrality was declared, and this with such vigour that the Dutch, who had also been inclined up to then to support the claim of Maria-Theresa, were obliged to have second thoughts and prudently wait to see what else might unfold. 'As long as George II persisted in maintaining the neutrality of Hanover, they saw no reason for declaring war in a cause that affected them but slightly.'[15] While there was no active threat to the security of the Austrian Netherlands, where Holland maintained several garrisons guaranteed under the Treaty of Utrecht (the Barrier Towns), the Dutch were well inclined to stay out of things, and did so.

France was assured, in this way, of British and Dutch neutrality in the quite probable event of renewed conflict between Prussia and Austria – so much then for solemn and binding undertakings given by an earlier generation of rulers and leaders. All the same, informed opinion in Great Britain was firmly in favour of Maria-Theresa, and the convention of neutrality was widely derided as unworthy, with Parliament in London voting a large cash subsidy to Vienna, which at least enabled Maria-Theresa's soldiers to be paid for the time being. Given the state of finances in Austria, this was something of a novelty, and further monies would be provided as time went on. Frederick II, meanwhile, having failed to induce Maria-Theresa to come to terms (even though George II advised her to do so), agreed a treaty with France, in so doing adding his support to the claim of Charles-Albert. In return, Versailles recognised Prussian sovereignty over that part of Silesia already occupied by the king's troops. In July the elector, seeing Vienna's apparent weakness, occupied Passau, a Habsburg enclave in Bavaria. Meanwhile, the Elector of Saxony had under French pressure declared his support for Charles-Albert, proving to be just another neighbour hoping to enrich himself with what pickings were to be had, and in September his troops quietly occupied Linz in Upper Austria.

Matters looked grim for Maria-Theresa and her cause by November 1741 when Charles-Albert's Bavarians, together with de Broglie's French and Saxon troops, advanced against ill-prepared Austrian opposition and reached not Vienna (although passing tantalisingly within 30 miles of that city) but Prague, the capital of Austrian Bohemia. The city was taken against only slight opposition – any support that Maria-Theresa hoped for from Russia was not forthcoming, as on 4 August 1741 Sweden, again encouraged by France, declared war on her neighbour, in a curious replay of the Great Northern War of the early part of the century. In this way the attention of the Russians was, for the time being, directed away from the problems in Vienna and central Europe.

Contrary to all expectation, the tide of fortune dramatically turned and there appeared to be at least one ray of sunshine for Vienna. On 25 June 1741 Maria-Theresa was crowned Queen of Hungary in Bratislava – her spirit and resolution in the face of calamity won many hearts and much admiration, and the staunch Hungarian nobility and their fine troops rallied enthusiastically to her cause. 'Amid all the disasters, the courage of the young queen, rooted as it were in the belief that right must triumph, remained unshaken.'[16] Moreover, the Sultan of Turkey, abiding by the terms of long-agreed treaties, unlike a number of his western European counterparts, sent messages confirming that he would not enter the hostilities, so that Austria as a result need not fear for her eastern provinces. Frederick II was inclined for the time being to keep quiet and count his gains, at least until the end of the year, so that Austria was freed from concerns on that front for the time being. As a result, faced with unexpectedly reinvigorated opposition, de Broglie's overly extended and now rather dispersed army was obliged to fall back and concentrate once more on Prague.

The French and Saxon troops who had been ravaging Bohemia were shut up behind the stout walls of the city, a long way from their depots and magazines, and invested by the Austrians under command of Archduke Francis-Stephen and the able veteran campaigner Field Marshal Königsegg-Rothenfels (referred to generally as Königsegg). It was found, however, that there was no senior officer in the Austrian army with the necessary skills to undertake a formal siege, but as it turned out this did not matter too much. With his troops facing starvation, Marshal de Belle-Isle managed to beat off an Austrian attack in August, but with no hope of relief he decided on 16 December on the desperate measure of breaking out with just what he could carry. Leaving behind 4,000 sick and wounded French and Saxon soldiers, he began a gruelling retreat to the westwards with his bedraggled army through the snow. Their grim march was undertaken in bitterly cold weather, harassed by Austrian regulars and irregulars on the blizzard-swept road, and inevitably involved losses in men who could not keep up with the line of march, baggage and materiel. French prestige was badly damaged as a result of the débâcle. Of the 15,000 soldiers who marched out of Prague, some 10,000 reached sanctuary together with their guns, having seen nothing short of a dismal end to the ill-judged and poorly managed campaign. Some reports state the French losses to be much higher, but these seem to represent men who fell out from the line of march and rejoined their units later. Whatever the true figure, this whole episode was a major defeat for both France and Saxony, and Maria-Theresa, for the time being, had recovered her strategic balance. Meanwhile, British and Austrian diplomatic pressure had succeeded in bringing Piedmont-Sardinia (Savoy), usually close to French interests, into the war on her behalf.

Austrian troops under Field Marshal Khenhuller invaded Bavarian territory, brushing aside only light resistance, and occupied Munich on 12 February 1742, while Charles-Albert was away happily attending the imperial Diet in Frankfurt and congratulating himself on being elected as emperor the previous month. This much he had achieved, but whatever satisfaction he derived from the success must have been heavily tempered by events in his own country. The princes and electors of the empire, having elected him, then ignored his plight over the fate of Munich, and France was not much more help. Despite this hopeful sign for the eventual success of Maria-Theresa's claim, an Austrian army was beaten once more by Frederick II at the battle of Chotusitz on 17 May 1742, but her troops fought well and Prussian casualties were disproportionately heavy for what limited success was gained. Largely as a result, Frederick decided that he had seen enough of this expensive war for the time being – the effort was too great, and he had achieved enough; a cessation of hostilities, in effect a truce, was agreed at Breslau on 11 June. The king managed to hold on to most of his ill-gotten territorial gains, however, and laid plans to further consolidate his success when the moment was right. Saxony also came to terms with Vienna under the same flimsy agreement.

Meanwhile, in London King George II and his ministers had undergone a collective change of heart, and saw advantages to be had in once more offering assistance to Maria-Theresa and her husband. However, 'The British supported Maria-Theresa only to embarrass France; and they supported her only to the extent to which it was in their interest to do so.'[17] That much may have been true – and no worse a reason for it being so, national self-interest is not to be lightly set aside – but although nothing so mundane as a declaration of war against France would be made, it was resolved to send 16,000 British troops to the Austrian Netherlands to act in concert with Hanoverian and Hessian detachments already there. Their actual status would be that of auxiliary troops, operating in support of Austrian units in the service of Maria-Theresa. Dutch troops would not yet be actively in the field, but would simply garrison the fortresses in the region, thus freeing Hessian regiments to operate elsewhere with the British and Hanoverians. The British commander of this force, known as the Pragmatic Army, the elderly John Dalrymple, 2nd Earl of Stair, formed a rather fanciful plan to invade France, occupy the port of Dunkirk and even go on to attack Paris, but fortunately this scheme was not taken forward and 1742 passed with relatively little activity in the north.

For Louis XV this lack of action on the ground was timely; the Low Countries might prove, as they had in the past, an ideal ground on which French armies could operate with relative ease, but the region also posed the greatest potential threat to the security of northern France. The king's armies were heavily engaged elsewhere. There were few major natural barriers, apart from rivers which any competent army commander could bridge almost at will, and many of the major fortresses designed and constructed by Marshal Vauban at the behest of Louis XIV fifty years before were now in Dutch and Austrian hands, although rather dilapidated. The border was neatly described as being 'The most important, the most exposed, and yet for a long time the most neglected of the entire kingdom.'[18] Such a lull in active campaigning would not last long though, and almost inevitably the scene was set for some of the most notable campaigns, and days of acute drama, of the war.

The new year saw considerable posturing, marching and manoeuvring between the opposing French and allied armies, but only in June did they face each other with real intent, not far from the small town of Dettingen on the river Main in north-western Germany. The 40,000-strong Pragmatic Army (composed of British, Austrian, Hanoverian and Hessian units) was commanded in person by King George II, an able and active campaigner in his youth under the Duke of Marlborough, but now elderly and portly. His second son, 25-year-old William Augustus, Duke of Cumberland, was at his side. Their French opponents were under the command of the capable Duc de Noailles, who had laid a trap, aware that his opponents must fall back on their depots at Hanau before too long to replenish their depleted supply trains. Not concerned by any thoughts of an offensive move by George II, Noailles rashly split his army on 27 June 1743 and sent his nephew, the Duc de Grammont, with a 26,000-strong force to cross the Main at Seligenstadt and occupy Dettingen, while the main French army crossed at Aschaffenburg to threaten the rear of the allies. It was on the face of things a good plan that promised much, so long as the two parts of the army acted in concert.

What might have been a perfect classic encirclement was ruined when de Grammont advanced prematurely and without proper support on to open ground. He claimed afterwards that he thought he was attacking the allied rear-guard only, instead of the whole army. He was shown to be an impetuous and inexperienced subordinate commander, and Noailles could only watch from the far side of the river in disbelief and exasperation as the Gardes Françaises pushed ahead through the village of Dettingen and across the Forbach and Hoggraben streams to engage their opponents. The prospects of the French troops were gloomy, an observer commenting that amongst their commanders there was not a single officer that knew how to properly manoeuvre his brigade.

After hard fighting de Grammont and his outnumbered troops were beaten down by the allied fire, and pushed back through the village and into hurried retreat. Two newly recruited Walloon battalions in the Austrian service proved their mettle under fire, in the process reminding many who saw them stand their ground of the fine performance of these excellent troops in Marlborough's day. For all de Grammont's mistakes, the allied success was certainly not easily won, and the cavalry action in particular was a brutal affair, in which the intrepid Mary Ralphson, dressed as a dragoon, took an active part. George II remarked to Sir Andrew

Agnew that he had seen 'the [French] cuirassiers get in among your men this morning, colonel', to which the cool reply came, 'Aye, your majesty, but they did not get out again.'[19] French losses were about 4,000, while those suffered by the allies were less than half that number. An undoubted success was had, qualified it is true and owing much to French errors, but very welcome and of course famously overseen by the last British monarch to actively take the field of battle. The king was naturally delighted in the fact, although his precise role in the activities of the day are a little uncertain, being at one point hardly able to control his horse, which showed an inclination to bolt. Little was otherwise achieved, for there was no proper pursuit of the French in their scrambled withdrawal, and in a way they were shepherded off the battlefield rather than driven off.

It rained heavily, which may have dampened some of the martial ardour of the victors, especially as the allied troops were separated from their tents and baggage, and had to spend the night wet and shivering in the open. The chance to really hobble the French effort in the war for the throne in Vienna was accordingly let go begging, but the allied army had no viable supply and support system in place to allow for any such pursuit. Few commanders at the time would take on board the notion of making such a rapid, even reckless, movement, heedless of the security of flanks, communications and supplies. As it was, the Pragmatic Army, having avoided defeat and happily achieved an unexpected victory, was not really in a fit state to attempt a vigorous movement for the time being. Their organisation was in fact so shaky that little attempt was made to recover the 400 or so allied wounded lying on the battlefield, and their care was left to their beaten French opponents, who, it should be said, did their best for them.

At last, on 15 March 1744, France declared war formally on Great Britain, and six weeks later did so against Austria; Holland, legally, was still not yet at war. The French declaration against the British detailed perceived grievances that gave rise to the regrettable necessity for war, in particular that the king (George II) had:

> Sought to provoke France by molesting her maritime commerce, in active disregard of international law and solemn treaties. Personally a foe to France, he has endeavoured to stir up other enemies against her on all sides. So many repeated insults and outrages have at last exhausted his majesty's [Louis XV] patience.[20]

Two weeks later the British response was typically blunt, accusing the French of violating the terms of the Pragmatic Sanction, attacking

Maria-Theresa as Queen of Hungary, and offering help to Spain in their war with Britain. 'Notorious breaches of treaties' were cited, in particular that:

> The affront and indignity offered to us by the reception of the son of the Pretender [James III/VII] to our crown in the French dominions, the embarkation actually made at Dunkirk of a considerable body of troops notoriously designed for an invasion of this kingdom.

For some time, Louis XV and his ministers had considered launching an invasion to place the Stuart Pretender on the throne in London. Marshal Maurice Saxe was placed in command, but winter storms ruined the enterprise which had never seemed to be wholehearted other than as a way to distract British attention from the Low Countries and the affairs of Maria-Theresa.

Not until June did the allied army take the field in an active fashion, General George Wade having about 50,000 troops under command, although he declared that far fewer were effectives. After a grand review near Oudenarde on the Scheldt, reinforcements were received from Great Britain, and the theoretical allied strength rose to 64,000, but only some 38,000 of these were British and Hanoverian troops, thought to be most useful. 'The Dutch army contained a large German element.'[21] Quite why this should imply that they were in themselves unreliable is not clear, as such troops had always proved themselves to be sturdy campaigners, even when hired out to foreign masters. The French, on the other hand, could deploy 62,000 troops, concentrated for the time being on the city of Lille. On 17 May 1744 they divided into two contingents, with Marshal Noailles going to lay siege to Menin, while Marshal Saxe moved to occupy Courtrai. Menin fell on 4 June, a success witnessed by Louis XV, who had accompanied the army. Noailles went on to lay siege to Ypres, while Saxe covered these operations from Courtrai, and Mauberge on the river Sambre was also secured. The garrison in Ypres submitted on good terms on 25 June, and Fort Knocke and Furnes followed suit soon afterwards. All this took place while the allies attempted very little to disrupt things. A British officer wrote of his dismay at this procession of French successes: 'To see the French taking all the towns with so much ease, scarce meeting with the least resistance, and we are not in a capacity to act, or likely to be in one.'[22]

Marching here and there by the opposing armies took up most of the campaign season but the British commander, newly promoted as Field Marshal Wade, did not come to grips with either Saxe or Noailles, a major failing despite the excuses he offered. The French had managed to secure several useful stepping-off points for a future move deep into the Austrian Netherlands, while Wade perhaps lacked sufficient strength to conduct an effective campaign. Large numbers of Dutch troops were still unproductively engaged in manning other fortresses that were under no real threat. A vague plan was formed to again move to threaten Lille, but the French got wind of this and quickly reinforced the garrison there, and nothing came of the notion. The onset of cold weather in October saw the troops in both armies make their way gratefully to their winter quarters.

Wade was predictably much criticised for what was regarded as inactivity, and he at last gave up the command of the allied army in the Low Countries, handing matters over to the capable Sir John Ligonier. Wade tried to pass the blame for the tepid conduct of the campaign in 1744 on to Dutch intransigence and reluctance to spend money on supplies and ordnance, in particular their reputed failure to provide heavy artillery. 'We hear that everyone in England is dissatisfied with our inactivity, but there is nothing we can do without cannon.'[23] Still, this was little more than making excuses for his own lacklustre behaviour, while he did find the time to agree with the French a table of cartel prices to be paid for the return of prisoners taken, ranging from £2000 sterling for a field marshal to a modest £4 for a captain of cavalry. The allied soldiers, in the main, were not impressed by what had gone on, with a great deal of apparently pointless marching and counter-marching, and one wrote with marked sarcasm that 'I don't like all this moving about, I should not be surprised if some day we were to fall in with the enemy'.[24]

Holland, oddly enough, was not yet at war with France in a formal sense, and her troops were still regarded as auxiliaries in the service of Maria-Theresa. As long as the borders of the republic were under no direct threat, the States-General in The Hague were not willing to get too deeply involved. Meanwhile Frederick II had re-entered the fray, sparking what became known as the Second Silesian War. The emphasis in the conflict seemed to swing towards central Europe, but Prince Charles of Lorraine led an Austrian army on a raid into Alsace, occupying Lauterburg and Wissenburg, and causing alarm in Versailles – of necessity many French troops were diverted to meet the threat, hampering any attempt to make the most of their gains in Flanders.

At a diplomatic level it now seemed to suit the parties to the allied effort, including the States-General, to combine their energies. On 8 January 1745 an alliance was agreed between Great Britain, Austria, Holland and Saxony (whose elector had been induced to change sides) to push forward the war against France and by virtue of that endeavour also against the cause of the Elector of Bavaria (Charles-Albert/Charles VII) in favour of Maria-Theresa's claim. A substantially increased cash subsidy, largely from British sources, was granted to shore up the perennially shaky Austrian finances, and amongst other provisions there was agreement that the overall command of the allied army in the Low Countries should in future be exercised by George II's son, the Duke of Cumberland. The young nobleman arrived at The Hague to take up this appointment on 17 April, from where he proceeded to join his troops, with his fellow commanders the Austrian Field Marshal Königsegg (not enjoying robust health) and the commander of the Dutch troops, Karl-August, Prince of Waldeck-Pyrmont.

Fate took a hand that spring when Charles-Albert, elected just two years earlier by the Diet as emperor, unexpectedly died. In theory supported by both France and Prussia, in fact he had almost been ignored as the military fortunes of the Bavarian forces waned. The thrust of the war had turned by then and Austrian troops had overrun Bavaria, while despite ardent promises of assistance real French support was lacking. The deceased elector's 17-year-old son Maximilien had no ambitions in this regard and, aware of Bavarian military weakness, agreed to peace terms offered by Vienna on 15 April. With his allies falling away, and the matter of the disputed succession apparently resolved, Louis XV had his ministers put out feelers for peace, but the terms suggested were so unsuitable that the war had to go on for the time being. The soldiers in northern France and the Low Countries would have to set out once more, to tramp the roads that led them in time to the fields and copses around Fontenoy.

Chapter 2

The Art of War in the Eighteenth Century

*It is not the big armies that win battles,
but the good ones.*[1]

Almost all the military campaigns fought in western Europe in the early to mid-eighteenth century were of a consciously limited nature. In part this was a matter of deliberate policy stemming from a reaction to the horrors of the Thirty Years War that had ravaged much of the continent in the previous century. There was, also, the remorselessly grinding cost in treasure, manpower and human suffering of the Nine Years War (1688–1697) and the War of the Spanish Succession (1701–1714), with a general desire that they would not be repeated. An earnest, if overly hopeful, attempt was made in what was called the 'Age of Reason' to civilise in a way what was inevitably a pretty uncivilised business. The intention was understandable and laudable, even if the application was patchy, and there was still plenty of violence on the battlefield and ruthlessness in all campaigning. When things came to a head, of course, an opponent had to be killed or rendered inactive in one way or another, and in that respect the manner of making war did not change very much.

Army commanders, most particularly but not exclusively the French, had established a technique of 'eating up' a country so that an opposing army could not subsist in that same region – an effective if brutal tactic that had an inevitable impact upon the unfortunate civilian population, who would face starvation and destitution as the sad result. There were relatively few regions in western Europe rich and productive enough to sustain campaigning armies (the Low Countries being one such), and so the repeated depredations inflicted by campaigning armies were concentrated in a most unfortunate way. To be fair, this way of carrying on was not just the French way of doing these things; other commanders could be just as ruthless when it was thought to be necessary, and an army on campaign would as a matter of course always assume priority when it came to seizing forage, horses, cattle, crops and supplies.

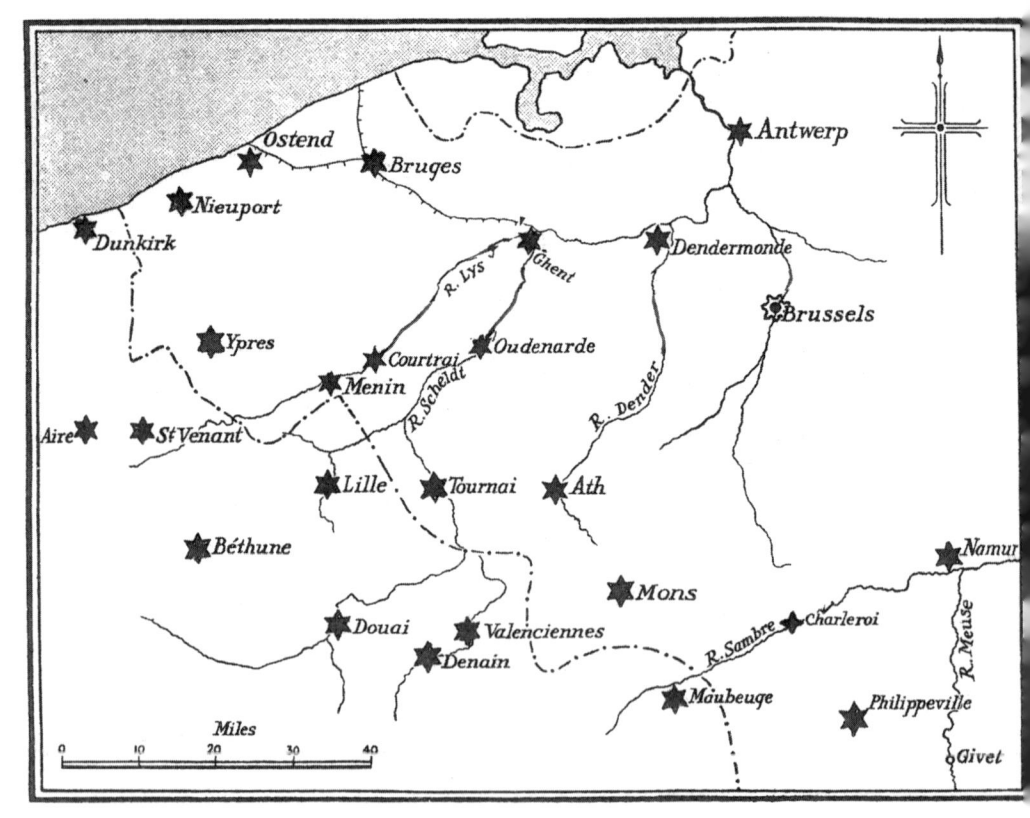

The fortresses of northern France and the southern Netherlands, 1745.

It should also be said that the Duke of Marlborough, well known for his humane concern for the welfare of his own soldiers, undertook almost exactly the same course of action before the battle of Blenheim in 1704. He attempted, despite the protests of his fellow commander, the Margrave of Baden, to force the then Elector of Bavaria to abandon his alliance with Louis XIV and come to terms. Despite the widespread and deliberate destruction, no such agreement was reached with the elector, but Bavaria had been so picked clean by Marlborough's raiding cavalry that neither of the opposing armies could have spent the winter there. Once again, inevitably, the common people would starve in consequence of the duke's actions – a not uncommon occurrence in warfare down the ages; clearly even what passed for limited war was grim enough.

A comparatively slight but reasonably telling tale of such destruction by passing soldiers, and the consequent hardships endured by the local people, is given by a priest during the 1747 campaign in Flanders, just a couple of years after the battle at Fontenoy: 'The English troops drained at least fifty to sixty village ponds ... the reason for the drainage is simple, the hungry soldiers just had to pick up the fish.'[2] Callous and thoughtless, bordering on vandalism perhaps, and it would be wrong to suggest that such conduct by soldiers was either typical or actively encouraged by their officers, but it was not uncommon. If it was done without real authority it was still done, and often not punished – that punishment for such offences was often commented on indicates not that this happened regularly, but on the contrary that such measures to actively enforce discipline were quite unusual. Perhaps so, although there are certainly more than a few accounts of soldiers in the armies on both sides of the conflict being hanged, or more often flogged, for pillaging and looting, as an example to their comrades to behave a little better.

It was also fairly common for local civilian labour to be impressed by passing armies to help repair roads, rebuild bridges and undertake hazardous work in digging siege trenches, often without payment. Of course, to pay for the labour had an associated benefit, as the men conscripted in that way would then be less likely to try to abscond, and many commanders understood this simple point. But the work required was nonetheless onerous and much disliked, and to be avoided if at all possible. All the same, civilian labour at many levels was 'bought in' by commanders to enable their armies to operate effectively; importantly this included those contractors who supplied the stores necessary to feed and sustain the troops and their horses, and the drivers for the hundreds of carts and wagons needed to transport stores, fodder, munitions and materiel and to move the cumbersome guns of the artillery. These specialists, for such they were and so regarded themselves and acted accordingly, were of high value and not to be trifled with, even though quite understandably they were often reluctant to get too close to the firing line where their particular skills would probably be wasted. After-action accounts of civilian drivers making off to a safe spot are usually highly critical of such conduct, but they miss the essential point. These men were paid contractors, not soldiers, and they would simply be acting according to the terms they had agreed when accompanying a campaigning army. The drivers of the allied gun teams at Fontenoy did just this: they went away from the line of battle and were criticised for so doing, but wrongly. If those civilians had no wish to stand the French shot, then that was their right, and if the system allowed them to do so and that arrangement was not adequate for the purpose, then the system had to change, as it eventually and slowly did.

Any army on campaign, by the very nature of its moving across an area, would cause a great deal of nuisance and destruction, whether intentional or by accident. This was almost inevitable and so armies were usually unwelcome, even though they might be 'friendly' and consist of soldiers native to the region or district. As a consequence, the troops were well advised not to stray too far, or alone, from their encampments, as they would sometimes be set on, often with considerable brutality, by outraged locals. Those people rarely had any direct interest in whatever great matter was being fought over, and that the troops in the neighbourhood might be of the same nationality and religion would often not lessen their depredations upon flocks, herds, crops, grain stores and occasionally the farmers' daughters. Once in the territory of an opponent, then those constraints that were in place, however imperfectly, were loosened, either deliberately or by simple neglect. A soldier recalled that, 'Our soldiers knowing that we were now in our enemy's country, used it accordingly ... they plundered the houses of everything.'[3] The useful if ruthless concept of 'eating up a country', as demonstrated in Bavaria in 1704, took a long time to fade away.

If campaigning on a day-to-day basis could only just be termed limited, whatever hopeful intentions there might be, then neither could it be said that the war aims of the great powers involved in the contests of the time were that constrained. Often these aims centred on the redrawing of national boundaries (France with Alsace and Lorraine, for instance), establishing or reinforcing dynastic rights (the wars for the thrones in Madrid and Vienna), or the securing of vital trading opportunities (Jenkin's Ear), and as time went on hungrily expanding empires on a worldwide basis. In this latter endeavour France and Great Britain were particularly busy, and the contest spread to North America and Canada, the West Indies, and the Indian sub-continent with the Carnatic Wars of the eighteenth century – it would not be clear for a long time who would gain the ascendancy in this deep affair of empire building.

Any such considerations of limited warfare must really only be applied to the conduct of wars carried out in northern and western Europe, where an attempt at restraint was made to one degree or another. The Great Northern War (1701–1721) which pitched Sweden against her Baltic neighbours, and eventually and disastrously also Russia, was marked with a great deal of routine brutality, which tended to be more prevalent the further east the campaigns drifted. If that drift was into south-eastern Europe then the fighting was usually against the Ottoman Turks, whose way of war was marked with systematic ruthlessness, both to opposing armies and local populations, and what attempts had been made to civilise warfare in the west had little place. Nonetheless, when the *sublime porte* in Constantinople entered into a treaty, its terms tended to be adhered to – a practice that did not always hold sway in western Europe, as the young

Maria-Theresa found on the death of her father in 1740, when the one near neighbour she did not have to fight was the Ottomans.

Still, limited warfare to a certain degree was made a necessity as it was simply not possible in the eighteenth century to maintain large numbers of troops in the field over extended periods. There was the inevitable and mundane problem of obtaining adequate finance from reluctant legislators and tax-payers, and equally cautious suppliers. Such difficulties were not easy to overcome even for absolute monarchs such as Louis XIV (and to a lesser degree his great-grandson Louis XV and the Prussian King Frederick II). Finding enough young and fit men to fill the ranks was no simple matter, even in those countries where conscription or impressment from the local militia was common. In Great Britain there was a long-held aversion to having a standing or regular army: memories of civil war and the rigours of Oliver Cromwell and his way of doing things were long and remarkably fresh eighty years later. It was feared that such troops, if maintained on a regular basis, could be used to suppress civil liberties, and so Parliament in London was reluctant to provide the funds to maintain a decent-sized army in anything other than extreme circumstances. The glory days of the triumphs of the Duke of Marlborough had perhaps understandably faded from popular memory, and even he had fought with large numbers of hired foreign (usually German and Danish) troops under his command, so it was thought in the coffee houses in London that this was perhaps the best way of doing things. That the keen cutting edge of the duke's army had perhaps inevitably dulled in the long years of comparative peace after 1713 was not yet apparent.

France had a long and well established military tradition, of course, even if this had been rather more than slightly battered by Marlborough and Prince Eugene in the opening decade of the eighteenth century. A large standing army was common, but with such a substantial population (some 18 million) at the time, France could not be said to be an overly militarised nation. Holland had a fine military tradition, dating back to the long struggle with Catholic Spain to gain independence. Years of ruinously expensive war with the France of Louis XIV had made the Dutch cautious over such matters and, with a thriving civil economy and burgeoning overseas trade, that military tradition had faded, with increasing numbers of foreign troops filling those ranks once held by stout-hearted Dutchmen. Not that foreign troops were ineffective: the princely states of Germany and the cantons of Switzerland had their own long tradition of hiring out their excellent young men to foreign service, and they enjoyed a fine reputation both for their fighting ability and, often, for their devotion to the cause of their employers. Austria of course had fought long and hard against the Ottomans in eastern Europe, but the experience was often one of frustration and occasional defeat and the very disparate nature of the Habsburg empire made difficult cohesion between the constituent parts, such as the independent-minded Hungarians who were in revolt from time to time. Holding together such a vast enterprise as the empire both diluted military and diplomatic effort and mentally and physically wearied the government in Vienna – and, coincidentally, devastated its finances.

No matter how the nations sought to further their interests, the raw material in the armies that trudged out on campaign was remarkably similar, even if obtained in different ways. With some inevitable local variations, all soldiers would be dressed and equipped very much alike; the well known tricorne hat comes easily to mind as the most common headgear for those not deemed fortunate enough to merit the tall grenadier cap or the looser bonnet of the dragoon. These troops out on campaign were once rather unfortunately and mistakenly described as the scum of the earth, but this was neither warranted nor fair, for the raw material was good. Sturdy young men, raised in the main from communities working on the land, made for good soldiers. Recruiting parties were strictly instructed not to accept men with physical issues such as hernias or rotten teeth, although in truth such niceties would sometimes be winked at, especially in times of war when the need would be most pressing. While many would not welcome the tap on the shoulder of the impressment officer, or were reluctant to step up to the table and accept the shilling from the recruiting sergeant, others were often inclined to enlist as they did relish the odd life of a soldier. 'The truth was, that going for a soldier appealed to the kind of men who wanted to liberate themselves from dull routine or escape from some intolerable domestic situation.'[4] Not all were fleeing from rural poverty, romantic entanglements and prospective fathers-in-law, or to avoid debtors' gaols. Samuel Bagshawe, a young man of good family, enlisted as a private soldier in 1731 and shouldered a musket for seven years before being able to purchase his commission. He eventually rose to become a colonel and raised his own regiment, at considerable expense, to fight for his king – not a common example, perhaps, but equally certainly he was not unique.

Even when an army was formed, manned, armed and provisioned, and put into the field – an enormous and time-consuming business at the best of times – the overriding imperative was that the good dry campaigning weeks were really only those of late spring, summer and early autumn. In those few precious weeks the almost universally unmetalled roads of the time would, with luck, be dry enough for armies to travel along with relative ease accompanied by all their baggage. Soon enough, in the wetter days leading to winter, those same roads would become like muddy ditches and the armies would struggle to march and manoeuvre – even to move camp was difficult, and commanders would have to seek shelter for their men when this late season approached.

Time in which to push matters to a favourable result in the year's campaign season was therefore limited, unless an army commander was bold enough to operate in winter – few took the risk and did so, notably Marshal Turenne in the late seventeenth century, Marlborough (once), Prince Eugene and the Swedish King Charles XII in the early eighteenth century. There was an almost complicit understanding between opposing commanders that it was just not practical to operate in winter, and the likely outcome was almost certainly not going to be worth the effort. Far better to pack up for the season, put the troops into quarters of varying comfort and quality, and – by courtesy of passports sought and usually obtained without difficulty from opponents who hoped with good reason for the same courtesies – go home to settle affairs and play at politics while making plans for the next year's campaign. Such an arrangement seemed to suit everyone, and probably did.

Closely tied to the handicap imposed on marching troops by the poor roads of the time was the inexorable problem of logistics: how to pay, feed, clothe and supply large numbers of troops when on campaign. The growth in the size of national armies in the period was notable, and whereas 40,000 men might take the field in the mid-seventeenth century, it was not uncommon for armies of twice that size and more to be employed by the time that Marlborough and Eugene fought Marshal Villars at Malplaquet in 1709. The ability to pay for these necessaries was paramount, and one of the weaknesses of France, having enjoyed such major military successes over the decades, was that of the exhaustion of national finances resulting from the long wars engaged in by Louis XIV. Having the army live off the land partly supplied the need, but only just and overall this was an unsatisfactory way of proceeding. Marshal Tallard arrived in Bavaria in the summer of 1704 having forced his way through the Black Forest, but he had advanced without a fully provisioned supply train and his troops, particularly his splendid cavalry, were far from their best for the experience. It was also notable, in that same famous summer, that the allied army brought south from the Low Countries by Marlborough had the ability to pay in advance for the supplies necessary, and were all the better for it. The period of relative peace which followed the close of the War of the Spanish Succession – almost thirty years of peace between France and Great Britain, although others were not so fortunate – was due in no small measure to the need for Versailles to re-establish the national finances, while adroitly pursuing French interests in other, less costly, ways.

To the enormous practical difficulty of maintaining such numbers in good order was added the simple problem of how a field commander, however gifted he might be, was to control such a mass of men on the battlefield. Carefully thought-out plans would be made in advance, of course, but as is well known no such plan survives contact with the enemy and so the uncertainties of the battlefield would soon take over. Then, well practised procedures and drills, the discipline of both men and subordinate officers, and the way in which commanders at all levels knew one another and to what degree they trusted each other, came into play. In this regard it is not out of place to comment that the Duke of Cumberland and Brigadier General Sir Richard Ingoldsby certainly knew and liked each other, and presumably there was a good element of trust between the two men. That Ingoldsby should so fail the duke in not grasping the essential task he was given at Fontenoy is a tantalising puzzle. Their relationship was reportedly why Ingoldsby was selected for the important task in hand in the first place, but it seemed not to solve a pressing problem on the day of battle. As would be seen then, and on many other occasions, messages and orders at the time were almost always given verbally and delivered face to face – hastily scribbled notes on scraps of paper, where employed, were little more reliable, with all the potential for misunderstanding and confusion that might result. The content of those same messages would often be framed by a commander not in full possession of the relevant facts, or relying on facts that had become irrelevant as events rapidly unfolded, and were probably therefore leading to trouble. The experience of Cumberland and Ingoldsby comes to mind yet again.

Inevitably an army commander would have to rely upon the services of subordinate officers, often men of lesser calibre and more limited understanding, who would be directed this way or that by verbal messages and instructions carried in haste through the thick of the fighting by mounted aides and orderlies. Given the hazardous nature of such occasions, these messengers might never arrive at their intended destination. The army commander might not know, any more than the men he led, until perilously late, if at all, that his orders had not been received and accordingly were not about to be acted on. More than one rear-guard died in place as their opponents closed in grimly with musket butt and bayonet, never knowing that the order to withdraw was tucked into the gloved sleeve of an officer lying dead in the mud only some dozens of yards away. This was all part of the rigours of the battlefield. Inevitably, a commander with a surer touch, having the invaluable ability to 'read' the battle's progress and maintain composure under pressure, would be at an advantage over a less gifted, or perhaps less experienced, opponent.[5] It follows, therefore, that a commander with more experience, more refined skills and a better feel for the battlefield with all its uncertainties would be at an advantage over an opponent not so endowed.

The basic units, the building blocks, for all armies was the infantry battalion (about 600 officers and men strong), the cavalry squadron (200 strong) and the four- or six-gun/howitzer artillery battery. Once out on campaign, these units would be formed into groups ready for the task in hand, in effect put into ad hoc brigade-like formations under an appointed senior officer (often entitled the 'brigadier general' for the occasion). There was no formation corresponding to a modern division, but these brigades, once formed, would in turn be grouped into either a left or right 'Wing' (similar in many respects to a modern army corps) to allow greater command and control. The appointed commander of each Wing, always a man of rank and seniority, experience and standing, would in turn report to and receive orders from the army commander. The Wing was big and strong enough to stand a general action on its own for a limited period, perhaps while the other Wing manoeuvred for a better position, but this was not its true role. The two Wings of an army moved and fought together, complementing each other with their strength, the one ideally providing depth and a fresh echelon of uncommitted forces for the other. For an opponent, of course, a prime aim was to isolate an enemy Wing, either by blocking manoeuvres or by driving it on the battlefield, and so to destroy the formation as it stood unsupported. The surviving Wing could then be dealt with in turn, if it had not already made its escape – a fine example of this as 'Grand Tactics' could be seen in practice at the battle of Blenheim in August 1704.

The terms 'right' and 'left' must be used with some care, as they are indicative only, and depending upon circumstances the left Wing might be moving up on the right while the right Wing held the left flank secure!

As it happened, at Fontenoy the left Wing of the allied army was commanded by the Prince of Waldeck, on the left of the line, while the infantry of the right Wing was commanded, on the right, by the French-born Sir John Ligonier, who, when he advanced, was accompanied by Cumberland and his staff. The duke's opponent, Saxe, having disposed his troops in an almost formal defensive position with little likely scope for manoeuvre, did not feel the necessity to operate a Wing system on the day of battle, although the command of his reserves on his comparatively exposed left flank was entrusted to a subordinate.

The cavalry and infantry, when formed into brigades on a temporary basis for a certain operation, would in turn be grouped into a First Line and a Second Line, each with a commander reporting to the officer commanding the Wing; once again this was intended to aid tactical command and control. The First Line would, as custom dictated, be considered the post of most honour, in a way not dissimilar to the most senior unit being on the 'right of the line'. The intention, and often the reality, was that the First Line would receive and deal with the initial shock of contact with the enemy and then the Second Line would move forward to take advantage of whatever had been achieved. The pressing need to have an uncommitted second echelon of troops, able either to bolster a sagging line of battle or ready to move forward to exploit hard-won success, depending upon the fortunes of war, is no modern military concept. Furthermore, a commander who neglected this simple necessity was one who ran a considerable risk of failure. As the Duke of Cumberland would find, it was also necessary that such a second echelon, if it was to be used to good effect, should be so placed as to usefully move on the battlefield at the height of combat and at the appropriate time.

Having alluded to the limited nature of eighteenth-century warfare, it has to be said that there was little that was limited in the conduct of an actual pitched battle when those infrequent occasions arose. This is very much in the nature of these things, given the liking of many young men for some occasional unbridled but licensed violence from time to time. The relatively simple tools of the soldiers' trade at the time – the smoothbore musket of the foot-soldier, the smoothbore field gun or mortar of the gunner, and the sabre, carbine or pistol of the cavalryman and dragoon – were of quite short effective range, and necessitated that troops closed with their opponents to achieve their intended purpose to best effect. The use of black-powder in muskets and field guns would very rapidly cause a build-up of smoke, hampering observation and the ability of officers to exercise proper command and control of their men. The use by officers of the side-drum and the cavalry trumpet to transmit instructions, rather than having to rely on shouted commands, was therefore of huge value – thus the opponents' drummers and trumpeters, always distinctively dressed, were prime targets in order to shut down this essential means of communication. Officers waving their arms would always attract the same deadly attention, and the casualty lists often bear this out.

Both sides in a battle would of course labour under the same handicaps, so overall there was a levelling effect, with the more astute commander, fortunate enough to lead better trained and equipped troops, most likely to achieve success. The neat serried ranks of an army of the time are familiar from the many artistic depictions of these dramatic occasions, and the long red wall that was British troops in the field is a stirringly familiar sight. However, the need to control large numbers of men and horses in the midst of a confusing battle, clouded usually in drifting smoke, meant the use of formal formations was usually necessary as a practical tool for commanders at all levels. Not all was rigid formality, though, and what became known as light infantry tactics and the use of scouts and outposts were commonplace; skirmishers were also used, although 'light' troops were rarely employed in formed units at the time. Notable exceptions at Fontenoy were the French *Grassins* present in the woods, who gave the attacking allied troops so much difficulty on their right flank, while on the same day the impetuous charge of the nimble Highlanders of the Black Watch against the French defenders of that village gave a tantalising glimpse of what might have been achieved if the allied commanders had employed a little more imagination.

Cavalry had for many decades been regarded (and certainly regarded themselves) as an elite, the decisive arm, using rapid movement and shock tactics to sweep an opponent to destruction. This shock action, with massed horsemen cantering forward 'en muraille', as it was known, was what only the cavalry could do, and in the right circumstances, especially when employed against a disordered or ill-trained opponent, this classic tactic could be devastating and might prove to be no less than a battle-winning asset for an army commander. However, good horsemen were expensive to obtain, train, maintain in camp and in the field, and employ in war. By the mid-eighteenth century most armies in western Europe had about a quarter of their strength in cavalry and their closely associated comrades, the less well paid dragoons. The use of dragoons – initially mounted infantry armed with muskets and bayonets, and able to be deployed for action either in the saddle (on smaller horses than the real cavalry) or on foot – was increasing by this time, a trend that would grow and eventually all but erase the difference between the two types of horsemen.

A significant factor that bore down on the employment of this elegant and expensive mounted arm was the increased effectiveness of the oft-derided infantrymen they faced, and the ability of cavalry to dictate the pace of a battle was progressively diminished. The introduction of the bayonet by the close of the previous century – initially a rather crude 'plug-in' knife that could be inserted into the muzzle of the musket, and later the more effective socket variety which allowed the soldier to continue to fire his weapon while the bayonet was in place – produced the means for the foot-soldier to combat his mounted opponent. The horsemen, not yet being armed with the lances so familiar in Napoleon's army (at least in western Europe), could not easily outreach with the sabre or cavalry broadsword the 42-inch-long musket with an 18-inch steel bayonet securely attached. Such effective use against cavalry depended upon good discipline in the infantry, of course, with the required training and ability to stand their ground in tight formation, most often in the well known infantry square. It was plainly essential not to allow the enemy cavalry to get amongst the ranks of the square and break up the formation – when that happened, then all was chaos and the cavalry were once more in the ascendancy, capable of hacking down their opponents almost at will.

Training, determination and discipline, like so much when engaged in battle, were key. The Bavarian infantry withdrew from the field at Elix-heim in 1705 by adopting just such a great square, with the grenadiers posted at whichever corner was under most immediate threat as the manoeuvre was undertaken. The cavalry of the Duke of Marlborough, for all their dash and courage, could not interrupt the remorseless progress of the square, and an admiring British officer who watched the Bavarian regiments in action wrote: 'This shows what the foot are capable of doing against the horse.'[6] For all that, infantry squares were not necessarily invulnerable, and much depended upon the robustness of the foot-soldiers in the formation and their ability to keep their allotted positions. It might also be noted that at Garcia Hernandez in 1812 the cavalry of the King's German Legion broke four French squares, even though they occupied good ground – this was a notable achievement, but this was by no means the only occasion when an infantry square did not hold firm.

The use of the infantry square, allied to the effective employment of the bayonet-tipped musket, stripped away from the cavalry the advantage they previously enjoyed, and greatly diminished the battle-winning effectiveness of the mounted arm. Infantry caught while still in line, with their flanks relatively open to attack, were of course highly vulnerable to a cavalry attack. Over time, the most effective use of the cavalry became to fight other cavalry, as neither side's riders would wield a musket with attached bayonet (the analogy of modern battle tanks' main role being to fight other tanks, rather than supporting infantry against barbed wire and machine guns, which was their original intended purpose, comes to mind). Nonetheless, the cavalry remained an important and effective arm with the valuable ability to scout and to cover ground at a good pace which the infantry could not match; the ability to warn of hazards, and protect the flanks of an army while on the march and when forming for battle, was of great value. After all, in the right circumstances the cavalry could still overwhelm an opponent with a tightly controlled charge, and go on to harry to destruction a disordered enemy in flight, and these abilities, for all the cost of the cavalry, remained a highly useful asset for any army commander.

All the same, for the cost of one fully equipped cavalryman, a general could have three trained foot-soldiers, and arguably would get a better bargain for practical use. Only the infantry, then as now, could take and hold ground, whether operating in open cornfields, tangled hedges, woods and copses, close village streets, houses and cottages, or muddy ditches and siege trenches. Principally, the ability of trained infantry to maintain a good and effective rate of fire with their muskets, directed and controlled by tap of side-drum, was important. Drills for this purpose were devised and well practised, while the innovation at the turn of the eighteenth century of various kinds of platoon firing, rather than firing by whole ranks together, enabled disciplined foot-soldiers to keep their opponents under an unrelenting lash of musketry with little hope of respite.

To achieve this rate of continual galling fire, a British battalion, for example, would be formed of sixteen platoons, each of approximately thirty to thirty-five men, allowing for casualties, the sick and so on, and two grenadier platoons. In theory, the grenadiers comprised the taller and stronger men in the unit, and wore the distinctive mitre cap. These eighteen platoons would be formed into three 'firings', each of six platoons, and each firing would discharge their muskets together on the given command or riff of the side-drum. They would then reload their muskets while the second and third firings were in action, making ready for the next volley. The platoons about to give fire would take a smart step forward to do so, the men in the second and third ranks discharging their muskets over the right shoulder of the man to their front (at some risk to his hearing, of course). Having given fire, the firing would take a step back and the next firing would step forward, and so it would go on, a neat drill that reminded the men in the mist of the smoke and noise of battle that they were, or were not, about to fire their muskets. In this way the enemy was kept under continual fire, and the officers and NCOs were better able to ensure that their men were not firing too high, a circumstance not easy to manage if a whole rank was in action. The spontoons and canes carried by the officers and the halberds of the sergeants were used for this purpose, alerting the men not to let the muzzles of their muskets get too high in the excitement of the moment. Good discipline and training were clearly necessary to achieve the best result with this technique, and no doubt after several volleys the neat arrangement described here must have become at least a little ragged. Still, most armies in western Europe used this drill, devised in the 1690s, in one form or another, although the French, curiously, were slower than most to do so, not even adopting it formally until after the close of the war for the throne in Vienna.

A foot-soldier carried his rounds of ammunition, each consisting of a musket ball (about 1 ounce or 28 grams in weight) wrapped in a paper cartridge together with the powder charge. The British troops at Lauffeldt in 1747 went into action with twenty-eight such cartridges each, an interesting comment on what volume of fire was expected, but they had to be quickly resupplied as the fighting intensified. The need to bite off the end of the paper cartridge before pouring the powder down the muzzle of the musket, with the ball and wad of paper to follow, made it essential for soldiers to have a good set of front teeth, and it was an offence to remove these teeth, however rotten they might have become due to the indifferent dental hygiene of the day. The charge and ball would have to be securely rammed into position to ensure a good shot, and the introduction of iron ramrods to replace the more fragile wooden versions helped in this. Concern was expressed, however, both at the cost of the iron ramrods, and their tendency to rust in wet weather. Some soldiers, in their haste, simply banged the butt of their musket on the ground to seat the cartridge charge and ball, rather than using the ramrod. In the rain, of course, the effectiveness of the black-powder was impaired and the flint held in the cock to ignite the charge on firing might not give a good spark, although the use of the pre-packed cartridge did help to overcome the difficulty.

For all the apparent crudity of the weapons used, in practice well drilled and disciplined infantry could build up truly devastating rates of fire. The drill for loading, cocking and firing the musket would be well practised and, even allowing for the fairly poor effective range of the weapons, and given that individuals were not taught to take aim at any specific target (relying instead upon delivering fire *en masse* in a given direction for effect), large numbers of stricken soldiers would fall from the ranks as the close-range fighting developed in intensity. Some commanders still felt that the musketry delivered was less effective than closing with the cold steel of the bayonet, and on occasions poor training and drills did mean that a volley had little effect. All the same, there are plenty of examples of a close-range volley being devastating, and the contrasting experiences of the British and French guards in May 1745 does point exactly to this fact.

The infantryman's smoothbore musket was usually only effective, to a degree, at ranges of no more than 80–100 yards. Even this was hard to achieve when too-hot-to-hold barrels became encrusted with burnt black-powder residue making reloading difficult, and simultaneously increasing the recoil of the weapon into the shoulder on firing. The tendency of the soldier to anticipate this and flinch when firing was a common result. 'Its range was very short, inspiring tactics based on blocks of infantry which fired away at each other at close range in a contest where the rapidity of fire and the steadfastness of the firers were of prime importance.'[7] All the same, when this was tested in practice (admittedly without the inconvenience of an active enemy firing back), it was found that at a range of 150 yards almost 40 per cent of musket shots hit their target. The target was a large one certainly, but this does not really indicate a lack of accuracy when the soldiers put their minds properly to what they were doing.[8] To add to this thought, it was recorded that during the preliminary skirmishing before the onset of the Jacobite charge at the battle of Culloden in April 1746, Private Newman of Sempill's Regiment took careful aim at a Highlander who was making a nuisance of himself and shot him dead. The actual range was not given, but again inaccuracy of the musket as a weapon was certainly not in evidence on that occasion.

The prime duty of the foot-soldier, then, was to keep his place in the line and his musket in working order, with a good flint applied and a ball cartridge properly rammed home ready for firing when ordered. The principal killing and disabling effect of musketry was achieved by the soldiers firing all together in this disciplined way, although the use of sharpshooters was growing, with the ability to pick off suitable targets – once again officers, colour-bearers and drummers were favourite candidates for this deadly purpose. However, King Frederick II of Prussia had his soldiers fire off their muskets at ranges of up to 300 yards, hoping in this way to intimidate their opponents in the process, but whether such lavish expenditure of expensive powder and ball was justified is far from clear.

The smoke obscuration caused by the use of black-powder would soon build up with sustained firing, making observation difficult for the commanders of all armies when in action. The pressing need to close quickly with the opponent became obvious. Such combat at close range could and often did produce appalling casualties amongst men kept in tight formation to allow for necessary command and control exercised either by shouted orders or by the riffs and flams of the drummers. The bayonet was, of course, often the weapon of final resort and could inflict ghastly wounds if both sides stood their ground long enough to come to grips at close quarters. Such grim contests were sometimes seen but not that often, one side usually being beaten down by the superior musketry of the other and not waiting around to cross bayonets. In fact, reports of numerous bent and broken bayonets after an action are common, indicating that the quality of the steel in use was not that good, and driving home the blade – 'putting him to the point' as it was known – was an uncertain business, but they looked to be fearsome weapons and were intimidating enough for all that. The bayonet was also useful as a spit when part roasting meat over a campfire, or, with the point driven into the ground, the socket could be used to hold the stub of a tallow candle. At all events, it was certainly of more practical use than the cheaply made and ineffective hanger-type sword still carried by many infantrymen.

The employment of artillery, the 'god of war', as a military science had progressed significantly through much of the seventeenth and early eighteenth centuries. The pieces were no longer so cumbersome that moving them on the field of battle was almost an impossibility, even if their employment in a more mobile role was still unusual, while the horse artillery as an arm was developing only slowly. By the mid-eighteenth century, although light 'battalion' guns would be trundled about the field, the usual practice was still to have the artillery batteries dragged into the most promising position and used from that point throughout the action. These guns were expensive and prestigious pieces, and few commanders were mentally robust enough to put them in harm's way where they might fall into the clutching hands of an opponent. As with captured infantry colours and cavalry standards, to seize an opponent's guns was a distinct mark of military success, and their display would always be a focal point for victory parades.

For all their destructive power, the artillery personnel who served the guns were few in number compared to the cavalry and infantry. At the start of the war for the imperial throne in 1741, Great Britain had only 593 officers and men in service in the Royal Artillery, in all theatres of war and in garrisons at home and overseas. At the Treaty of Aix-la-Chapelle some seven years later this total had risen to just 1,025. 'Since the artillery was a service of recent origin, it lacked the prestige associated with the far older and more conventional infantry and cavalry. Its appeal was different.'[9] Frederick II's army was similar, with his gunners numbering a mere 1,201 at the end of the war, and it is fair to assume that other armies were in a similar position.

The guns would be served when in action by their crews; that much is obvious, but the teams of horses, and occasionally of oxen used to move the heavier pieces, were led by civilian contractors hired for the purpose campaign by campaign. These men were experts at their trade and valued by their employers for their skill, but not surprisingly they had little taste for the risks of the battlefield itself. As already mentioned in the context of Fontenoy, there was a tendency for them to make off to a quiet spot with their teams once the fighting began, although, as with the movement of guns around a battlefield, there were occasions when the teamsters showed remarkable devotion to their calling and to the troops they supported.

The two classic roles for the artillery – siege operations and firing in open battle – remained, of course, and the image of round-shot, the easily recognised cannon-ball, careering across a packed battlefield strewing death and mutilation in its path is easily conjured up. When employed well such missiles could be certainly be devastating, particularly when fired in enfilade from a flank so as to shoot down the long lines of opposing troops, knocking the unfortunate men down in a manner not unlike falling skittles. Such opportunities were uncommon, however, and the shot would more commonly bounce and roll across the ground – less dramatic to see but in many ways just as deadly. Inexperienced soldiers had occasionally to be stopped from putting out a foot to intercept the passage of these projectiles – they often retained surprising force, and broken and mangled limbs could be the result of such idle playfulness.

Just as deadly, in some ways more so, was the employment by gunners of canister shot, munitions formed by packing dozens of musket balls into a canvas bag backed by a powder charge, rammed into the artillery piece and then fired across the battlefield in a manner similar to a giant shotgun. This was best employed at short range and the effect on packed troops, whether cavalry or infantry, could be appalling; canister could also be used to good effect against light barricades hastily made up of carts, doors and general lumber. The use of grapeshot is often referred to (even by soldiers who had been under that fire), but it was usually canister shot, as grapeshot was a naval munition using larger but fewer balls (as in 'grapes') to rend rigging and sails and to sweep with brutal efficiency the quarterdeck of an opponent's ship.

Howitzers, short-barrelled field pieces and mortars, each with the ability to fire at a high angle trajectory, were mostly employed in siege operations, rather than in the open field, although at least one allied howitzer battery was in action at Fontenoy. Their ability to search into dead ground, for example against troops sheltering behind defensive ramparts and buildings, was valuable. Explosive shell was often used by the howitzers and mortars, ignited by fuzes and with the useful ability to both air-burst and to set buildings alight, depending upon the length of fuze cut by the gunner prior to loading. Fired from a static wooden bed, the mortar was plainly too immobile for field use, although the howitzer was not quite so constrained. The smaller mortars, known as perriers, were used to fire showers of fist-sized stones against enemy defenders – a quaint and almost comic-sounding technique but one which in reality was ferociously effective, with the missiles seen to be able to penetrate 6 inches or more of packed earth while brutally 'flaying the ground' and those soldiers cowering round about.

The wounds suffered by the participants in these pitched battles were often gruesome, and the effect of a lead musket ball, usually distorted in shape on impact, smashing through flesh and bone and frequently carrying filthy fragments of clothing into the wound cavity meant as often as not death or permanent disablement due to blood loss and infection. The ability to bring the wounded man to a surgeon's care counted for everything, and frequently this happened too late; although battlefields would be cleared, both of debris and the fallen, this often took place days after the action. Still, rapid extraction of the missile, cauterisation of the wound, or amputation of a mangled limb could save the wounded man (and occasional woman).

Soldiers are, generally speaking, a tough lot, and cases of recovery from terrible wounds were not uncommon: Sergeant George Depp survived for fourteen years with a stomach wound resulting in a massive prolapsed colostomy, while Irish-born Peter Drake had his brain *dura matter* exposed by a sabre sash at Malplaquet in 1709, and remembered that the after-effect was mainly that it was difficult thereafter to wear a hat with comfort. Although the medical services available on campaign appear to us to have been rather crude, all regiments had the services of a surgeon and surgeon's mate to call on, and even making allowance for the special hazards of the trade, a soldier generally was no worse provided for medically than his civilian counterpart, whether apprentice, servant or ploughboy. Not all soldiers were that convinced of the merit of the surgeons and their assistants, however, and one British veteran wrote many years later that:

> I have known wounded men often to be three days after an engagement before it came to their turn to be dressed, and it may be safely calculated that one-half of those men were thus lost to the service. Those medical men we had were not always ornaments to their profession. In the field they did more mischief, being but partly acquainted with anatomy; there was enough for what medical men call *bold enterprise*. In cutting down upon a ball for the purpose of extracting it, ten chances to one but they severed an artery they knew not how to stem.[10]

There was also a macabre kind of self-selection in such matters. Men who were terribly wounded, perhaps with serious bleeding from their injuries, would in all likelihood expire while lying on the field of battle waiting in vain for assistance. Those less severely hurt, or perhaps in more robust overall health, would be more likely to survive until given some form of attention, rough and ready though it might well be. Inevitably, for a wounded soldier to survive, he had to be resilient and Surgeon John Buchanan of The Blues wrote after Fontenoy of 'Corporal Orford of St James' Troop, who was not dressed for ten days after I amputated his forearm. The part stank abominably, but [he] did well with proper care.'[11] For many, the chance of survival lay with the devotion of friends who, once matters had calmed down, might go looking for fallen comrades. Then there were their women, coming forward from the camp when the firing died down, to try to find in the fading light a fallen man lying neglected on the battlefield after great events had moved on, or in some crowded makeshift field hospital hoping for the attention of an overworked and exhausted regimental surgeon.

There had been a sharp reaction to the heavy casualties suffered at such occasions as the costly battle of Malplaquet in 1709, so that losses of this kind were to be avoided if at all possible. The end was held not always to justify the means, and the attainment of a military aim would have to render very great and tangible advantages to justify a large butcher's bill. This restraining hand on army commanders was in many cases not unwelcome, for campaigns had in any case often been unproductive of decisive action and clear-cut result. Instead, they came to focus on elegant and complicated manoeuvres intended to put an opponent at a disadvantage, and perhaps bring them to withdraw (giving the heartening appearance to their opponent of success) or to seek terms. Otherwise, there was the option of engaging in siege warfare with a clearly defined and tangible objective of real value – in western Europe this was often a major fortress of the complex and intricately formidable design of the French engineer Marshal Vauban or his Dutch counterpart Meinheer van Coehorn.

Such a course had the attraction of seeming (only seeming) to be less expensive in casualties than taking part in the hazards of an outright battle. Contests in the open field were risky and unpredictable affairs, and potentially costly to carefully crafted reputations, whereas the seizure of an important fortress would be an undoubted achievement and one to be rightly celebrated; it was sometimes even possible to invite one's monarch to be on hand for the happy occasion, to take the keys of the place from suitably submissive magistrates and claim the victory for themselves. Such things would go a long way to establishing, or further embellishing, a military career. Siege warfare was, however, a slow and somewhat sedate business, conducted through well established procedures, and with the requirement for vast amounts of munitions and materiel to be accumulated. Nor was it without risk, quite apart from the casualties inevitably incurred in the siege trenches and in attempts to over-awe the garrison and overwhelm the defences. To threaten an important fortress, the loss of which might entail strategic disruption and loss of prestige to the opponent, could well induce them to make an attempt to disrupt the siege operation and in the process bring on a major battle, as indeed happened in May 1745 outside Tournai.

Of course, major fortresses were prime assets and were not to be neglected or given up lightly. So, to use the siege of such a place as a lure to entice an opponent into the open was a tactic which had certain merits. The alternative, of having to watch an opponent besiege and eventually capture such a place, with nothing being done to disrupt matters, would do little for an army commander's reputation and not much either for the morale of his troops. Commanders therefore had to balance the cost, the opportunities and the risks when deciding whether to let matters run, or to force a contest in the open field to lift the siege. Any campaign focused on limited objectives and modest risk could escalate rapidly into something more drastic, with the opposing armies confronting and grappling with each other. Such matters were finely balanced, and a commander with a robust attitude to weighing the considerations of both the shadow of risk and the brightness of opportunity might conclude that the former was just too great and that the loss of the fortress was, after all, the better price to be paid.

Such an approach was not to be scorned, for no fortress was able to withstand a formally conducted and adequately resourced siege for ever. To endlessly endure was, in any case, not the role of the fortress, the true worth of which was its ability to hold out for a certain period and by doing so to buy time for armies still in the field, which could, in the breathing space provided, manoeuvre and gain a suitable advantage, or even to take the road to the negotiating table. In a similar way, a captured fortress, unless it was a part of some redrawing of national boundaries (such as Lille in the 1670s), was a useful bargaining tool to tender at those negotiations. No commander of a besieged fortress was expected to resist to the last extremity and force the besieger to storm the place 'sword in hand' with all the butchery and pillage that would be entailed. Emperor Napoleon, brilliant in so many ways, required his fortress commanders to withstand at least one storm before submitting, but that was at variance with an understanding of the true purpose of the besieged place. Outlying defences, ravelins, bastions, crown and horn-works and so on would be attacked and occupied by the besieging forces, but this would be to enable the artillery breaching batteries to close up to the main defences to commence their role in breaking open a 'practicable breach' – one capable of allowing an armed soldier with both hands on his musket to enter unaided.

If that breach could not be sealed and kept shut, the garrison commander would know that the defence was fatally compromised and the time to ask for terms and submit had come. In those circumstances good terms would usually be given, and the honours of war granted to the garrison, who would be permitted to march out with their arms, colours and equipment, and go on parole to a neighbouring town, there to remain, not engaging in active campaigning, until formally exchanged with a like number of their opponent's men held captive. Such terms of parole were hardly ever misused, and if they were, the culprits could expect little sympathy if apprehended. The circumstances of such a submission could occasionally give rise to misunderstanding and ill-will, as once more reputations might hang on the outcome. A garrison commander who was not granted good terms, and was instead taken into captivity as a prisoner rather than being given parole, might be suspected of not having done his best to defend the fortress. On one such occasion in 1711 Louis XIV himself got involved, wrote to enquire about the precise terms offered for a capitulation, and tried to argue the issue, unsuccessfully as it turned out.

Siege warfare becoming such a common feature of campaigns was due in part to the relative lack of nimble mobility of the armies involved, but also to the aversion to risk of the commanders whose carefully nurtured reputations were not lightly to be put in jeopardy by the uncertainty of open battle. Sieges were usually conducted according to generally well understood procedures, and there was a certain comforting stateliness about these things – Marshal Vauban himself had set out a model 48-day programme for such an operation – while the avoidance of needless casualties was generally appreciated by both attacker and defender alike. This did not mean that the defending garrison and the attacking army did not exert themselves, but rash and ill-prepared attacks and counter-attacks with resultant heavy loss of life were frowned on and often criticised as unworthy and unprofessional when they took place. The civilian populations of the beset towns were themselves, to a certain degree, shielded from the worst excesses of the siege operations, although this protection was necessarily of a limited nature – if the fortress had to be stormed through some miscalculation by the senior commanders in the garrison, then nothing was left safe. Bergen-op-Zoom would be stormed and sacked soon after Fontenoy in a notorious lapse in military practice and discipline.

Any formal siege would be undertaken by an army in two complementary parts: the investing force which actually carried out the operations to reduce the fortress to the point of submission, and the field army covering those same operations and protecting them from enemy interference. Without that arm's length cover, no formal siege could really proceed. It had been a generally accepted practice for besieging armies to construct two defensive lines around the beleaguered fortress, one facing inwards ('contravallation') to guard against sorties by the garrison, the other facing outwards ('circumvallation') to ward off any relieving force. The besieging army would be able to encamp in the security afforded between the two lines. This formal and laborious procedure, common in the seventeenth century, was, however, fading as the next century progressed (even in 1709 Marlborough did not bother to construct lines at Mons, and nor did Marshal Saxe at Tournai). A lot, of course, depended upon the judgement of the commanding general of the besiegers, and whether he felt his opponents would pose a serious enough threat to the proceedings to make the effort worthwhile. It says a great deal for the analysis of the threat they faced that neither Marlborough or Saxe did so.

Mobility for any army is a key factor, even when a campaign was centred, as many were in the eighteenth century, on the prosecution of the siege of key towns and fortresses. An army that can move and manoeuvre with relative ease is a dangerous and living thing, while the commander who in contrast is handicapped by poor roads, broken bridges and water obstacles that cannot be easily crossed will often flounder and fail. So, a prime aim was always to obtain and maintain mobility, and by employing counter-mobility tactics – felling trees across roads, flooding areas of land, breaking down bridges and so on – to strip that vital asset away from the enemy. Corps of military engineers were in general not yet formed, but officers skilled in engineering tasks, usually in addition to their normal regimental duties, were active in all armies and by using soldiers and paid (or impressed) civilian labour these men could achieve a great deal in ensuring the easy movement of troops while hampering those same movements to those on the other side of the tactical hill.

A prime asset for all army commanders was the pontoon bridging train, the invaluable 'tin boats', which would be carted along with the marching army and under the practised eye of the engineer officers and the civilian wagoners (well paid for their trouble and expertise, of course) could be laid across rivers and canals at surprising speed. Once the army had crossed more or less dry-shod, the pontoons would be picked up, packed up and put back on the wagons and taken forward ready for the next water obstacle to be encountered. With such an asset, an army commander would not be hampered in his movements by rivers, canals or marshes, or by those broken bridges which his opponent had left behind. Accordingly, to lose an army's bridging train to an opponent during a campaign was a serious matter (Marlborough achieved this seizure at least twice, in 1704 and 1706), impacting severely on the whole ability of an opposing commander to operate with any effectiveness.

The essential task for army commanders remained to keep their forces viable and in the field in trying circumstances. Supply (and the maintenance of supplies) was a key consideration, and this necessity has already been discussed. The administrative 'tail' of any army would stretch for many miles behind the sharp tactical spear-point formed by the fighting troops. No commander could lightly risk that 'tail' being exposed to serious attack, interruption or interference, and accordingly the ability of any army to manoeuvre entirely freely was always limited. The security of both the mobile supply trains and the lines of supply and communication back to major depots in cities like Brussels and Lille was an important consideration. Such tempting targets for an opponent's cavalry were not, in practice, that vulnerable, as any raiding force would have to be of such a size that its presence and progress would be quickly detected and countered. Should an army commander try to move his main force on such a task to intercept his opponent's supplies and communications, then the focus of the whole campaign would shift significantly.

Both sides wrestled with the problem, of course, an issue that was as old as warfare itself. The more astute commander, having chosen his line of approach and taken post on carefully selected ground, could then observe what counter-moves were being made, and given the right moment and circumstances move to threaten lines of supply and communication to hamper or neutralise the opposing army. It might even be possible, by actually severing those lines, to oblige an opponent to stand and fight in disadvantageous circumstances, but that sort of event was not too common – once again, the reluctance to risk all in outright battle was a consideration. Of course, a commander with real drive and confidence might be less concerned with his own lines of supply and communication, judging that the best way to protect them was by moving against those of his opponent. A really intrepid commander might even consciously abandon his lines and turn his army into a kind of gigantic flying column for a while, and move to fall on his less mobile opponent. Such instances were rare, but just who was actually dictating the pace of a campaign was overall a factor in these judgements.

No army could operate in an area that could not provide a major part of the supplies needed for the day-to-day subsistence of the soldiers and forage for the horses. A properly formed eighteenth-century army of say 60,000 men would require no fewer than 40,000 horses for cavalry duties and supply functions. Such numbers imposed a formidable strain upon commanders, and upon their ability to operate freely. Supplies could be hauled forward, of course, but this kind of undertaking was difficult and again fraught with the risk of hostile interception. The use of canals and rivers would greatly ease the difficulty, and the security of these waterways would always be in a commander's considerations. It followed therefore that relatively few parts of western Europe were suitable for active campaigning, but the southern Netherlands and north-eastern France comprised one such area in which much might be achieved. That so many battles would be fought in the region, rather than in the wooded Ardennes or the constricted Moselle valley, is not too surprising. In addition, well populated areas would provide not just rich pickings for the commissary parties of the contending armies, but also important fortified places – Tournai was a good example – which offered tempting targets to any opposing commander.

Armies on campaign had a certain self-contained nature about them, the fighting troops being accompanied by a large number of people not in uniform but providing essential ancillary services. The use of civilian contractors to haul the gun teams and pontoon trains has been mentioned. The provision of rations was also in civilian hands, the contractors bidding for permits to provide supplies at the start of a campaign, although foraging and trying to live off the land was always a common feature; however, this was an uncertain process, not least because local farmers would do their best to avoid having their crops, flocks and herds taken by passing soldiers. Many commanders took steps to reduce such depredations by their troops, and much produce acquired in this way was paid for, but by no means all of it, campaign-hardened soldiers having a convenient tendency to 'find' things.

As well as the drivers, wagoners, sutlers and other associated personnel accompanying an army, there were the women, usually the wives (whether formally married or not) of the soldiers. These redoubtable females, faithfully following the drum, provided cooking, washing and nursing services for the troops as well as those obvious comforts of a more personal nature. In the aftermath of battle they were often the only nurses available to aid the regimental surgeons striving amongst the wounded. Their offspring usually accompanied them on the march. 'Many tender women and young children marched with us,' one of Cumberland's officers wrote, 'were never on horseback, nor carried on wagons. One of the troopers' wives in Germany marched thirty-six hours with the child in her arms the fourth day after delivery.'[12] Often not 'on the strength' of a regiment, and having to shift and make do for themselves as best they could, Black-eyed Nancy and her sisters had their counterparts in all armies, providing a rude measure of homely comfort for those men who followed the strange trade that is the life of a soldier on campaign.

The Size of the Armies at Fontenoy

Why fight at Fontenoy at all? Pitched battles were infrequent affairs, heavy with risk, and as a result they understandably did not take place very often; many commanders, made cautious as their careers progressed and prospered, actively avoided them, and that approach to campaigning was not necessarily wrong. To seize territory and the occasional fortress would pay handsome dividends for use as bargaining counters in the eventual (and almost always inevitable) negotiations for a peace settlement. It followed therefore that the commanders of opposing armies had to feel they had something worthwhile to play for in offering and accepting the hazards of a battle in the open. The cover and protection of the troops engaged in the prosecution of a major siege might, on the one hand, provide just such a valid reason, while the chance to disrupt and drive off that same besieging force and so relieve the beleaguered fortress could, on the other hand, be an equally pressing goad for the opponent. Bloody Malplaquet was one such example of this, with Louis XIV insisting that Mons was to be saved, and Fontenoy thirty-six years later, fought with such severity for the security or otherwise of Tournai, was another. The capture of any important fortress was a laudable aim, for which risks might be run, and offering other opportunities in the wake of its fall. In a wider sense, if an army commander was shrewdly calculating that he could draw out his opponent and force a confrontation on advantageous terms, then to lay siege to that fortress might do the job very well. It is not too difficult to conclude that Marshal Saxe had just that in mind in the late spring of 1745.

The two opposing armies on 11 May 1745, leaving to one side the Dutch garrison in Tournai and the French troops investing that fortress, were in total some 110,000 strong, although estimates of the actual numbers of the men in each army who actually engaged in combat do differ. Precise numbers are hard to come by, as most contemporary accounts list units only, and the strength of these could vary to a fair degree depending on casualties, sickness, stragglers and so on. The general consensus, summed up by the great historian on the British army, Sir John Fortescue, gives Marshal Saxe 56,000 troops in the field with seventy guns, while the Duke of Cumberland could deploy on that same day 50,000 men with ninety guns (Skrine mentions a figure of 46,500, which appears to be too low).[13] The imbalance in artillery strength is noticeable; again numbers vary, although many of the guns in service were light 'battalion' guns not especially suitable for counter-battery work. It is perhaps not possible to be too precise on this point, but the figures mentioned as troops deployed for battle (as opposed to containing the garrison in Tournai) appear to be appropriate. The essential fact was that Cumberland was the weaker in bayonet strength when he attempted his attack, while his apparent superiority in artillery, on paper at least, was more than countered by the stout entrenchments that Saxe had time to construct in which to shelter his troops.

Chapter 3

The German Marshal – Maurice Saxe

I am all in favour of bastards.[1]

Arminius-Maurice de Saxe was born in October 1696 in the small town of Goslar in the Hartz Mountains of western Germany. His 34-year-old Swedish-born mother, Countess Maria Aurora von Konigsmarck, had not been able to take the prudent step of marrying his father, Frederick-Augustus, Elector of Saxony. The elector, who would one day become 'Augustus the Strong' and King of Poland, had no intention of marrying his latest mistress, having quite recently acquired as his wife the agreeably wealthy daughter of the Margrave of Bayreuth. The countess's family background, it should be said, was not without its shadows, as her brother Philipp Christoph had been widely and notoriously known as the lover of Sophia Dorothea, wife of George, Elector of Hanover, and reputedly he paid with his life one night for the illicit dalliance. Maria Aurora was not above conducting her own affairs on the side as it were, nor was she that discreet about it; rebuked for her lack of fidelity by Augustus, who declared angrily that Caesar's wife should be above reproach, she tartly replied that he was certainly not Caesar and she for that matter was not his wife. Despite all this, the elector was undoubtedly pleased with his new young son, albeit he was born on the wrong side of the blanket, and he remained fond, in a casually respectful way, of the mother too.

Perhaps unsurprisingly, the young Arminius-Maurice was taken into his father's household, along with other half-brothers and sisters, in a turbulent period during which the new King of Poland was first thrust from his throne by King Charles XII of Sweden and then managed to recover the title. A contingent of Saxon troops was committed to fighting with the Grand Alliance against France in the War of the Spanish Succession, and the young man, while still only 12 years old but with an interest in military matters, was sent to accompany their commander, Count Matthias von Schulemberg, on campaign with the Duke of Marlborough and Prince Eugene in the Low Countries. His position as the king's son, however, was not supposed to hold too many privileges, the instructions from his less-than-doting parent to the Count being to 'Keep him on his toes and don't coddle him. Toughen him up. I want you to make him march on foot to Flanders ... and don't let him pay other soldiers to do his guard duty for him unless he is seriously ill.'[2] Von Schulemberg was a good soldier, and a thoughtful tutor, and interpreted these instructions in a sensible way.

The immensely strong French-held fortress of Tournai, so central to the later telling of the story of Fontenoy, of Marshal Vauban's innovative design, endured a grim siege by the allied army for several months in the summer of 1709, with the French garrison commander only submitting on 5 September after a valiant defence. This was Maurice's baptism of fire in active warfare. Six days later the terribly expensive battle at Malplaquet was fought. 'An access [excess] of mental rage seems to have taken possession of both sides simultaneously.'[3] The Saxon regiments were heavily engaged in the attacks through the tangled copses of the Bois de Sars on the allied right flank, dragging their heavy guns through the thickets to engage the French cavalry, but Arminius-Maurice spent much of the day safely out of the way, rather to his chagrin, helping to guard the baggage train. The ghastly casualty roll made a deep impression on him, however, and he strove never to repeat the bitter slogging match that the battle became before the allied commanders could force their opponents away and claim a rather heavily qualified success for the day.[4]

Two years later Frederick-Augustus at last formally acknowledged Arminius-Maurice as his son, after he had completed further campaigns in Flanders, and accorded him the title *Graf von Sacshen*; it was under this title that he became best known, as Maurice, Count of Saxony, or just simply Saxe. His father's repeated attempts to reinstall himself as King of Poland saw the young nobleman campaigning in Pomerania against the Swedes, taking part in the capture of Treptow and Peenemunde, an unsuccessful attempt to seize Stralsund, and the capture of Stade. In December 1712 Saxe fought with the Saxon cavalry at the battle of Gadebusch and, although they were compelled to withdraw from the field, their Swedish opponents were too exhausted to pursue and make the most of their success. His father was sufficiently impressed with his conduct under fire to appoint Saxe, although still only 16 years of age, to the command of the prestigious King's Own Regiment of Cuirassiers. Life on campaign continued, for which the young man had shown a strong liking, and the capture of Usedom on the Baltic coast in 1715 indicated a decline in Swedish influence and power; this was compounded when Stralsund was taken from them by a force of Saxon, Danish and Hanoverian troops.

Saxe was keen to go east to join Austria's latest campaign against the Ottoman Turks, but Frederick-Augustus would not permit this until late 1716 when the young nobleman joined Eugene's army on the Danube. At the siege and capture of Belgrade the following spring he played a notable part, and on his return to his father's court in Dresden was invested with the Order of the White Eagle of Poland, an unusual honour for so young a man, even if he were the king's son. Saxe would, all the same, never be more than on the side-lines as just one of the king's many natural offspring, and the restlessly ambitious young man sought his fortune elsewhere, leaving Dresden (and his affectionate new young wife, Johanna-Victoria) for Paris in the spring of 1720, apparently intending to study mathematics. To no one's great surprise, nothing came of this commendable but rather academic notion.

Saxe instead pursued his military career, with the financial support of his royal father, as it was believed that in the French service 'He can learn the business of war better than he can in Saxony, which is not at war, and which hopes to remain at peace.'[5] In August 1720 he was appointed *Maréchal de Camp* in the army, a rank lying between that of a brigade commander and a lieutenant general, and the following year he purchased for a considerable sum of money providentially provided by Frederick-Augustus the colonelcy of the German-speaking Greder regiment, henceforth to be known as the Saxe regiment. Saxe proved to be a sound drillmaster and thoughtful disciplinarian, and it was soon commented by other senior officers that all troops should be drilled to deliver their musketry in the way that he insisted his men did. The French inability to do so at Fontenoy many years later would indicate that this was a lesson that took a long time to sink in. Saxe was, of course, a quite seasoned campaigner by now at the age of 24, and took a particular interest in the nature and science of fortifications and siege warfare. These disciplines were often the key to successful campaigning at the time, as the opportunity and relish amongst senior commanders for outright battle was generally rather limited.

Restless by nature, in 1725 Saxe obtained leave and was on his way to Courland on the Baltic coast (south of the Gulf of Riga, in present-day Latvia) where the throne to that duchy had fallen vacant on the recent death of the last Grand Duke. The region had been devastated by Russian troops during the Great Northern War, yet Tsar Peter still had designs on the strategically important peninsula, sitting so close to the approaches to the growing naval port of Kronstadt. Saxe's permission from his father to embark on the adventure was withdrawn, though, as current unrest in Poland might have been made worse as a result. The young man went ahead all the same, and arrived in Mitau to find a warm welcome from the Courlanders who, if it could be managed, wished to be ruled neither by a Russian or by a Pole. A grand charter was signed by the Courland nobility in July 1726 confirming Maurice's election as ruler-designate but after a period of apparent success, Russian intervention and Polish hostility proved deadly to his hopes. The following summer he was forced to flee the duchy, although he continued rather optimistically to style himself 'Duke-Elect of Courland and Semigallia' to the end of his long life.

Frederick-Augustus, King of Poland and Elector of Saxony, died in February 1733 and the tricky question of the Polish Succession immediately arose. The French preference was for the candidacy of the governor of Poznan, Stanislaus Lecsinsky (coincidentally and rather conveniently the brother-in-law of King Louis XV), rather than the late Elector's eldest son Frederick-Augustus III, who had the tacit support of Austria. With that strong French backing, in September Stanislaus was duly elected in Warsaw. Young Frederick-Augustus, of course, did not accept this quietly; Saxon troops occupied the city and the following day he was duly confirmed as the elected monarch by the assembled nobles, worthies who clearly understood what was expected of them. Stanislaus had to withdraw with his supporters to Danzig on the Baltic coast, where he sent for French military and naval assistance.

War having been declared on 10 October 1733 (the War of the Polish Succession), French and Austrian forces, on behalf of the respective candidates for the throne, were soon engaged in hostilities in Lombardy and on the upper Rhine. Saxe served once more as *Maréchal de Camp* under the veteran campaigner James FitzJames, Marshal Berwick. He accompanied the French army in an advance on the strategic crossing points over the Rhine. As Austria and Saxony were allied in the cause of the Polish succession, Saxe was fighting against his own countrymen, but he appeared to feel that his principal loyalty lay with the French under whom he held his formal military rank, even though this was contrary to the aspirations of his own half-brother. Such an odd-seeming conflict of interest and loyalties appeared to cause few qualms or comment in either Austria, France or Saxony, nor were relations between the two men apparently strained.

The hard-fought siege of Kehl, covering the right bank of the Rhine opposite Strasbourg, saw Saxe overseeing the construction of a pontoon bridge over the wide river so that Berwick's main army could cross, and his participation in a failed general assault on the defences three days later. The Austrian garrison commander submitted shortly afterwards to avoid further bloodshed, but the lateness of the season prevented the French from exploiting their success. The next spring Saxe was with the Duc de Belle-Isle at the capture of Trier in the Moselle valley and the subsequent attack on Trarbach, but he then went south to join the Duc de Noailles in forcing the Lines of Ettlingen not far from Rastadt. Marshal Berwick, however, decided against a general advance against the outnumbered Austrian army led by Prince Eugene, until the major fortress of Philippsbourg, held by General Wutgenau, was taken. The siege went forward in poor weather, and Saxe was once more active in repulsing a smart Austrian sortie on 7 June 1734, being described by the director of siege operations as his right-hand man. Five days later Berwick was decapitated while in the trenches by a round-shot fired by the defenders of the fortress (in less than a week his old comrade, Marshal Villars, died in Turin in the same room and the same bed in which he had been born eighty years before).

In the round of promotions following the demise of these renowned commanders, two of Saxe's supporters, Noailles and the Duc d'Alsfeld, were made Marshals of France. As a result, the young count's influence increased proportionately, although formal promotion for the moment eluded him. General Wutgenau capitulated Philippsbourg in mid-July and Eugene's army fell back, enabling the French to move against Mainz, where in the castle of Neiderulm on 1 August 1734 Saxe received the news that Louis XV had appointed him to the rank of lieutenant general. As the campaign languished with the cooler autumn weather, news also came that Stanislaus had been forced to abandon his hold on Danzig and withdraw to Prussia, where in Königsburg he formally abdicated his claim to the Polish throne; he went on to accept the Duchy of Lorraine instead (courtesy of Louis XV, and firmly displacing the husband of Maria-Theresa in the process). The following year saw inconclusive campaigning and an armistice was declared in November 1735, rather to Saxe's regret, as apart from some sharp skirmishing he had found little opportunity to shine in his new rank.

The Duchy of Courland had once more become vacant, on the death in 1737 of the reigning Duke William, so the enterprising young nobleman hastened to once more put forward his claim to the title. The Russians, however, quickly advanced the merits of their own preferred candidate, a native of Courland, Ernst Biren (reputedly the lover of the late Tsarina Anna). The electoral college in Mitau was bullied into accepting Biren's nomination, and there was little that Saxe could do about it as he lacked support from his half-brother, now the King of Poland, who was in no position to lightly offer offence to the Russians just to oblige him.

Temporarily with no active service to perform, but with expensive tastes and in consequence habitually short of money (despite a generous allowance from his half-brother), in 1739 Saxe suffered a severe injury in a fall from his horse, which left him with a broken knee and reopened an old wound from his youthful campaigns. His health quickly began to deteriorate, his robust constitution degraded by enthusiastic and frequent indulgence in wine and women and occasional hard soldiering. In the summer of 1740 Ernst Biren was deposed from the Ducal throne in Courland, reputedly on account of his overbearing manner, and Saxe went to Dresden to press his case, but a substitute approved by St Petersburg, a young prince of Brunswick, was already in place – once more nothing could be done. More pressing matters, however, were in hand on a much wider stage, for Emperor Charles VI of Austria died without male issue and, as discussed in a previous chapter, war over the Austrian succession was the result. 'Here is a muddle,' Saxe wrote rather approvingly to a friend, 'and I have a part to play in it.'[6]

The apparently unstoppable French and Bavarian advance on Vienna in the summer of 1741 saw Saxe in command of the vanguard, confidently brushing aside an Austrian blocking force at Ulm on the river Danube. Then, missing a fine opportunity, the French turned away from Vienna and went onwards into Bohemia. Early in November Saxe stood before the fortified walls of Prague, and he met in the Saxon army encampment no fewer than three of his own half-brothers (natural offspring of their prolific father): Count Rutowski, Count Cosel and the Chevalier de Saxe. Together they hatched a plan to seize the city. Overcoming the objections of cautious French and Bavarian generals, Saxe took advantage of a diversion made by the Saxon troops to storm one of the city gates under cover of darkness. The daring attempt was successful and the French and Saxons broke in against little opposition and joined hands in the centre of the market square – the cost to the attackers was trifling compared to what had been achieved, with just fourteen men killed and twenty-two wounded. Saxe was rightly accorded the credit due for his outstanding exploit, and was then active in preventing any looting taking place.

By the early spring of 1742 Saxe had been summoned to push forward the languishing siege of Egra on the river Eger. The defences were strong, but the French heavy guns blasted gaps in the fortifications and the garrison commander capitulated on 19 April, good terms being granted to the Austrian troops who were paroled. With two real successes to his credit, at the capture of both Prague and Egra, Saxe found that the French army commander, the Duc de Broglie, was now rather envious of his growing reputation as a skilled commander, and a perceptible rift developed between the two men. Obtaining leave of absence from the army, Saxe took himself off to Moscow, to press once more his increasingly improbable claim to the Duchy of Courland. He was warmly received by the Tsarina Elizabeth Petrovna, who at one time in her adolescence had been considered a suitable wife for him, but was offered no help or support in his quest for the duchy, and had to return to campaign in Bohemia. The French forces there were isolated now that Prussia and Saxony were no longer active in the war, and Saxe took part in the effort to relieve Marshal Belle-Isle and the Duc de Broglie and the troops still shut up in Prague. His energy at this time was sorely needed as the French higher commanders appeared to be in a fatal state of lethargy, with one observer writing, 'If we lose Count Saxe, who is obliged to take everything on his shoulders, I do not know where we shall be.'[7] He was critical both of de Broglie, who left his troops during the withdrawal from the city to hurry onwards to safety, and of Marshal Maillebois, who was supposed to be covering the march in the freezing weather of mid-December but failed to do so effectively.

Saxe was appointed in the spring of 1743 to command the French army in the Palatinate, taking over command of de Broglie's forces shortly afterwards. An initial attempt by Prince Charles of Lorraine to force the line of the Rhine was frustrated at Briesach, and at other crossing points over the river, but Saxe was instructed in October to hand over his command to Marshal Coigny; when he returned to Paris he was accorded a warm welcome from the king for his achievements in that dismal year for French fortunes, a year that had notably seen the wholly avoidable defeat at Dettingen in northern Germany. In late March 1744 Saxe was raised to the rank of Marshal of France – one of only twelve such notables at the time, a signal and unusual honour for a comparatively young man (he was 47 years old), especially one who was German born and in the delicate matter of religion a Protestant.

The newly appointed marshal was sure that France had the most to lose by inaction, and he was amongst those who advocated an offensive campaign into the Low Countries in 1744 to throw their opponents onto the defensive. In May he accompanied the king and Marshal Noailles on an inspection of the army in the north-east, and once the campaign began Saxe drove the allied forces from Ghent and Bruges, but adverse conditions in Alsace obliged Noailles to go there with reinforcements and the French offensive in the north stalled. The threat soon passed, and in mid-November 1744 Louis XV appointed Saxe, despite his declining health, to the command of the main French field army in the north.

> His Majesty appears to have decided to entrust you again next year with the direction of the army which you have recently commanded to His Majesty's satisfaction and that of the troops. ... You can then return to Flanders at the beginning of February to carry out the plans we will have worked out. If you agree with this I can then inform His Majesty, who, I can assure you, will be very pleased to see you.[8]

The scene was set for the marked success that Saxe would achieve in the fields around the village of Fontenoy, early in May 1745. In the warm afterglow of that battle he would in effect be the hero of the hour, the shame of French defeat at Dettingen expunged, and he was laden with honours by a grateful king, which included an additional annual stipend of 40,000 livres and tenancy for life of the royal Chateau de Chambord.

Although increasingly unwell, Saxe remained active as a campaigner and by the end of that autumn his army was in possession of most of the Austrian Netherlands, although the allied garrison in Ath had held out until October. Rumours abounded that the marshal had suffered a stroke and was too ill to return to Paris to rest over the winter months but in January 1746 his army thrust forward again, seizing a string of provincial towns before forcing the capitulation of the garrison in Brussels on 20 February. In March Saxe returned to Paris to receive the acclaim which was his due, with a patent of naturalisation as a French citizen, and to take part in the council of war in Versailles for the coming campaign season. Despite his protests, a cautious strategy was once more decided on, and he returned to his army in rather low spirits, having to contend with two princes of the blood (Conti and Clermont) leading French troops concurrently and ineptly in the same theatre of war. Saxe and the two high-spirited and opinionated young noblemen inevitably clashed during a campaign that consisted mostly of minor sieges, although admittedly Clermont neatly took Antwerp while Conti captured Mons in July. In the end a sharp formal note from the king was required to make Conti and Clermont understand that they really were under the orders of the marshal and should act accordingly.

Saxe began a siege of British-held Namur on the river Meuse in September, and after some manoeuvring on 11 October he beat the Anglo-Dutch army at Rocoux near Liège, which fell to him soon afterwards; the conquest of the Austrian Netherlands was in effect complete, and Holland was laid open to French invasion if that course were chosen. He returned to Versailles, and on his late arrival the king, who had already retired for the night, most unusually got up again and came to greet the ailing marshal with sincere warmth. The German-born soldier was appointed Marshal General of France, the most senior post of that select body, last held thirty years earlier by the great Villars. 'They have made me Marshal General, the equivalent of the German General Field Marshal. It makes me the first general in the realm, above all the marshals of France. I cannot hope to rise higher.'[9]

Campaigning for 1747 began in April, with Saxe out-marching the Duke of Cumberland and then defeating his army at the costly battle of Lauffeldt on 2 July. All parties were tired of war now, and the marshal general's reception on his return to Paris was noticeably cooler than before, in part because of reports of excessive looting and outrages at captured towns such as Bergen op Zoom. Even so, he was appointed Commandant General of the Austrian Netherlands in January 1748. Moving forward once more with his loyal troops, Saxe feinted to the west against Breda and Tilburg and then swooped on Maastricht, which fell to his army on 10 May, even though it was known that a general armistice leading formally to peace had already been signed.

With that peace, Saxe had really nothing more to do and returned to Chambord with its seventy-four staircases and 440 rooms. He conducted himself there in some state as the duke-elect of Courland should, although his subjects were just the tenants on his estate and a hundred or so minor local gentry, farmers and peasants. He also wrote, and had published, his 'Reveries' – his rambling and rather unreliable thoughts on the conduct of war. In 1749 the unemployed old soldier visited Dresden for the last time, before going on to Potsdam, where he was received at Sans Souci by Frederick the Great, who wrote 'I have been entertaining the hero of France, the Turenne of the age.'[10] Once more in retirement at Chambord, and confined to bed with a severe head-cold in November 1750, Maurice suffered a stroke and despite (or, indeed, perhaps because of) insisting on drinking liberal quantities of strong cider, which he seemed to consider beneficial to his failing health, died on 30 November early in the morning.

It is not easy to find a parallel military career of such vaulting ambition, brash opportunism, dash, daring and simple skill as that of Marshal Saxe; undoubtedly he was a great man, quite out of the common mould. At the king's direction, the funeral and interment of this notable soldier of France was carried out on 7 February 1751 in Strasbourg, where a large proportion of the citizens were Protestant and so many of whose young men had served in the renowned Saxe regiment.

Chapter 4

Billy the Martial Boy – Cumberland, the last Captain General

You would have loved him, if you had not feared him.[1]

There is no immediate reason to suppose that the son of a monarch should be a natural-born soldier or a good field commander, or for that matter, that such a monarch himself (occasionally herself) should even have such rare gifts. However, throughout much of history it has been the lot of such young princes to be given command of armies, and accordingly, for good or ill, to hold in their hands the hazards, well-being and lives of many men. Perhaps surprisingly, on frequent occasions this trust has been well merited, and great things have been accomplished at relatively modest cost. On others, of course, a grimmer result has been obtained, when more suitable but less well born alternatives have been available but not deemed elevated enough for the role of commander. On infrequent occasions the son of a monarch has proved to be not a great commander but a good soldier in a broader sense, and the Duke of Cumberland was just such a one.

William Augustus, second and certainly most favourite son of King George II of Great Britain and the Elector of Hanover, was born in the evening of 15 April 1721 at Leicester House, London. His grandfather, George I, was still on the throne, and the mutual antipathy between the king and his own son, heir to the throne, was well known. The little boy's mother, Caroline of Ansbach, had a strong and vivacious personality, and took great care over the education of her numerous children, even though Frederick, her first-born boy, spent much of his childhood in Hanover. At the age of 5 William Augustus was created a royal duke, with the resounding title of Duke of Cumberland, and two years later his father ascended the throne when George I had a stroke and died in Osnabruck in Westphalia while on the way to visit Hanover. The years of youth passed quickly for Cumberland, indulged by his father unlike his older brother; he proved particularly adept at riding and his great sporting passion was always hunting. In the spring of 1740, as the likelihood of war shadowed western Europe once more, the young royal duke was nominated to the colonelcy of the 2nd English Foot Guards. Despite his lack of previous practical military experience, he was well read on the lives and campaigns of the great commanders, had studied the drill manuals of the day, and quickly made himself known to his officers and men at their encampment on Hounslow Heath to the west of London. The duke was generally popular and soon active in instigating improvements in camp routine, discipline, food and training. The guards became, as one observer noted, 'An ornament and a safeguard, instead of being what they had too often been before, a nuisance and a terror.'[2] What Cumberland lacked in practical experience, he apparently had amply in both energy and common-sense.

Understandably keen to gain a reputation for active service, which the Foot Guards were not likely at the time to experience, in August 1740 Cumberland went to sea with the Royal Navy aboard HMS *Victory* (100 guns), the flagship of Admiral Sir John Norris. Instructed to intercept a Spanish convoy, Norris' squadron was delayed by foul weather from sailing from Portsmouth, and when it did HMS *Victory* collided with HMS *Lion* and was severely damaged. Transferring to HMS *Boyne*, Norris and his royal guest set off once more, but contrary orders were received from London to wait and embark troops for an attack on Saint Sebastian or Ferrol in northern Spain. Frustrating delays ensued and in late September Cumberland was instructed to return to London, as Norris was now under fresh orders to take his squadron to the West Indies, and the royal duke was certainly not going to be permitted to be exposed to the rigours of that unhealthy climate.

Promoted to the colonelcy of the 1st English Foot Guards in February 1742, Cumberland took his seat in the House of Lords and became a privy councillor soon afterwards. As George II made preparations to join his troops on campaign in the Low Countries, the duke was made major general, and father and son left England in April 1743, the first time that Cumberland had been abroad, other than his less than distinguished excursions on the high seas. The Prince of Wales had also hoped to accompany them, but not surprisingly this idea was refused, while Cumberland was taken to Hanover and enjoyed hunting in the royal parks and forests. The British and Hanoverian troops, and those Hessians in British pay, had assembled under the supervision of veteran campaigner the 2nd Earl of Stair,[3] and marched towards the river Rhine, but George II, concerned for the security of Hanover, ordered that he should not move forward of the river Main for the time being. The king and his son joined the army, and were confronted at Dettingen by Marshal Noailles. Cumberland was noted for being in the thick of the battle there, apparently enjoying himself in the action: 'He gave his orders with a great deal of calmness and seemed quite unconcerned.'[4] Struck by several spent musket balls, and rather more seriously by a canister shot in the leg, the duke was persuaded with some reluctance to leave the line of battle and be taken to a surgeon to have his leg dressed. He generously first insisted that attention be given to a wounded French officer, the Comte de Fenelon, who was lying nearby.

The wound to Cumberland's leg proved slow to heal; tendons had been torn, infection set in and the duke ran a high fever, so that, unsurprisingly given the medical methods of the day and the dread fear that gangrene would take hold, amputation of the limb was considered. This proved unnecessary and he rallied and gradually recovered, so that by late summer he could review his regiment on horseback (against the advice of his doctor), although he remained partly lame for the rest of his life. The young royal duke was, in fact, already showing a tendency to corpulence, despite having an energetic nature and being a keen rider to hounds. This hardly helped his complete recovery, and as time went on his weight contributed to a pattern of increasing ill-health.

War was formally declared by France on Great Britain but George II refused to allow Cumberland to once more join the Earl of Stair and his army in the Low Countries, aware that his son's injured leg had yet to fully heal. The year 1744, at any rate, passed without major incident, but the pace of war quickened after the death early in 1745 of Emperor Charles VII. After some adroit negotiations with the Dutch, Cumberland was appointed commander of the allied army campaigning in the Low Countries; he would have the veteran Austrian soldier Field Marshal Königsegg at his side to offer advice and guidance. On 6 March Cumberland was appointed Captain General of all His Majesty's Land Forces, and within a few weeks he was in the field with his army, making ready to confront Marshal Saxe. The events of the Fontenoy campaign, and the Jacobite adventure in Scotland and northern England, in which the duke played such a notable role, will be dealt with in detail in succeeding chapters.

In October 1746, while Cumberland was still in London, General Sir John Ligonier was roundly beaten in battle by Saxe at Rocoux, not far from Liège, on the river Meuse. The following February Cumberland returned to the Low Countries to resume his command of the now enlarged allied army. After some inconclusive small-scale actions and the French capture of Hulst on the river Scheldt, Saxe was well placed enough to lay siege to Antwerp and simultaneously threaten Maastricht. Unable to cover both places, Cumberland decided to concentrate his forces to protect the latter fortress, and by late June 1747 his army was encamped near Lauffeldt, close to Maastricht. There, on 1 July, Saxe and Cumberland fought each other once again; the French, after enormous effort, broke the allied line but once again failed to exploit their success. Both commanders appeared to have difficulty in controlling the very large numbers of troops engaged. Saxe's losses were significantly greater than those of Cumberland, and the marshal could not go on to mount a serious attack on Maastricht; although arguably outfought on the day, the royal duke had rather more significantly, and in a curious reversal of the fortunes of Fontenoy, achieved his aim. Once again he had been seen to be in the thick of the fray, deftly defending himself from the sword cuts of a French dragoon at one point, and a British officer wrote that 'The strength of his own arm saved him from being made a prisoner.'[5] The war to decide who would sit on the imperial throne in Vienna had run its course, and in April 1748 Cumberland signed the peace Preliminaries Articles, but his own forces were being reduced and Saxe used the intervening period to gain ground and seize Maastricht. The final Treaty of Aix-la-Chapelle was at last concluded in October.

With peace achieved, the duke turned his attention in London to army reform, taking practical and long-overdue measures to improve the standard of discipline, training, equipment, clothing and pay of the troops in the British army. He also took a keen interest in the welfare of the thousands of soldiers released from employment in the ranks now that their services were not required, and facing idleness and penury. Army reform has always proved controversial, with vested interests under threat, and when faced with predictable protests at the disbanding of a senior regiment that had performed poorly in the recent campaigns, the duke wrote, 'My reasons for proposing the reduction was to oblige the Old Corps to be more careful for the future and not to trust entirely to their seniority but their merit.'[6] His principled and well meant efforts were unpopular with many officers who resented the more stringent controls placed upon them and their activities. Despite this, the Act of Parliament necessary to implement reforms was eventually passed, although a proposal to abolish the purchase of commissions was considered too contentious and dropped, not to be resurrected until late in the following century.

A constitutional crisis broke out on 20 March 1751 when Cumberland's older brother, 44-year-old Frederick, Prince of Wales and heir to the throne, fell sick and died. The deceased prince's eldest son George was then just 13, and the question arose of establishing a regency should his grandfather, George II, die before the young boy reached maturity. Cumberland was the obvious choice for such a role and the king supported the suggestion, but Parliament would not approve it and so the dowager Princess Augusta, Frederick's widow, was nominated to be regent with the advice and assistance of a council, the head of which was, of course, Cumberland. The duke, however, rightly felt that he had been pointlessly slighted by Parliament. He found solace in his passion for hunting and horse-racing, and in making wide-ranging improvements to Windsor Great Park where he was Head Ranger, as well as being Lord Warden and Head Ranger of Windsor Forest. In November 1751 Cumberland suffered a bad fall from his horse, with the wags in the London coffee houses claiming that the horse had almost certainly just given up and collapsed under his increasing weight. Severe bruising and internal bleeding were the result, and the old wound to his leg gave renewed concern; for a short time his life was despaired of, but he slowly recovered.

Concern with what was regarded as French ambitions and encroachment in both North America and southern India grew during this period, and Cumberland arranged to send Major General Edward Braddock with two regiments from the Irish Establishment, to help counter the activities of the Marquis de Duquesne in the American backwoods. Braddock was carefully briefed by Cumberland on what was to be achieved, but it appears he paid little attention and his expedition came to grief – with Braddock killed and his force dispersed – in an ambush just 7 miles from his objective, the French-held Fort Duquesne. Outright hostilities between Great Britain and France having been renewed, attempts to defeat a French attack on the island of Minorca were unsuccessful, and Admiral John Byng was shot on the quarterdeck of his own flagship in March 1757 for the failure, for which he bore only partial responsibility. Cumberland urged clemency for the disgraced admiral, but in vain – an example was to be set to deflect criticism from the government of the day, and that was Byng's fate. Versailles, meanwhile, had agreed a treaty with Austria, and then with Russia; Frederick II of Prussia, under imminent threat of encirclement, acted first and invaded Saxony, and by doing so precipitated the Seven Years War. In effect, what had been a long and imperfect truce agreed under the Treaty of Aix-la-Chapelle fell to pieces, and the contending armies set out on campaign once more. Parliament in London having voted funds for the necessary defence of Hanover, plans were laid for an Army of Observation to be formed with British, Hanoverian, Hessian and Prussian troops stationed on the river Weser.

The duke had been active in preparing defences in southern England against a likely French invasion attempt, but on 10 April 1757 he sailed from Harwich to take command of the troops gathered to campaign in defence of Hanover. Despite a renewed period of ill-health, his old leg wound continuing to give trouble, the Prussian king had urged that Cumberland be given the appointment, and George II with some reluctance agreed. The duke was also hesitant, as the interests of Frederick II by no means coincided closely with the interests of either Hanover or Great Britain. Nonetheless, he landed at the mouth of the river Elbe and travelled overland to Hanover, where on 18 April almost nothing was found to be ready in preparation for active campaigning. The 'Army of Observation' as it was known comprised some 50,000 troops in all, and even when made ready to take the field the Prussian contingent was under orders just to defend their king's territory and nothing more.

The veteran French commander the Duc d'Estrées, newly created a Marshal of France, advanced with a 100,000-strong army on 1 May 1757, and Cumberland in response marched to confront them between Paderborn and Bielefeld in Westphalia. The French approach, for all d'Estrées' numerical superiority, was slow and ill-disciplined. For several weeks not much happened, but early in June Cumberland, while labouring under the handicap of a heavy asthma attack, had to fall back to avoid an attempt at encirclement by his opponent. Some Prussian regiments were mauled during the rearward movement towards Hameln on the river Weser, but a French advanced guard came on too far and too fast and suffered heavy losses in the scrambled fighting. All plans were upset when news arrived that the Prussian main army had been heavily defeated at Kolin by the Austrians, and every regiment Frederick II had under arms was under orders to be withdrawn from campaigning with Cumberland and gathered ready to defend the approaches to Prussia itself – any semblance of allied unity fell away as a result.

Stripped of such support, the duke faced the French at Hastenbek just to the south-west of Hameln. On 26 July 1757 the opposing armies clashed in a confused and piecemeal battle, where each commander variously considered himself successful or beaten as garbled and inaccurate reports came in. Cumberland was, of course, badly outnumbered, but the French marshal did not make the most of his advantage. The duke showed considerable skill in a hopeless cause on the field, holding d'Estrées off, but the French General Chevert turned his left flank with an innovative night march across unknown and wooded hilly country. The following morning Cumberland sent in a well handled counter-attack to drive Chevert back, and this was achieved after heavy fighting, but at the same time the batteries in the centre of his army's position were being overrun. Although counter-attacks restored the position more than once, Cumberland could see that his army was fought out and able to do little more. 'The Brunswick and Hessian troops were most exposed and bore for six hours the severest cannonade that all the generals say they have ever heard.'[7] Orders were given to withdraw, a movement which was accomplished in good order, with comparatively modest losses in the circumstances of some 1,200 casualties; d'Estrées failed completely to make the most of his hard-won success, and partly as a consequence he was soon replaced as the French army commander.

Cumberland's army fell back along its own lines of supply and communication towards the river Elbe. This much was sensible and showed appropriate caution, but the move in the process exposed to the French the available road to Hanover. The strategic aim to cover the electorate had plainly failed, but despite this George II wrote to his son in terms of clear regard and anxiety:

> I hear with great concern your leg is not well and your health not of the best. Pray take care of a life that is both so dear and so necessary for me; and when you have settled everything, come to a father that esteems and loves you dearly.[8]

Cumberland had already been granted wide powers to negotiate a truce, or perhaps even a permanent peace, to save Hanover, Brunswick and Hesse-Cassel from invasion and depredation at the hands of the French. His new opponent, the Duc de Richelieu, yet another veteran of Fontenoy, was still able to deploy troops in such numbers that he could no longer be seriously challenged. Negotiations between Cumberland and de Richelieu for a truce began on 3 September 1757, and five days later the terms of the soon-to-be-notorious Convention of Kloster Zeven were agreed. Despite the bleak circumstances in which he found himself, the duke achieved a good deal, saving his army from another almost certain defeat, with the Brunswick and Hessian soldiers permitted to return to their homes for the winter, although the Hanoverians had to find sanctuary in friendly Danish territory. At heart, though, Hanover was now laid open to the French as a means for directly marching onwards against Prussia, although as usual many of Louis XV's officers felt that the terms of the convention were unduly lenient towards Cumberland.

Within a week George II had heard of the convention and taken alarm at (and heeded bad advice over) the strategic situation in northern Germany. He wrote to urge his son to march his army eastwards to combine with Frederick II and continue the campaign. This was nonsense and bore no relation to the bleak facts on the ground; Cumberland had with much credit fought a hard campaign with insufficient resources, and could have done no more, short of courting a more complete disaster than it already was. All the same, when the king learned the details of what had actually been agreed at Kloster Zeven he was furious, though his son's viable alternative options were not at all clear, and concern that the Prussians were being left in the lurch had to be tempered when it was found that Frederick II was already trying to negotiate a separate peace for himself regardless of what happened to Hanover, Brunswick or Hesse-Cassel. 'If England should have the least mind of it all would be lost,' Frederick wrote to one of his ministers.[9] As it was, Prussian fortunes would revive, but Hanover and her immediate allies would, it seems, play little further active part in the war – as time would show, this was quite misleading.

Cumberland was understandably dismayed at his father's reaction to the terms of the convention, but was adamant that the fate of Hanover was now no worse than it would have been had no agreement been reached with de Richelieu, and instead his own army defeated and scattered. He was characteristically not bashful in expressing this view when he returned to London on 11 October, and seemed after careful reflection to feel no regrets at all at the course he had been obliged to take. After a furious altercation with his father, at which the older man stumped out of the room in a fit of temper when Cumberland refused to be brow-beaten and express remorse, the duke calmly resigned all his official appointments. 'There is nothing so difficult than to maintain a wise and disdainful silence under unmerited disgrace.'[10] Although Cumberland's political opponents, envious always of his hitherto strong popularity with his father, made much of the affair, many others thought the king's reaction to be overwrought, and the distinguished politician William Pitt commented on Cumberland's actions that he had full authority to do as he saw fit. Sir John Ligonier, a capable and safe pair of hands, was nominated to replace the duke as Commander-in-Chief of the British army, but there would never again, it proved, be a captain general.

George II soon regretted his intemperate outburst of anger with his son, but Cumberland was not to be easily coaxed back; the damage done went too deep and he refused the king's offer of reinstatement in his appointment as Colonel of the 1st English Foot Guards. By strange irony, of course, the Duc de Richelieu was much criticised in France for agreeing terms at Kloster Zeven that were too lenient, and that Hanoverian troops were, in fact, free to go on campaigning when they left Denmark and were fit to do so. The undeniably good condition in which Cumberland had left them meant that they could take the field again before very long, under the command of Ferdinand of Brunswick, the Prussian king's brother-in-law. 'The Duke of Cumberland always said that he had been most unjustly praised for Culloden, and most unjustly depreciated for his capitulation at Kloster Zeven; so upon the whole, he considered justice had been done to him.'[11] That William Augustus possessed a certain wry sense of humour, even in adversity, was evident.

The war trundled on, with British troops particularly active in North America, Canada and India, and what success they enjoyed owed much to the reforms hard-won by Cumberland against vested interests, both in the army and in Parliament, in previous years. That he was now aged just 36 and effectively in retirement was certainly regretted by many in the army and some in Parliament, and a pamphlet circulated amongst officers, a number of whom had once resented his efforts at army reform, read:

> Our army is greatly improved in points of discipline, for which we are obliged to the duke, and indeed nothing less than a person of H.R.H.'s authority could ever have removed our prejudice in favour of our licentiousness which we erroneously called liberty.[12]

Cumberland's ill-health plagued him more than ever – he was, of course, very overweight, asthmatic and suffering still from his damaged knee, so much so that he could no longer hunt comfortably from the saddle, although he took great interest in horse racing and the breeding of better English bloodstock, and was instrumental in the foundation of the Jockey Club.

The year 1759 appeared to be one of great achievements for British fortunes in the ongoing war, with successes in India and North America, and most notably perhaps at the battles of Minden in Westphalia in August, and along the Saint Lawrence river in French Canada that September. A fresh invasion scare arose when it seemed that the French might attempt a landing in southern England, but Cumberland refused any suggestion that he should take command of the militia, his reaction to the suggestion being both firm and heavy with world-weary cynicism: 'I do not believe that the command will be offered to me but when no wise man could accept it and no honest man would refuse it.'[13] As it was,

Admiral Hawke destroyed the French fleet in Quiberon Bay in October, and the prospect of an invasion was for many years no longer a viable prospect.

In August 1760 Cumberland suffered a mild stroke, and had yet to fully recover when he learned on 25 October that his father, George II, had died after a heart attack. The duke's young nephew, King George III, soon had to face war with Spain, the monarch in Madrid, Carlos III, having agreed on 19 December 1761 a Bourbon 'family compact' with Louis XV to enter the conflict against Great Britain. Whatever calculations the king and his ministers in Madrid had worked out proved to be faulty, and Spain fared badly in the fighting, losing Havana to a British expeditionary force in September the following year. Feelers for a negotiated peace were going out from Versailles in the meantime, and George III discussed the proposed peace terms with his uncle in detail. Cumberland found much to dislike in what had been tentatively agreed in Paris by the Duke of Bedford, in particular the lack of guarantees for Frederick II of Prussia, inconstant and self-seeking perhaps but still felt to be Great Britain's ally. Nonetheless the terms were agreed after a bitterly argued debate took place in Parliament in London, and the Peace of Paris was signed in February 1763.

The duke remained in official retirement, but offered well judged advice on the difficult political currents of the day. He still enjoyed racing and bloodstock breeding, and undertook to supervise further extensive landscape gardening at Windsor and Virginia Water in Berkshire and Surrey. Cumberland had another stroke in 1764 and, despite his doctor's advice, attended race meetings at Newmarket that autumn, but he suffered from increasing pain in his injured leg, which had developed an abscess; an operation to drain the wound of infection was necessary. Although only partly recovered, he insisted on attending a ball soon afterwards and had yet another stroke; despite this, he was able to assist the king in the forming of a new administration and to offer advice over the growing trouble in the American colonies. On 31 October 1765 the Duke of Cumberland complained of a pain in his shoulder, and then collapsed at his home in London and died, apparently from a blood clot to the brain, aged just 44. A man of many good qualities, highly regarded in his lifetime by allies and opponents alike, but little valued or well remembered since, passed from the scene. The duke's funeral on 9 November, as that of the son of a king, was a grand affair, with eight general officers bearing the canopy over the heavy coffin as it was taken to the Henry VIII Chapel in Westminster Abbey.

The Duke of Cumberland's reputation would in time be traduced unfairly, mainly by those with Jacobite sympathies – those who whimsically looked forward (or backwards) to the ruinous turmoil of a Stuart restoration in London, perhaps a return to the old supposedly sylvan days of clan life in the Highlands. The duke's great misfortune as a battlefield commander was, of course, to face Maurice Saxe at Fontenoy, plainly a far better and more experienced general. It would be absurd to suggest that the two men were evenly matched – still, that Cumberland for all his lack of a 'feel' for the battlefield came so close to success on that fateful day in May 1745 says a great deal for his abilities and courage, no matter what his merits or demerits may have been as an army commander. A witty anecdote by a French officer, who claimed not to wish to take the duke prisoner, as he was of more use to them by remaining in command of the allied army, may be taken with a generous pinch of salt – his conduct in command at Lauffeldt two years later attracted much praise, unlike Saxe. Someone could be a good soldier without being a great commander, and William Augustus, Duke of Cumberland, had energy and talent not only as a soldier, but also as an army reformer and administrator interested and active in promoting the well-being of his men. 'To transform the fashions of a profession is harder than to succeed in one hundred campaigns, for it requires an enthusiasm for the drudgery of detail.'[14] In addition, the duke had been of great assistance to his nephew, the young George III, at a difficult time of political turmoil. Arguably, Cumberland had done more than any other to prepare the British army for its many successes in future decades, and to that end he would be sadly missed and deserved to be better remembered. In truth, it could be said of him that he was 'Often impatient, sometimes haughty, occasionally guilty of misjudgement, he nevertheless served the crown and the country with indefatigable energy and sense.'[15]

Chapter 5

Gallant Lieutenants – Löwendahl, Waldeck, Königsegg and Ligonier

To fully appreciate the campaign and battle of Fontenoy it is necessary to at least glance in the direction of some of the senior subordinates who supported the efforts of the two army commanders, men upon whose diverse talents the fortunes of the day in large part rested. King Louis XV was on the field, of course, with his son, but his direction of the battle was at best slight, and he may even have got in the way, so he has not been included in these brief histories.

Marshal Saxe's principal subordinate in May 1745 was Ulrich-Frederick Waldemar, Count von Löwendahl (1700–1755). Born in Hamburg of Danish parents, and entering the service of the Habsburg Emperor Charles VI as a cadet at the surprisingly tender age of just 13 years old, he transferred to a Danish-recruited regiment, hired out to the emperor, the following year. In 1716, having attained the rank of captain, the young man fought at the battles of Peterwarden and Temesvar against the Ottoman Turks, and had already established a good reputation for skill and daring as a commander. He was naturally impetuous, but his deft and instinctive handling of cavalry was noted, and the following year he was present at the capture of Belgrade.

Five years later Löwendahl transferred to the service of the Elector of Saxony, with the rank of colonel. Partly due to the influence of Saxe, this skilled soldier of fortune progressed rapidly in the Saxon army, and by the 1730s had become the Inspector-General of Infantry. He served in the defence of Cracow during the War of the Polish Succession, and commanded the Saxon forces on the Rhine in 1734. After transferring his service to that of the Russian Tsar, he fought against the Ottomans once again at the battle of Khatyn in 1739, and then against the Swedes in the Baltic region between 1741 and 1743. Later that year Saxe was able to persuade Löwendhal to transfer to French service, although this entailed a drop in rank to that of Lieutenant General of Infantry, but he was authorised by Louis XV to raise a 'foreign' German-speaking regiment of his own.

The count's successes in Flanders in 1744, which included the capture of allied-held Menin, secured his reputation with the French and he fought valiantly and to good effect at Fontenoy in 1745. His competent handling of the reserve regiments on the left of the French position, and their effective deployment at the moment of crisis, contributed greatly to Saxe's success that day. Whatever crisis the marshal faced, he was sure that his left flank was in good hands. Löwendahl subsequently very successfully seized both Oudenarde and Ghent, where his quick thinking and rapid marching clearly outmatched the abilities of his opponents. However, in 1747 he proved unable (or unwilling) to control his troops as they stormed the defences of Bergen-op-Zoom and pillaged the town. Although this outrage attracted a great deal of criticism, Louis XV soon afterwards created Löwendhal a Marshal of France, only the second Protestant ever (after Saxe) to hold that rank. The king ruefully commented that he had either to promote him or sack him, after the disgraceful affair of Bergen-op-Zoom, and he preferred to do the former. The count was, however, ailing, worn out with hard campaigning, and died soon afterwards.

Commander of the Dutch troops at Fontenoy, Karl-August Freidrich, Furst von Waldeck-Pyrmont (Waldeck) was the second son of Freidrich-Anton-Ulrich, Graf von Waldeck-Pyrmont. He was born in Hanau in 1704, and like so many of his family before him entered foreign military service as a profession suitable for a nobleman without great prospects. Having served as a cadet in the French army, he transferred to the Prussian service, but in 1728 succeeded to the dignity of prince and count on the deaths of both his father and, unexpectedly, his older brother. Engaged in the War of the Polish Succession (1733–1738), the young nobleman fought alongside the redoubtable Prince Eugene in imperial service at the battle of Klausen in October 1735, and went on to serve against the Ottoman Turks in south-eastern Europe. In 1739 he was wounded in the dire campaign that led to Vienna's loss of Belgrade, although two years later he was made General of Infantry in the imperial army. Over the whole period the prince gradually established a good reputation as a commander, whose energy and tactical sense could be relied on.

In 1744 Waldeck was appointed to the command of the Dutch troops forming part of the allied army, a move that was not without controversy as a number of Dutch generals, with whom he would have to campaign, aspired to that same role. This friction, in particular that with van Cronstrom, led to less than perfect harmony and cooperation amongst the Dutch commanders, and contributed to some degree to their lack of success on the day of battle at Fontenoy. However, Waldeck had his own orders from The Hague to heed, not just those coming from the Duke of Cumberland, and having avoided excessive casualties in adverse circumstances he withdrew his troops in good order with the loss of no guns, even though the conduct of some of his cavalry was rather shaky. Despite criticism of his performance, he was created an imperial field marshal in 1746, remaining in command of the Dutch troops fighting on behalf on Maria-Theresa, and was present at the battle of Rocoux. The following year he fought at Lauffeldt, where his conduct was again criticised for no very good reason, and was subsequently and rather unfairly relieved of his command. Waldeck died in 1763.

Empress Maria-Theresa's commander in the Low Countries, Field Marshal Lother-Joseph-Dominik, Graf von Königsegg-Rothenfels (Königsegg), was born in May 1673 and educated at a seminary at Besancon in France. He began a career in the church in 1689 as part of the household of the Prince-Archbishop of Salzburg and was then sent to the Vatican to complete his training. Instead, in 1691 he absented himself and travelled to Hungary to enlist as a cadet volunteer, subsequently gaining a commission as an officer in the Hohenzollern cuirassier regiment, fighting in one of the frequent wars waged against the Ottoman Turks. After serving under Prince Eugene in northern Italy during the War of the Spanish Succession, and distinguishing himself at the relief of Turin in 1706, Königsegg was put in charge of the fortification of Mantua. At the close of hostilities in 1713 he proved to be a skilful diplomat, effective in maintaining Austrian interests during the complex negotiations to achieve the peace terms agreed at the Treaty of Rastadt (1714). Königsegg was then appointed commander of the imperial forces in what would become known as the Austrian Netherlands, a post he held until 1717.

In that year Königsegg was made General of Infantry, and served on diplomatic duties in Paris, Warsaw, The Hague and Madrid before becoming a field marshal in 1723 and Vice-President of the Imperial War Council in Vienna three years later. Campaigning in northern Italy once more, during the War of the Polish Succession, he gained initial successes against the French and Spanish but was defeated at the battle of Guastalla in September 1734 and forced back into the Tyrol region, where he resigned his command. On the death of Prince Eugene in 1736, he was appointed President of the Imperial War Council, but in 1737 went on campaign in command of imperial forces against the Ottomans. Severely defeated, Königsegg once more gave up his command and resigned from military duties. Largely through influence at court with Maria-Theresa, he managed to avoid the opprobrium and punishments that were meted out to some of his senior colleagues for the abject failures in the campaign, and served as the military governor of Vienna during the early part of the War of the Austrian Succession, adroitly negotiating the terms of the French withdrawal from Prague in 1743. Königsegg was sent to the Low Countries as the commander of the meagre imperial forces there the following year. In this role he was, in effect, an adviser to the Duke of Cumberland when he assumed the command of the allied army in April 1745, and he offered generally good advice, but was both elderly and infirm and well past his best when out on campaign. Despite this, he showed conspicuous courage under fire at the duke's side at Fontenoy and was unseated from his horse at one critical point. After the battle he largely retired from public life and died in Vienna in December 1751, an old soldier who had given good service but perhaps shone more at the diplomatic negotiating table than ever he did on the battlefield.

Prominent amongst Cumberland's commanders on the day was Lieutenant General Sir John Ligonier. Born Jean-Louis de Ligonier in 1680 in Castres near Toulouse, his family as Huguenots were obliged to take refuge abroad following the revocation of the Edict of Nantes in 1685 by Louis XIV. In 1702 Ligonier was naturalised as an Englishman, and by the following year had gained a captaincy in North and Grey's Regiment. He fought in all of the campaigns of the Duke of Marlborough, being awarded a bounty of £30 sterling for his services at Blenheim in 1704, and became a major after the battle of Ramillies in 1706. During the fighting at Malplaquet in 1709 twenty-two French musket balls reportedly passed through the skirts of Ligonier's coat but he remained unharmed.

In 1710 Ligonier was appointed to the staff of the British army campaigning in Spain, becoming a lieutenant colonel in Phillip's Regiment in 1711. The following year he was appointed Adjutant-General and then Lieutenant-Governor of Minorca, which Great Britain retained at the Treaty of Utrecht in 1713. Not actively engaged during the 1715 and 1719 Jacobite risings, Ligonier was made Colonel of the 8th Horse (Black's) in 1720, and largely due to his influence the regiment had a fine reputation for smartness and horsemanship. He enjoyed the trust and confidence of King George I, becoming a Gentleman of the Privy Chamber in 1724 and an aide-de-camp to his son when he succeeded to the throne as George II. Ligonier was also active in promoting the interests of promising young officers, and notable amongst these must be Jeffrey Amherst, subsequently famous for his victories in North America and Canada, who served as a young man in the 8th Horse and enjoyed Ligonier's patronage. Promotion to brigadier general came to Ligonier in 1736, and to major general in 1739, and three years later Ligonier was appointed to the command of the Danish and Hessian troops hired to assist in the defence of Hanover as the War of the Austrian Succession gathered pace. After serving at Dettingen as a lieutenant general, he was General of Foot under Cumberland at Fontenoy two years later and behaved with conspicuous and aggressive gallantry. Acting as commander-in-chief in Flanders in 1746, Ligonier fought at Rocoux, and was taken prisoner the next year at Lauffeldt, where his skilful handling of the cavalry rear-guard saved the allied army from catastrophe.

With the peace, Ligonier commenced a career in politics and became Member of Parliament for Bath in 1748, but was made field marshal and *de facto* commander-in-chief on the resignation of Cumberland in 1757, following the royal concern over the terms of the Convention of Kloster-Zeven. His well considered and impartial influence and advice were widely appreciated, and he established friendly relations in both government and military circles, being created Baron Ligonier (and subsequently Earl) in 1763. Although he never married, Ligonier was fond of female company and in time became something of an elderly roué and raffish man about town. He notoriously took an action against *The Times* newspaper for publishing his age in a report, and thereby apparently dashing his hopes of marrying a much younger heiress, but the action failed on the grounds that the paper had simply told the truth. Highly regarded, companiable, gregarious and with few if any real enemies, John Ligonier, the only ever French-born field marshal of the British Army, died at his home in London in 1770.

PART II
A MOST BLOODY BATTLE

Chapter 6

Tournai – the Great Fortress on the Scheldt

The Gateway into Flanders.[1]

Much attention in the year 1744 had been taken up with what proved to be an attempt to carry out an invasion of England on behalf of Prince Charles Edward Stuart, the Jacobite 'Young Pretender' to the throne of Great Britain. The prince would have arrived on behalf of his father, of course, the son of the late James II who had gone into exile in France in the 1680s. The plan was poorly managed and ill thought-out, and promoted principally by the French king's principal adviser, Cardinal Tencin. Whatever the prelate's spiritual virtues, he was no great strategist, seeming to firmly believe that a determined landing by French troops in England would spark a Stuart uprising to unseat George II and install a Stuart pro-French monarch in London in his stead. Such a fantasy would be shown to be nonsense in the following year, but all that was yet to come.

All the same, some 15,000 French soldiers were mustered and transports and naval escorts made ready at Dunkirk for the troops' embarkation, and Marshal Saxe was appointed to the command of the expedition. The veteran soldier perhaps understandably showed little enthusiasm for the project; in any case, the inconvenient presence of a British naval squadron patrolling off the French coast delayed plans for setting off even after the embarkation of the troops, and strong gales in the Channel added to the problems once the ships were under way. A number of the transports were driven ashore in the stormy seas, with some soldiers and sailors drowned, and the survivors limped back into Dunkirk in a sorry state. Recriminations flowed but, for the time being, any fresh attempt at invading the British Isles with a Stuart proxy as figurehead had to wait.

The Treaty of the Quadruple Alliance agreed in Warsaw in January 1745 to push forward the cause of Maria-Theresa and her husband in the war contained, amongst its many provisions, one clause which increased the subsidy to be paid to Vienna to £500,000 sterling. Such a magnificent sum for the time was expected to enable the raising, training and equipping of an additional 50,000 Austrian troops for the coming campaign. Holland was to provide 52,000 men, and Great Britain and Hanover 40,000 more, including foreign enlisted troops such as the ever-reliable Hessians. Rather inconveniently, Maria-Theresa had withdrawn most of her own regiments from the Low Countries in order both to bolster the defence of the Austrian heartland and to pursue adventures in northern Italy, so the defence of her territories in north-western Europe she quietly entrusted almost entirely to her allies.

Much criticised for his lack of determined action (not without justification), Field Marshal Wade retired to London in November 1744 and John, 2nd Earl of Stair, prudently declined to take up the post as commander – given his age and rickety state of health this was perhaps wise. He was also not an acceptable choice to the Austrians with whom he had a tendency to quarrel. The thorny question of who was to command the allied army in the Low Countries was settled by the agreement that this should be William Augustus, Duke of Cumberland. He would have at his side to assist and offer advice Sir John Ligonier, Field Marshal Königsegg-Rothenfels (longing for the comfortable retirement that Maria-Theresa would not permit), and the Dutch field commander, the Prince of Waldeck-Pyrmont. The subsidiary but implicit task of the last named two men was also to ensure that their own soldiers (rather few in the case of Königsegg) were not put at undue risk by the actions of this British commander-in-chief. General Joseph Wendt was also on hand to keep an eye on the well-being of the Hanoverian troops. Cumberland was, perhaps, a surprising choice, as he was only thirty-sixth on the British army's list of general officers, but he was the king's son and that counted for a good deal. As a royal prince he also had an implicit authority when dealing with allies, so the choice was not without its merits. The appointment of Cumberland was confirmed by an entry in the *London Gazette* on 12 March 1745 (OS). As often with coalition warfare, this arrangement between the four highly opinionated men, although apparently on the best of terms, would impose strains and restraints on the freedom of choice and action of any army commander, however gifted or otherwise. Marshal Saxe was not quite so constrained, although he would have his king at his elbow on the day of battle, not an unmixed blessing, and there were other inconveniences that would chafe him along the way.

Cumberland arrived at The Hague on 17 April 1745 to take up the command: 'I met with a very friendly reception from the government', he wrote, 'and was spared many points of ceremony which I should be very glad to dispense with.' Of his fellow commanders, the duke went on:

> My intentions are to imitate his [Königsegg's] example, as well as to follow his advice; and I persuade myself there is a sure foundation laid for a thoroughly good understanding between us. I have good reason to be satisfied with the Prince of Waldeck and [Hanoverian] General Wendt, and I promise myself great advantage to the general cause by their good disposition.[2]

Saxe, meanwhile, unwell with chronic dropsy (oedema swelling of the limbs) and thus short-tempered, had set out his plans for the campaign that summer. In an attempt to avoid the near stalemate of the previous year, he advised Louis XV that his intention was to provoke the allies at some sensitive spot, some prize worth fighting for, and by so doing to draw them out to fight in the open.

By taking the initiative the marshal expected to steal a march on his opponents, and fight them on ground of his choosing. Saxe understood that the aim of the war, at this point, was to divide the enemy forces in Flanders, to give the Dutch something to worry about, and cause George II to be concerned about his electorate of Hanover. The French king approved the plan outlined, and Saxe arrived in Valenciennes on 15 April; the Army of Flanders, having spent the winter in quarters around Courtrai, was then gathering in the vicinity of his new headquarters in the fortress town of Mauberge, not far from the site of the infamously bloody 1709 battle of Malplaquet in which he had participated as a young man, even if it had been from the security of the baggage park. On the face of things the French army was in good order, well equipped and with regiments that were fully manned, but many of the rank and file soldiery were newly mustered and rather lacking in experience.

Despite the trail of successes of 1744, the morale of the French army after the dismal failure at Dettingen was uncertain, although the worst example had surely been that set by the commanders on the day, and the marshal was not too sure that he could trust his troops to manoeuvre well under pressure. He had also to contend with a number of subordinate commanders whose reputations were suspect at the least – those who had held prominent commands at the débâcle at Dettingen ranked high amongst these, while others of limited ability enjoyed royal favour and had to be tolerated as a result. Such a problem was not unique to the French army of course, favourites being favourites and all that entails, but almost unique must surely be the Comte de Clermont, who was bluntly forbidden by Louis XV, under any circumstances and no matter what, to issue orders to the troops he had under command. At the same time Saxe had the services of such excellent men as Count von Löwendahl, effectively his second in command of the field army, with the Marquis de Lutteaux and the Vicomte de Chayla as senior aides. The marshal could also have asked for no better chief of staff than the dependable Louis-Hyacinth de Crémille.

Saxe was not alone in having to cope with strong-willed and even insubordinate officers; John Lindsay, Earl of Crawfurd, who would have to take the command of the British cavalry at Fontenoy, responded to one instruction that didn't immediately appeal to him, 'I shall obey orders when it suits most proper.'[3] For all that, Crawfurd was a gifted commander and held in high regard. Richard Davenport remembered of him that he gave great spirit and encouragement to his men, who would have followed him anywhere – that such capabilities should not be put to more use on 11 May 1745 remains one of the tantalising puzzles of Fontenoy.

On 18 April Saxe joined the army with his senior commanders, several promising options having presented themselves to his fertile mind: he could move eastwards along the line of the river Sambre and threaten Huy and Liège on the Meuse, while a tempting alternative was to go further and put the great allied depot and fortress of Maastricht at risk. However, to move that way would lay open the left flank of the French army to attack while on the line of march, and although with hindsight that appears to be only a faint possibility, Saxe was not yet to know that this kind of bold counter-stroke was not what his opponents would attempt. To move against Tournai on the Scheldt would avoid such a risk, while promising rich rewards, as the loss of that place would threaten to hobble the allied campaign, and might get them to stand and fight for its security. Of course, Saxe was not that anxious for such a confrontation, unless the odds were in his favour, as the performance of the French army at Dettingen had not given reason for optimism. Marshal Noailles had written after that defeat that his infantry had been under a murderous fire: 'The old officers had never seen anything like it, and so superior to ours one could not make any comparison.'[4] Alternatively, the French commander could strike deeper along the line of the river Scheldt, and menace Oudenarde. To best achieve that aim, though, the capture of Tournai on that river line was advisable, to remove it as a supply base for the allied campaign. Success there would also break open the allied dispositions, and allow the French to strike north not only to Oudenarde, but towards Ghent and Bruges.

The choice of Tournai as the initial objective in the campaign that summer was a good one, as might be expected of such a veteran as Saxe. To take the fortress would give his army almost unfettered access to the course of the Scheldt as it flowed northwards, with the enticing prospect of a subsequent advance. With the line of the river in French hands, the defence formed by the Ghent–Bruges canal (which the Duc de Vendôme had used to such good effect in late 1708) would be broken, and such important places for the allies as Ostend and Antwerp laid under threat. In that case, British communications with the ports in southern and eastern England would be cut, while the southern border of Holland was exposed. The marshal's initial aim in the campaign, therefore, was indeed to threaten Tournai, itself a masterpiece of design by the late Marshal Vauban. With an expected superiority in numbers, Saxe could, at least for the opening phase in the campaign, dictate the pace of operations. All this should not, in fact, have been a great surprise to the allies; a British officer who had read the intelligence reports brought into Ghent wrote early in February 1745, that 'Hitherto they are all very quiet, their usual way of talk is the same everywhere of all the great things they are to do ... they talk of attacking Tournai.'[5]

As a precaution, strong and well provisioned allied garrisons had been put into Mons, Tournai, Namur, Ath and Charleroi, although this inevitably reduced the strength of the field army, to just under 45,000 troops, even allowing for the belated arrival of some Hessian reinforcements. Cumberland, having made these arrangements, reviewed the assembled army at Anderlecht to the south-west of Brussels, and professed himself well satisfied with their bearing, equipment and training. Maria-Theresa still felt able to provide only six under-strength squadrons of cavalry and some independent companies of infantry to help defend her possessions in the Low Countries. 'We shall assemble the army early,' Sir John Ligonier wrote. 'If we are stronger, we shall immediately enter upon action; if weaker, we must try to hinder them from anything.'[6] Despite such rather optimistic good intentions, the French commander could at this point field many more troops than his opponents, and at least on paper outmatch whatever the allies could throw against him.

However, any advantage in numbers would be considerably reduced once the formal siege of Tournai or any other substantial fortress was begun, with large demands on available manpower being made to undertake the operations in the trenches themselves. An army that was engaged in a formal siege routinely operated in two complementary parts: the investing force to carry out the siege, and the army of observation to cover those operations. This dilution in the strength of the French field army by having to maintain substantial numbers in the siege trenches, even allowing for the use of impressed civilian labour, was offset by the necessity for their opponents to maintain several fortress garrisons simultaneously to ensure their security. These could only be drawn on once the actual area of most threat became evident, and quick decision-making and rapid marching would be needed to concentrate in full strength. The more active and enterprising the field army, however, the less need there was for maintaining large and immobile garrisons which may never hear a shot fired in anger, so in this respect it may be said that Saxe's way of thinking was rather ahead of that of his opponents.

Decision-making in the allied camp had so far lacked a deal of focus. Until the Duke of Cumberland came to take up his appointment as captain general and *de facto* army commander, the principal aim had been to simply protect the fortresses that in theory guarded the borders of Holland but did little else. Once the duke was in post, which did not happen until almost the same day that the French army set out on their advance into the Austrian Netherlands, a mistaken assumption amongst the allied commanders of their own numerical superiority led both Cumberland and Waldeck to adopt an aggressive forward posture. They aimed to brush the French aside, relieve Tournai or Mons, whichever was under most threat, and perhaps then move against some exposed French fortress, such as Mauberge, and so oblige Saxe to fall back. 'The allies concentrated in the neighbourhood of Brussels and had the pleasing prospect of endeavouring to hold not only Flanders and Brabant, but also Hainault and the line of the Sambre with a force far inferior to that of the enemy.'[7] Plainly, too great a front was being maintained with too few troops, and the allies by their miscalculations were strong nowhere.

So much for good intentions, for Saxe feinted successfully towards Mons, sending a detachment of troops under the Comte d'Estrées on that road, and Cumberland's attention was quite naturally drawn in that direction. The governor of Mons reported in some agitation that his outposts had been driven in by the French, and he expected that a siege of the fortress was only a matter of time. This was not so, as nothing happened other than perhaps a trifling affair, as the marshal then adroitly switched direction. Moving swiftly, despite poor weather which hampered the army's marching speed, by 28 April the very capable Duc d'Harcourt had invested the 7,000-strong Dutch- and Swiss-recruited garrison in Tournai. The Marquis de Dreux-Brézé was entrusted with the command of a subsidiary force that took possession of the left bank of the river in order to push forward the main effort of the siege, while maintaining contact with d'Harcourt on the right bank by means of newly laid pontoon bridges around the villages of Calonnes and Cherq. This much having been achieved, d'Estrées was summoned from his role in threatening Mons to join the main army. All this was well known to Cumberland within two days, although it is often reported that he was in some doubt for longer.

In Tournai, the joint Dutch garrison commanders, Baron van Dort and Major General van Brakel, were capable and honest men, but neither was very well and both were past their prime; certainly they had been taken by surprise by the sudden French approach. In fairness, it should be said that Cumberland, Waldeck and Königsegg were also initially taken unawares by this turn of events, although the sheer size and scale of the French siege train, with all its vast stock of stores and associated impedimenta, must have been hard to miss as it trundled slowly along the muddy country roads of Flanders towards Tournai. It is hard not to conclude that the allied commanders were less alert than was really required at such a critically early point in the campaign.

The French siege operation, initially under the overall command of von Löwendahl, formally began on the night of 30 April, with trenches being opened opposite the two massive horn-works covering the gates of Lille and Seven Fountains. The complex and laborious procedure began: the digging and preparing of approach and parallel trenches, and gun and mortar battery positions, and the collecting and stockpiling of munitions and stores. The French engineers clearly knew their business well, and matters proceeded swiftly until they had completed their second parallel of siege entrenchments. Seven batteries of siege guns and mortars began to pound the defenders, who, it should be said, responded as vigorously as their rather limited means allowed. Their cause was not helped by the defection on 9 May of the Dutch engineer-in-chief, Colonel van Hertslet, together with Sluice-master Schmidt (who regulated the level of water in the defensive ditch). Sabotage of the works under their care was evident, with the ditch being almost dry and at the very most presenting a mediocre obstacle to the French. There was plentiful evidence of gross neglect if not *actual* sabotage, and the evidence for either of these was pretty damning, as can be seen in a subsequent report on the deficiencies that were laid bare:

> He [van Hertslet] must have been aware that other shortcomings would come to light, for on May 9 he quitted Tournai, apparently for the French camp ... The day before the engineer's escape he directed

Sluice-master Schmidt, who followed him in flight, to remove six planks from every sluice on the side facing Hainault. He left open the great sluice below Tournai, and the water fell 3 feet, enabling the enemy to construct bridges of communication with ease. Then a great disaster occurred on Friday night, May 7, the citadel powder magazine was exploded, probably by a mine dug by a traitor ... two of our sappers have not been seen since the explosion. We all did our best to remedy our evil plight.[8]

The likely fate of the fortress and the garrison was apparently not a happy one, and the place would fall before long, unless some vigorous counter-stroke was made to drive the French away. In fact, this was an error in judgement by the allied commanders, for which there would be serious consequences, with the adoption of an unwise course of action and sombre results. The garrison in Tournai, and their veteran commander, all knew their trade and would prove their mettle, and be well worth their salt.

Nonetheless, by investing Tournai, Saxe had threatened a key point for the allies, and in the process had 'fixed' them, stripping down any choice of options to just one – how best to save the fortress. To lose the place would damage the whole allied strategic posture for the summer, put them at a disadvantage, and lay other of their fortresses, most particularly those along the Scheldt river, open to attack. Such a move would also in the process threaten to interpose a French army between the British forces and the Channel ports, and this would not have sat well with Cumberland, as his direct communications with southern England would be at risk. There was, it seemed, no comparable French fortress within practical reach that the duke could easily threaten in order to draw Saxe away from the intended siege, although Valenciennes, Mauberge or Le Quesnoy, even Arras, might appear to have been vulnerable to a really bold stroke. To do so might, it was true, lay open the allied lines of supply and communication to risk, but that same risk, if enough pressure were applied to the lines of the French in their advanced posture around Tournai, might have alarmed Saxe and his generals and yielded worthwhile dividends. Once again, much depended on who was dictating the pace of the campaign, and who was reacting to that dictation as best they could – by threatening Tournai as he had, Saxe had demonstrably taken away the freedom of action of the allied commanders, intent as they now were that the place should be relieved without delay.

Field Marshal Königsegg, with his long experience, did advise that a campaign of manoeuvre be adopted as the best course, but Cumberland was not convinced by this; it clearly weighed heavily with the duke that should the allied army stretch too far forward, Saxe might well move to cut across their lines of communication and supply back to the depots in Brussels and Antwerp. Given the well known reputation of the elderly marshal for daring, this was a possibility not to be taken lightly. It surely also figured in Saxe's own calculations of what his opponents would attempt – their natural sensitivity about those lines was bound to play a part in whatever approach they took. In any case, neither Cumberland nor Waldeck had the mental robustness and agility to really attempt such a course of manoeuvre, with any likelihood of ready success. Accordingly, just as their opponent expected, the one overriding necessity for the allies became to close with the French army covering the siege operations against Tournai. There they might either manoeuvre to turn a flank and so threaten French communications, obliging Saxe to withdraw and think again, or more dramatically engage him in battle and force his army away from the fortress. So much was obvious to a seasoned campaigner such as the marshal, and he judged rightly that Cumberland would not accept any advice to opt for the risks of manoeuvre. The duke would surely confront the French by the most direct route, and this, as it happened, lay on the road that ran through the small village of Fontenoy some 4 miles to the south-east of Tournai, and the marshal made his dispositions accordingly. His chief of staff, the able Marquis de Crémille, had already been tasked to carefully scout the ground on which the French deployment would take effect, and to direct into position a forward screen of troops to give warning of the expected allied approach.

A commander with more practical campaign experience than Cumberland would surely not have taken the course that was chosen: to attempt a frontal attack to drive a highly proficient opponent off a position which he had had time to prepare for defence. However, the duke's decision, one he shared with his fellow commanders of course, and in hindsight so questionable, can be seen to have more than an element of good sense about it. A glance at the map will show, as it must have shown the allied commanders, that to swing to the right and try to manoeuvre against the French left flank would have taken them to the road leading from Ath and Leuze into Tournai itself, and marching an army with all its guns and impedimenta across open fields would not have been practical. That road led into the heart of the French dispositions, so that far from manoeuvring Saxe out of position, such a move by the allied army would simply have shifted the focus of the coming general action from the vicinity of Fontenoy to the fields between the villages of Rumpigny and Ramcroix.

That such a shift would have been of any benefit to the allied army is not at all clear, given that Saxe could move his own troops to his left, using shorter interior lines, to counter any move of the kind. A move to their own left would have led the allies to the waters of the Scheldt.

That a wider campaign of manoeuvre might have been attempted misses the essential point: for the allies the overriding concern was that the siege of Tournai was to be lifted as soon as possible. Over all these considerations may also have hung the general feeling of distaste for the lack of vigour in the allied campaign the previous year, when so little had been attempted, let alone achieved, and for which so much criticism had both justly and unjustly been earned. A heavy hand lay, metaphorically, on the shoulders of the allied commanders, pushing them to get on with things and not dither.

For all that, whatever might have been the perils and concerns over a campaign of manoeuvre to relieve the fortress of Tournai, they surely faded in comparison to those risks adopted by the allied commanders in their chosen course of action. Frontal attacks, with no clear superiority in numbers, were not usually successful. Nor could the 'usages of war' really be cited as justification for their decision; to relieve a besieged fortress was clearly a good thing to do, but not at the expense of all other considerations. The 1st Duke of Marlborough conducted numerous difficult sieges during his career as Captain-General but never once did a French commander deem it to be expedient to attack his covering army; it was judged better to save their field army for another day and let the garrisons in the fortresses fight on for as long as they could manage. The troops in the garrison, moreover, would be fighting on ground of their own choosing, always an important military consideration, selected and prepared well in advance, so that the advantages did not always sit with the attackers. In any case, at this time the purpose of any fortress was not to hold out indefinitely – that was understood to be impossible in all but the most unusual circumstances – but instead to impose delay upon the opposing commander and thus narrow his available options and constrain his campaign. Tournai, even with its ill-maintained defences, could be said in the early summer of 1745 to be doing just that, if only Cumberland and his fellow commanders took advantage of the fact. The Dutch, however, were anxious that the fortress, the 'gateway to Flanders', should be relieved as soon as possible, and this seems, in addition to the need to be seen to be taking action, to have been the overriding consideration. A French observer wrote: 'On the news of the siege of Tournai and at the insistence of his Dutch allies, he quickened his pace [march].'[9] The allies were doing just what Saxe expected and probably hoped for, but that was not yet entirely apparent.

That Cumberland realised that his appreciation of the tactical situation over these testing days was faulty can be seen in letters he subsequently wrote, admitting that he would have been better served to have held off from an attack and instead allowed the enemy to waste their strength by throwing men against the defences. The decisions were dictated by the belief that the garrison would have to submit quickly unless relieved. In fact, the Dutch commanders in Tournai, although both hampered by ill-health and with decrepit defensive works, would put up a good fight, one that was highly commendable given the poor circumstances in which they found themselves.

These things are so simple and self-evident in hindsight. Cumberland had certainly been misled by the pretended French move against Mons, and had written to London, 'By all the intelligence I have from the different parts, the real design of the enemy is to besiege Mons.'[10] Little could be done until Saxe's true intentions were revealed but, on learning of events at Tournai, the duke was pressed by the Dutch to do something quickly to relieve the place, and his reaction was commendably prompt. He had his army on the march on 30 April, the day after news of the investment of the fortress was received, although his cavalry apparently celebrated their departure on campaign rather too well and made something of a spectacle of themselves in trying to get out of Brussels in good order: 'We have many accidents and much confusion in passing the gates,' an officer wrote, 'attended with many inconveniences, carriages are overturned, broke down, men hurt and horses lame.'[11]

Despite this inauspicious start, the troops passed through Halle to the south of Brussels and moved on to Soignies, where Cumberland was joined by additional Dutch troops and a few squadrons of Austrian cavalry and *freikorps*, released from the garrison in Mons. That there was lingering concern for the security of that fortress was evident, as this road was not the most direct route from the allied concentration area, but it gave Cumberland the chance to switch the direction of his approach if Mons and not Tournai should, even at this late stage, be attacked by Saxe. That Cumberland had paid at least some heed to von Königsegg's suggestion of a move to threaten Mauberge can, perhaps, just about be seen in this initial move towards the south. Saxe could hardly have ignored such a move, of course, although he might well have counter-marched, as 'His main source of supply was at Mauberge, some 50 miles away, and ... the best chance of success lay in cutting this communication with Mauberge.'[12] Such a course changed once the allied army left Brussels, as soon as it became clear that a formal siege of Tournai by the French had indeed begun. To say that the allied commanders were dancing to a French tune would be to exaggerate, but without doubt Saxe was still dictating the pace and shape of the campaign, and his opponents were having to react to whatever he did. The common feeling remained that something urgently had to be done to save the fortress, at whatever cost, and a British officer wrote afterwards that:

> The siege advanced so fast, that there was no time to be lost; whatever was to be done towards obliging the enemy to raise it, was necessarily to be put into execution immediately. The generals of the army looked upon raising the siege as a point of the highest concern ... though the enemy was advantageously posted, *as well as superior in number* [Author's italics]'.[13]

With progress slowed by rain, the allied army moved from the use of a single muddy road, with all the congestion and delay involved, to three parallel country tracks, and better time was made. A French advanced detachment was pushed away from Leuze-en-Hainault on 7 May, and Cumberland moved on to Moulbaix where additional Hanoverian and Dutch infantry from the garrison in Ath joined the field army. This force now comprised some 50,000 men with ninety guns, disposed in two 'wings' of broadly equal strength under the respective commands of Cumberland and Waldeck.[14] Although the pace of the march cannot really be said to have been rapid, the duke seemed to feel that his confident approach would induce Saxe to raise the siege and fall back. 'I cannot bring myself to believe that the enemy will wait for us ... they have withdrawn their baggage over the Scheldt.'[15]

The decision having been taken to force the issue in front of Tournai, by 9 May the allied army was in close proximity to the French forces covering the siege, and a major clash became inevitable. Sir John Ligonier wrote with wry humour, and perhaps only slight exaggeration, that 'We begin the war where the Duke of Marlborough left it.'[16] Perhaps so, but the lack of real urgency amongst the allied commanders, who at times seemed almost to be waiting to see what Saxe would do in response to their approach, enabled the marshal to further entrench his troops firmly in position. Cumberland was almost edging forward, while his opponent was settling into position.

The allied army went into camp late on 9 May in the cornfields between the villages of Maubray and Baugnies, where the gently rising ground enabled the soldiers to see the French army encampment very well, with the towers and spires of Tournai clearly visible against the setting sun behind. That the siege operations were still busily in progress was evident from the sound of heavy artillery that carried easily to the soldiers. What was not clear to the observers was the precise nature of the French dispositions, so Cumberland and his fellow commanders rode forward with their cavalry escort through a shower of heavy rain to get as good a view of Saxe's dispositions as they could. It was soon apparent that French troops held the outlying villages of Bourgeon and Vezon, about 4 miles or so out from Tournai, and a lively French cavalry screen prevented any closer inspection, so the party returned to the allied camp. The duke's mind seemed to be firmly made up all the same, and from his headquarters in the village of Brussoel he gave orders that the French forward positions should be cleared the following morning in readiness for a general advance by the army. Some of Waldeck's Dutch troopers tried to scout the outlying copses of the Bois de Barri off to the right, but they were driven off by French fire from a battery of light 'Swedish' guns. That the woods were held by Saxe's troops was evident, but what conclusion was drawn as to how to deal with them was not clear. Still, that the copses would have to be cleared at some early point must have seemed plain enough.

Parties of allied pioneers, strongly supported by infantry, began work early on 10 May to open the approaches through the orchards and gardens around Vezon; these led onwards to the French main positions on the open ground around and behind Fontenoy. The allied soldiers had to repair the tracks, as the French outposts had neatly dug them up. 'We moreover rendered the approaches difficult by breaking up the roads and where it could be done with advantage, by pulling down houses, old walls and trees.'[17] The French troops in Bourgeon and Vezon wisely did not stay long to dispute the villages – that was not their role – and, after skirmishing for a while and firing a few shots almost as a gesture of defiance, they withdrew on the approach of British troops led by the 1st English Foot Guards, with the 3rd, 8th and 11th Regiments of Foot, all supported by Hanoverian and Dutch cavalry. French pioneer Sergeant Tulipe employed his flint and steel to good effect, and ensured that the combustible material piled up in the cottages of Bourgeon was set well alight before making off to rejoin his comrades behind their prepared defences. 'We had seen the enemy burn a little village somewhat short of Fontenoy, which they had fortified.'[18]

Cumberland moved forward and established his fresh headquarters in the village of Maubray, but although his attention was again drawn by Colonel Neville Hatton, his assistant quartermaster general, to the French troops clearly visible in the outcrop of woods sitting on the allied right flank, the duke did not take the trouble to secure those copses. This oversight was surprising and, as experience would show, most unfortunate, and all despite the additional urging of John Lindsay, Earl of Crawfurd, who clearly saw what a threat French troops securely lodged in the thickets might pose to any further advance. Crawfurd also suggested that a move around the woods to envelop the left flank of the French position might be preferable, but Cumberland was not persuaded. He did, however, screen the approaches to the Bois de Barri by placing the Highlanders of Murray's Regiment of Foot (the Black Watch), previously with the army reserve, on his right flank.

Of course, to attempt to force the light French troops out of the woods that evening might well have prompted a firm response from Saxe to restore the security of the left flank of his army. In the process this could have brought on a general action prematurely, with the allied army not properly formed to deal with such an event. Such things have a tendency to tumble out of control, and Cumberland had the firm, and outwardly cautious, intention to fight in a formal manner, once the allied army was properly in place and ready to do so. A brawling encounter engagement, relished perhaps by more experienced field commanders with all the enticing prospects of the unexpected that might ensue, did not suit him, nor Waldeck and Königsegg for that matter. Such a judgement would always be finely balanced, and it is hard to say whether the outcome in that case would have been any worse for the allies than that which actually took place the next day.

In the time that Saxe had at his disposal before the arrival of Cumberland's army, he had taken care with his commanders to carefully inspect the ground in the immediate neighbourhood, and to choose and prepare the field on which his army, still an instrument which he felt was of doubtful quality, would confront their opponents. The marshal's health continued to trouble him and his doctor was in close attendance, but he declared that he was 'Improving by leaps and bounds; yesterday I was four hours in the saddle, even though the ground was hard as iron, without feeling the least ill effect.'[19] While such an assertion may be doubted, he made his dispositions with all his usual care, although understandably still rather distracted by the affliction of dropsy that eventually made necessary his occasional use of a small wicker carriage drawn by a pony to get about the field. It was even reported in the allied camp that he was 'in so low a state that his death is daily expected'.[20] This happy thought was not to be, and he had good warning of Cumberland's approach. Saxe judged correctly that his opponents would not try to turn the left flank of his army now he was firmly in position to cover the approaches to Tournai, as that would expose their own left to attack while on the march. He could not, all the same, help feeling a certain nervousness about the possibility of such a move, and posted a strong force of horse and foot to cover his left just in case Cumberland should prove to be more enterprising than expected. The more direct approach to the French position, using the old Mons road, seemed the most likely course and that indeed was to be the route taken by the allied army. Apart from a possible overly wrought concern for the left flank of his army, Saxe's appreciation of the situation appears to have been spot on.

The Marquis de Dreux-Brézé remained in the siege works with 15,000 men, which enabled Saxe to deploy some 56,000 troops (129 squadrons of horse and dragoons, and 66 infantry battalions) for the coming battle, should Cumberland try to force the issue. The French field army had settled into position on the open ground, a mile and a half wide and half a mile deep, between the Bois de Barri on their left and the village of Antoing on the river Scheldt. The key to the whole thing for Saxe was the village of Fontenoy in the French centre, the loss of which would break open the whole position. The place was put into a strong state of defence, emplacing infantry and guns, with three stout earth and timber redoubts constructed, and linking the village with the cottages of Antoing, and more artillery was dragged into place able to sweep the approaches and the open fields of now trampled grass and wheat on either side.

On the other side of the field two strong redoubts were constructed at the edge of the outcrop of the copses of the Bois de Barri, with guns in place able to cover much of the front of the French position. Some of Saxe's generals scoffed at the suggestion that their soldiers needed such entrenchments to counter an allied attack, but he understood that a few hours' work with a spade could often save a lot of grief. In this the marshal had the full support of Louis XV, who arrived on the scene on 7 May with his eldest son, the dauphin, and an appropriately impressive escort of courtiers and guards, all of whom had to be accommodated, fed and watered, without adding one jot to the bayonet strength of the army. The elegant entourage had travelled in some haste, passing through Compiegne and Douai on the way, so as to be present on the day of the battle.

Despite the complaints at the effort involved, the entrenching work was carried out during 9 and 10 May, and an already good defensive position was made formidable in the process. Concerns were still brought to the king at the labour of the entrenching work, and more validly perhaps the wisdom of standing and offering to fight with a major river obstacle at their back. These thoughts were brushed aside, and he told Saxe that 'I intend that everyone shall obey you, and I will be the first to set an example of obedience.'[21] The marshal was assured that there would be no squabbling or dabbling in his well thought-out plans, but he did not take the trouble to construct a further redoubt in his centre to cover the approaches to the open ground on which the army would deploy its main strength. This appears to be strange and, as with Cumberland's subsequent neglect to secure the woods on the French left, an almost negligent omission that, if exploited to the full, invited disaster. If Saxe's intention was, in fact, metaphorically to 'leave the door open' to entice Cumberland into a carefully laid trap, then he was running a considerable risk in doing so. Had that really been his intention, then the forces made ready to deal with things as they unfolded were inadequate, so the puzzle remains just that. Also, the covering force under the command of the Marquis de Dreux-Brézé keeping an eye on things in Tournai was probably over-manned for the task, although some of his mounted squadrons did help to cover the road from Leuze.

The three redoubts between Fontenoy and Antoing were manned by the Crillon- and Swiss-recruited Dieback and Betten regiments, while Antoing itself, anchoring the extreme right of the French army, was occupied by the Royal la Marine and Piemont regiments under the command of the Comte de la Marck. Fontenoy village was held by four battalions of the Dauphin regiment commanded by the Marquis de la Vanguyon. These units were supported by the squadrons of dismounted dragoons from the Bauffremont and Mestre de Camp regiments. There was also on the far right the shield of the swift waters of the Scheldt, which could not be turned or crossed with ease, in case of success with the army holding firm, but threatened disaster in the event of a defeat and the need for a rapid withdrawal. A battery of heavy guns was emplaced on the far bank, but the range was rather long for effective shooting, although the intimidating impact of such flanking fire would soon be evident.

On the other side of the French position, past the sharp angle presented by Fontenoy and the long open slope, cut across with a sunken lane and leading up to the open plain in the rear, the most prominent redoubt on the edge of the Bois de Barri was occupied by two battalions of the d'Eu regiment, from which the emplacement took its name and became infamous. 'Near the wood', a British officer wrote, 'a fort mounted with cannon, where five or six hundred men might be lodged.'[22] Command here was exercised by the Marquis de Chambonas, and the underbrush had been cleared to give good fields of fire, with hedges of sharpened branches, known as abattis, laid in the approaches to hinder any attackers. A regiment of light troops, keen men with a taste for work in close country and known as the Arquebusiers de Grassin (*Grassins*), manned the edge of the woods in support of the d'Eu and the nearby de Clermont-Prince regiments, and the gunners in the two redoubts 'Le bois de Barry sera défendu par des troupes légères appelées Grassins, du nom de leur créateur.'[23]

In case of a serious reverse to his army, with a hurried withdrawal from the scene becoming necessary, Saxe placed four battalions of Royal Grenadiers, under the command of the Comte d'Hérouville, together with eight guns, to hold the bridges at the crossing points over the Scheldt at Calonne. These would be vital in such an extremity: 'Le pont de Calonne est fortifié, ses aborde garnis de batteries.'[4] Saxe deployed his remaining troops, the bulk of his army some 33,000 strong, on the open ground between and in rear of the line Fontenoy–Antoing on the one flank and the Bois de Barri on the other. The point likely to meet the first shock of any attack was clearly that acute angle at Fontenoy itself, facing towards the village of Vezon, a place now securely held by the advanced guard of allied troops.

Covering this most likely avenue of approach, the marshal deployed three battalions of the du Roi regiment, with one battalion each from the Aubeterre and Courten regiments. To their left were four battalions of Gardes Françaises in their laced blue coats, with two battalions of Gardes Suisse in red prolonging the line of battle, and twelve guns in support. These batteries were not emplaced behind prepared defences, unlike those between Fontenoy and Antoing, indicating, again, that the French commander might have been leaving a door open to tempt his opponent to step incautiously inside. Saxe was, of course, careful to keep a fairly strong reserve in hand, although with an emphasis still towards his left flank which was comparatively less formidable in defensive scope than the fortified position around the villages on his right. The lingering concern, if a little distant, over a possible move by his opponents along the road leading from Leuze to Tournai, can be discerned.

Here, under the overall command of the very capable Count von Löwendahl, was deployed the 4,000-strong Irish brigade, émigré troops of fine reputation, long renowned in the French service and comprising the red-coated regiments of Clare, Ruth, Berwick, Bulkely and Dillon, together with a cadre battalion raised by the Comte de Lally-Tollendal (in part drawn from deserters from the British army). The Royal Corse, de Angoumois and Normandie regiments extended the line to their left and slightly to the rear, providing an element, at least, of a handy reserve, in addition to the Hainault, Royal Vassieux and Traisnel regiments behind the Irish troops. The marshal could be reasonably sure that the left flank of his army was relatively secure, although his anxiety in this direction would always remain and to a degree hamper his actions on the day. Saxe placed his guns with due care, manning the stoutly constructed redoubts with the heavy 8- and 12-pounder pieces, and distributing the lighter batteries in the open to obtain the clearest fields of fire. A reserve of twelve guns was kept in hand to deal with any emergency that might occur, but the ability to move these pieces when in action was, as with most artillery at the time, rather limited.

Several hundred yards behind the infantry stood Saxe's cavalry, in two lines of battle and amounting in all to some 15,000 troopers: 'La cavalerie est derrière l'infanterie, deposes sur deux lignes.'[25] This fine body comprised the household cavalry – the Maison de Roi – with the Noailles, Charost, Villeroy and d'Harcourt companies of the Gardes du Corps, the Gens d'Armes de la Guard, the fiercely moustachioed Chevaux-Légers (known rather derisively by others as 'The Virgins' for never having lost a standard), the 1st and 2nd Companies of Mousquetaires, and the Grenadiers à Cheval. Eight squadrons of the Gendarmerie stood nearby, along with ten squadrons of the Carabiniers du Roi. In support were seventy-one squadrons drawn from the regiments of the Colonel-General, Brancas, Fitzjames (Irish-recruited), Clermont-Prince, Fiennes, Royal Cravates, Royal Rousillon, Prince Camille, Chabrillant, Royal Etranger, Noailles, Pons, Berry and Royal. In all, this was a most formidable and magnificent array of horsemen. As a reserve, Saxe kept the regiments of Orleans and Rohan, the dragoons of Septimanie and Egmont, and the hussars of Lynden and Beausobre in hand but closer to the siege works around Tournai, just in case the garrison commander should attempt to interfere in things. From all this can be clearly seen the depth of the tactical position that Saxe adopted, not simply with the formidable defensive works that his soldiers had laboured to construct, but in the placing of his brigades to cover the likely eventualities. His arrangements were made judiciously and with care, with evident concern for the ability, or otherwise, of his troops to manoeuvre effectively in close proximity to an active opponent.

On the other side of the tactical hill, Cumberland was still not too sure of the actual strength of his opponents in numbers of troops, or of the layout of the position he faced. However, the evident gap that was presented to the allied commanders, lying between Fontenoy and the nearest point of the Bois de Barri, was certainly plain, but was only just over 700 yards wide (Fuye says 1,000 yards but that seems to exaggerate). It was clear that unless the village, or the edge of the woods opposite (preferably both, of course), could be taken or neutralised as strong-points, any advance on the main French position would have to be made through a defile covered by the fire of their opponents on either flank. That an attempt must be made to open this defile and free any advance from such a galling cross-fire was clear, and it should have been (and perhaps was) a key part of Cumberland's plan to force Saxe off the position and away from Tournai.

The approach taken by the duke showed little imagination (and viewed in a critical light indicates a lack of careful consideration), his line appearing to be that the allied army would step smartly down the road and hit Saxe as hard as could be wherever he was found, and hope that that would be enough. For this lack of thought, Cumberland does not bear the blame alone – Waldeck and Königsegg were equally complicit, and while the veteran Austrian field marshal suggested manoeuvre as an alternative, he does not seem to have pressed the point. Of course, to bring an opponent to battle in good time and almost regardless of the odds was not necessarily the wrong way to proceed. Still, while a subordinate commander might do this, at some risk, in order to fix the enemy and hold his attention while other forces manoeuvred to close with them and bring about their defeat, the notion that the whole army should try to both fix and destroy, in one gasp and with no superiority in numbers gained locally, was suspect military logic.

The lie of the land of what became the battlefield was deceptively simple, consisting as it did of a gently undulating plain bordered on the one side by the river Scheldt and on the other side, only about a mile and a half distant, by the tangled copses of the wood of the Bois de Barri. Beyond those woods lay the road leading to Tournai from Leuze and Ath. While appreciation of ground has always been an important factor in any military planning process, neither of the opposing commanders showed it to great advantage. The silent deception, one played on both men, was the degree of dead ground in front of the plain around Fontenoy on which Marshal Saxe chose to position the bulk of his army and fight. This dead ground, always so dangerous for a soldier, hid from easy view the approach of the allied army until it got to quite close quarters. Their approach would be no real secret, of course, as Saxe had outposts in place, but his field of vision and fields of fire, particularly for his strongly emplaced artillery, would be limited while his opponents prepared to give battle. The deception for the Duke of Cumberland and his fellow commanders was that the same limited ability to view the French army in position gave little hint of the way that any attack that developed between Fontenoy and the Bois de Barri was, in effect, to be going forward into a gradually narrowing bottleneck with no obvious or immediately practical way out. Ease of movement would be constrained, and yet that same stretch of ground would be swept with deadly flanking fire from both sides. Any determined drive into this bottleneck, unless supported on the left flank, and with the French troops in Fontenoy suppressed, or perhaps even a sweep around to the right with cavalry to pin French reserves in position, would be akin to pushing a door that is stuck against a carpet: the harder the push, the greater the difficulty.

The duke was able to deploy some 50,000 troops (including 14,000 cavalry) with ninety guns, divided broadly into two component parts: the British and Hanoverians on the right wing, with the Dutch and the much smaller Austrian contingent on the left. The British infantry, under the command of Sir John Ligonier and William, Earl of Albemarle, had in the first Line the 1st and 2nd English Foot Guards, the 3rd (Scots) Foot Guards, and the 1st, 8th, 21st, 25th, 31st and 33rd Regiments of Foot. Major General John Campbell commanded the second line, with the 3rd, 11th, 19th, 20th, 23rd, 28th, 32nd and 34th Regiments of Foot, while General Thomas Eberhard von Ilten had the Hanoverian regiments of von Sporken, von Oberg, Campen and Alt Zastrow under his command. To this force could be added Brigadier General of Infantry Richard Ingoldsby's recently formed brigade, with the 12th and 13th Regiments of Foot, Murray's Highlanders (the Black Watch), and von Borschlanger's Hanoverian regiment. Cumberland's British cavalry, led by the elderly Lieutenant General James Campbell (like so many others that day a veteran of Marlborough's campaigns), comprised a Household contingent of the 3rd and 4th Troops the Horse Guards and the 2nd Troop the Horse Grenadier Guards, the Blues (actually the 1st Regiment of Horse, but always referred to as 'The Blues'), the 2nd (King's) Regiment of Horse, the 8th (Black) Regiment of Horse, the 1st (Royal) Dragoons, the 2nd (Royal North British) Dragoons, the 3rd (King's Own) Dragoons, the 6th (Inniskilling) Dragoons, and the 7th (Queen's Own) Dragoons (with the army reserve).[26]

The Prince of Waldeck's Dutch troops (many of them German- and Swiss-recruited) comprised in the first line of infantry the Gardes te Voet (Hollandaise) and the battalions of the regiments of Cronstrom, Bentinck, Rijsel Grenadiers, Schaumberg-Lippe, Salis, Oranje Stad en Lande, Oranje Vriestand, Buddenbroek and Ayla. Their second line was formed by the regiments of Constant-Rebecque (Swiss), Sturler (Swiss), Bronkhorst, Smissaert, Broekhuizen, Dorth and Waldeck. Waldeck's cavalry was composed of squadrons from the regiments of Hopp, Buys, Lijnen, Sandouville, Rechteren-Overjissel, Schack, Ginckel, Hesse Homburg, the Nassau Dragoons, the Carabiniers, the Garde Dragoniers, and the Schlippenbach Dragoons (with the army reserve). Field Marshal Königsegg's rather modest detachment of Austrian troops was formed by squadrons of the Ligne Dragoons, Styrum Dragoons, Karoly Hussars and Belezney Hussars, together with some *Freikorps* companies of infantry.

Back on the other side of the field, Saxe's plan, simple in essence almost to the point of over-caution, was apparently to invite Cumberland to thrust his army into a well prepared killing zone. There it could be safely battered to pieces in attacking the defensive works so carefully constructed, while judiciously sited reserves would be on hand to deal with any local allied successes. The risk of fighting a major action with a wide water obstacle at his back – a risk that most commanders would usually view with great caution – was accepted, although it did concern his senior officers. The marshal had learned not to expect too much of the ability of French troops to manoeuvre successfully and in good order when under pressure and, given their lacklustre performance at Dettingen two years' earlier, he may be excused for having this doubt. His plan therefore was not to ask too much more of them but to stand and fight, and the prepared redoubts and their firmly emplaced guns would surely do much of the work required. These prepared defences were not makeshift affairs, but well-entrenched redoubts faced with stout timbers and packed earth, and the villages had been similarly fortified and barricaded, with loop-holed cottage and barn walls. French military engineering skill was renowned – the memory and legacy of Marshal Vauban lasted long – and Saxe had been allowed the time to properly fortify an already good position.

It seems, however, that he intended from the start to fight a limited action, as little attention was given before or later to the ability to mount a telling counter-stroke, other than to restore a local setback, or perhaps to take advantage of any weakness in his opponent's arrangements once battle was joined. In this can be seen once again the marshal's lack of confidence in the abilities of his own troops, other than in a tightly controlled set-piece defensive action. In accepting this limitation on his capabilities, Saxe formed no real *mass of manoeuvre* with which to strike his opponent once they were off balance – a major error surely, which does the veteran commander little credit, although the constraints under which he laboured do offer some explanation. It might even be suspected that Saxe, while not anticipating a defeat, was actually fighting for a draw and would be content to just see Cumberland off so that he could get on with the siege of Tournai in peace.

The dispositions that the marshal made, and the course of the battle itself, were heavily dictated by the course of the river Scheldt. The river provided a convenient and most important protection for the French right flank, bent back at a sharp angle from the left as it was; no move by their opponents in that direction could be effective, other than a frontal assault on the long line from Fontenoy to Antoing, for which good defensive preparations had been made to counter. With that element of security in place, French reserves were placed to watch for any move by Cumberland against the centre of the position and the left flank, past the woods of the Bois de Barri in any attempt to interpose between the covering army and the troops investing Tournai. There was still a chance, however slight, that Cumberland would attempt to march around Tournai by way of the road from Leuze and envelop the French position. Saxe was still taking a distinct risk: if he failed in the coming fight his army would be pushed to destruction as it attempted to retreat in haste across the few bridges over the Scheldt. Those chances were weighed against the opportunities presented, and the risks balanced against the alternative, which was to withdraw behind the river and in effect allow the garrison in Tournai to be relieved. The marshal, with his long years of experience of command, considered the odds, decided accordingly and stood his ground.

By curious coincidence, Cumberland's plan was also one that showed little subtlety, given that he had decided against trying to manoeuvre Saxe out of position. The intention was first of all to attack and carry the salient point formed by the fortified village of Fontenoy, with the Dutch corps supported by the Austrians advancing on the allied left, to secure the village and redoubts leading towards Antoing. In doing this they would both unhinge the French defensive line and fix those of their troops in that part of the battlefield and, it was presumably hoped, force the commitment of part at least of Saxe's reserves to holding back the attack in that sector. Meanwhile, the British and Hanoverian troops, having cleared the redoubts on the edge of the outcrop of the Bois de Barri to secure their right flank, would advance from the vicinity of Vezon with infantry closely backed by their cavalry to penetrate between those copses and Fontenoy, and attack the French main force in position on the open ground leading towards Tournai.

If all went well, with Waldeck punching on the left and Cumberland thrusting on the right, an encirclement in position of the main French infantry force should be the outcome. To avoid this, Saxe would have to fall back from his carefully prepared position, with the Scheldt, immediately to his rear, to contend with; as a result, the French commander would be in a difficult dilemma. This was all well and good, despite the duke still not fully appreciating the strength both of Saxe's army and of the position it had adopted. However, the necessity of clearing both the woods to his right and simultaneously the village of Fontenoy to the left of his advancing troops was of singular importance; if the village remained in French hands, then the two wings of the allied army would increasingly diverge as they advanced, diluting effort and making mutual cooperation difficult. This being so, Saxe could turn to confront and counter-attack either of the allied wings with little fear of immediate interference from the other. A skilled commander of such experience might be able to defeat his opponents' army in detail, with the one part unable to help the other in good time. Certainly the ability of Waldeck's troops to achieve their task against the fortified villages of Fontenoy and Antoing and the intervening redoubts was perhaps taken for granted too readily by Cumberland, while the clearing of the Bois de Barri outcrop would prove soon enough to be simply a mishandled affair. It may be asked whether the duke quite appreciated the importance of driving French troops from at least the redoubt d'Eu; its necessity seems clear, and several of the duke's officers drew it to his attention, but the operation to achieve this laudable aim held the simple appearance almost of an afterthought rather than a necessary preliminary, the absence of which would throw much else awry.

By the evening of 10 May the two armies had formed up ready to meet the adventures and perils of the following day. On that evening Louis XV was noticed to be in jovial mood in the royal tent at Calonne. He dined, of course, with his senior officers and looked ahead with keen anticipation to the day ahead – for the first time since the action at Poitiers in 1356 a French monarch would be present at a pitched battle, but this time at what he was clearly hopeful would be a victory. Marshal Saxe, feeling ill and tired, almost tottering with fatigue, was in no mind for such talk and excusing himself went to his camp bed early. The troops in the two armies settled down to eat a meal of sorts, and sleep was attempted: for most men this meant lying on the hard ground, a rough couch surprisingly comfortable enough when tired out, in the few hours that remained to them before the riffs of the drums and chivvying shouts of their sergeants called them stiffly to their feet in the chill half-light of the new day. A fortifying and warming nip of rum, Genever gin or brandy was served out to the men, as this was a legitimate part of their daily rate of pay and few must have begrudged them the ration as they fell sleepily into line.

Chapter 7

A Breaking-in Battle

The battle, Sir, is not to the strong alone.[1]

The Duke of Cumberland was in the saddle by 4.00am on 11 May 1745. It was a misty morning and, had he known it, both Louis XV and Marshal Saxe were up at the same time, just a few hundred yards away across the fields to his front. The duke rode down the line of his mustering troops to where the Foot Guards formed on the right of the allied army's deployment. Here, the pressing need to clear the redoubt d'Eu on the edge of the Bois de Barri, before any general advance was made, was once more pointed out to him. 'An irreproachable tactical conception,' as one French observer drily noted, 'but applied without haste.'[2] Brigadier General Richard Ingoldsby, of the 1st English Foot Guards, had been detailed the previous evening to carry out the task with his brigade, with troops drawn from the 12th (Duroure's), 13th (Pulteney's), 25th (Rothes/Sempill's) Foot, Murray's Highlanders (the Black Watch, detached from the army reserve), and von Borschlanger's Hanoverians.

One of Cumberland's staff officers wrote afterwards that 'The idea of attacking the fort [redoubt d'Eu] near the wood was entirely H.R.H.'s, and he had chosen for the service Brigadier General Ingoldsby as a man in whom he had confidence.'[3] If that really were so, then the actual execution of such a key task remains puzzling and apparently inept. With this force of some 2,000 men, Ingoldsby was initially given very specific orders by the duke to march straight up to the French redoubts and seize the guns. A detachment of British gunners would accompany the attack, to turn the French pieces on their owners or otherwise to spike them if this was not possible in good time. It was a seemingly straightforward task of high importance that begged of no discussion, with a force that, at first sight, was quite adequate. The mission could have been taken on sooner, of course, but as previously mentioned this might have brought on a premature general action that the allies were not ready for. Saxe might after all have been better placed for such an eventuality, and have delivered a sharp rebuff to upset all of Cumberland's plans.

The battle of Fontenoy, 11 May 1745.

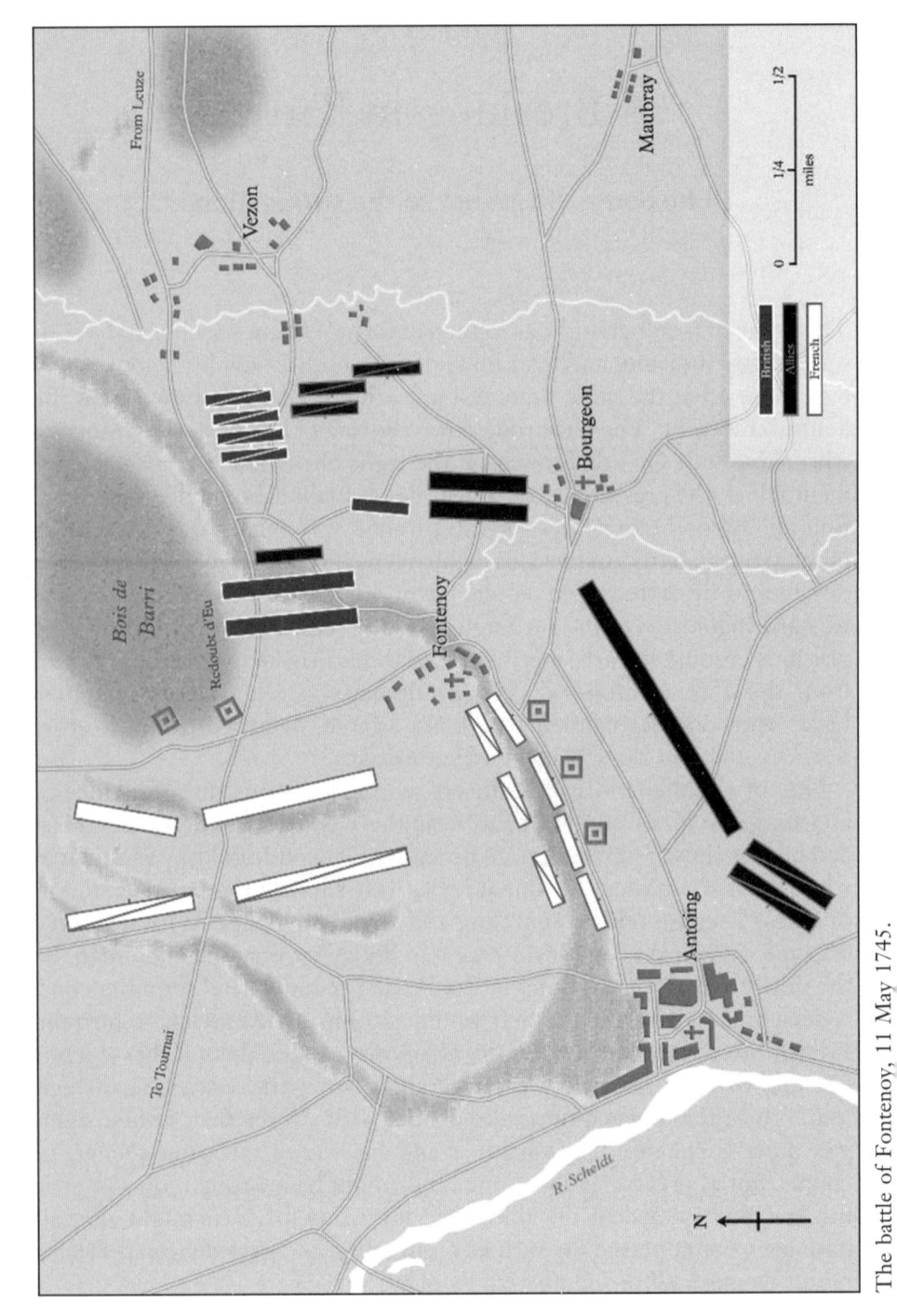

Although delayed while the Hanoverian soldiers moved into their new position, Ingoldsby set off at about 6am, but soon halted in front of Vezon, as 'He observed the enemy had a strong detachment in the wood, and that at that juncture were marching several parties towards it; particularly one which lay down flat in the corn about forty yards from the flank of the wood.'[4] Clearly in growing concern at the scale of the task he had been given, and for the security of his own flank as he moved forward, Ingoldsby sent an officer on his staff, Major Bernard, back to Cumberland with a request for light guns to accompany his force. The request was not unreasonable, but should have been foreseen, and while these pieces were being brought forward a lively discussion ensued in the chilly dawn light as to the best way to approach the redoubts. Colonel Robert Munro, commanding the Black Watch, suggested that his light companies should clear the wood, work for which they were well suited, while the remainder of the brigade, more cumbersome in their formation, advanced in support alongside the edge of the thickets. His men had, at their own expense, provided themselves with broadswords in addition to the more usual musket and bayonet, and could be expected to use them to good effect in such a close quarter action. This course of action was agreed, but Ingoldsby was intent on waiting for the guns to arrive before setting off, which they eventually did after a frustrating delay – three 6-pounders came up, more effective than the light battalion guns, but slowly and clumsily dragged along by sweating soldiers under the command of Captain Mitchelson.

Ingoldsby, despite having orders that appeared to be plain enough, still seemed unsure how to proceed, but the duke came up and instructed Mitchelson to commence firing on the edge of the Bois de Barri with canister shot. Return fire from the redoubt was immediately received but the advance of the brigade at last got under way, with the Highlanders in the lead, moving out of the sunken lane which had been the forming-up point in front of Vezon. Cumberland, satisfied that matters were now at last in hand according to his orders, rode off to rejoin his staff. The advance, however, soon slowed to a halt as what seemed to be large numbers of the light French *Grassins* could be seen moving in the wood-line 'Waiting in front of the redoubt.'[5] These men opened a disconcertingly effective musketry on Ingoldsby's leading troops, the foremost French soldiers, sharpshooters selected as the best marksmen, having loaded muskets passed forward for their use by comrades to the rear, a not uncommon practice at the time that ensured a good rate of fire. Ingoldsby, impressed with the bold front with which he was presented, and almost certainly over-estimating the strength of the French in the wood, apparently felt that he still had insufficient troops for the task, and sent back for fresh instructions. Cumberland's exasperation at this new delay was understandable, but his hurried response to the brigade commander was both ambiguous and unhelpful, being to 'Defend himself if attacked, but by all means to see and attack the enemy.'[6] A gunner officer, Colonel Jonathan Lewis, standing near the duke, recalled that he actually said that Ingoldsby was to 'Attack the battery in the wood, and to maintain himself if he could; if not, to make the best of his way off.'[7] This perhaps indicated the duke's exasperation and annoyance, but was unfortunate – a cool head was called for at such a moment; a more helpful reply might have been along the lines of 'Look, I have told you what to do, please just get on and do it.'

As it was, such vague instructions as given by Cumberland can only have made things worse, and at such a crucial moment were hardly a clear clarion call for Ingoldsby to make better time with things. 'The Fort [redoubt d'Eu] near the wood should have been attacked,' a report subsequently published in London read:

> and if that had been done, as his royal highness ordered, it would, in all probability, have been carried, which would have greatly contributed to our further success. But by some frailty Brigadier Ingoldsby did not attack the fort, notwithstanding the repeated orders sent to him.[8]

Shortly afterwards, Lieutenant General James Campbell was instructed to take his leading fifteen squadrons of cavalry, some 2,000 horses and their riders, along the Mons road through the bottleneck of Vezon village. Campbell sent Captain Forbes of the 2nd (Royal North British) Dragoons forward to enquire about the progress of the operation to clear the woods over to the right. To his dismay, the captain found most of Ingoldsby's brigade still in the sunken lane leaning on their muskets, having made almost no progress, and he reported as much to Campbell. Word was sent to Cumberland, who, instead of sending a staff officer with a smart message to everyone to stop dithering and get on with things, chose to go forward again to the lane to urge Ingoldsby on.

Despite this lack of progress on the right of the army, the planned general advance could no longer be delayed, and at about 7.00am four blank cannon shots were fired in quick succession; at this agreed signal the Dutch cavalry in two columns surged forward towards Fontenoy and Antoing. Simultaneous with this advance, Campbell led his own squadrons forward, picking their way past Ingoldsby's troops, to take position at the edge of the plain lying between the woods and Fontenoy. With the French gunners in the redoubt d'Eu still active and untroubled, this was clearly hazardous, and the thickly gathered ranks of allied horsemen were almost immediately met with a sharp shower of round-shot. Their conduct under this fire was admirable and they stood the casualties and ordeal well, but Campbell, so prominent and dashing as a young dragoon with his swordsmanship at Malplaquet, was struck on the thigh by a round-shot – the limb was badly broken and almost carried away; he was lifted from his horse and taken from the field mortally wounded.

The loss of Cumberland's cavalry commander at such an early point, an officer with whom he had presumably discussed his intentions in some detail, was unfortunate. Command of the leading British and Hanoverian squadrons was taken up by the Earl of Crawfurd, who, although highly capable, had it seemed no clear instructions as to what to do should he have to assume this role – he prudently drew the troopers back out of the French artillery fire and with some difficulty reformed them to the rear of the waiting British infantry. Cumberland made no attempt to interfere with this move, but any appearance of confusion is rather misleading; the squadrons could have done little good where they were while the French batteries were still active, as the French cavalry screen had already fallen back. The allied horsemen, unless they were to press forward onto the plain, would only serve to get in the way of the duke's infantry as they deployed, while providing the French gunners with a large and very tempting target to practise on. The main problem, one that would become steadily more apparent as the day wore on, was the constricted nature of the ground which allowed little room for cavalry and infantry to deploy and manoeuvre to mutual benefit.

While the allied army was arranging itself for battle in this way, Louis XV had crossed the Scheldt at Calonne together with his son and the Comte d'Argenson. He took up a position with his retinue towards the centre-right of his troops, near the Notre-Dame-aux-Bois calvary at a crossroads formed by the Mons road and the lane leading from Antoing to Ramcroix. Two squadrons of Gardes de Chèval stood nearby as close escort. Saxe, while properly deferential, was not at all appreciative of the distraction caused by his royal guests, and prudently made sure that the convenient route back across the Scheldt was kept open with the guard of Royal Grenadiers firmly in place, in case the king and his royal party should have to make their exit from the field in a hurry.

The marshal was so unwell that morning that he could not bear the weight of the steel cuirass that he usually wore in action, preferring instead to don a light quilted taffeta version. He had to suck a musket ball to assuage the thirst which afflicted him, and his fortitude and stamina on the day commanded, and still command, much admiration. Unable at first to mount his horse, he sat in his wicker wheeled chair and was conveyed in this rather undignified manner to his command position close to the redoubt d'Eu – his concern that Cumberland might even yet make a move to turn the left flank of the French position was evident. Orders had been given that as soon as the morning mist cleared sufficiently for fields of fire to be had, the gunners were to engage the allied units as they approached, and by now this artillery exchange was well under way. The actual effect of this bombardment and counter-bombardment was, however, limited, apart from killing and maiming some scores of soldiers, of course. The French gunners failed to prevent or even slow the allied deployment for battle, while the allied artillery did not suppress or disrupt the opposing defences and emplaced batteries very much, if at all. Any slackening in the rate of fire of the guns seems to have derived from a desire to save ammunition for more tempting targets, rather than because the gunners themselves had been killed or driven off. Orders had been given in particular to augment the supplies of round-shot and powder available to the batteries in Fontenoy, but these seem to have gone astray. As the officer responsible for this lack did not live to see nightfall, no explanation was ever offered.

Soon after 7.00am Sir John Ligonier began to move his first line foot-soldiers forward from the crowded orchards and gardens around Vezon, forming them on the gently undulating rising ground; Fontenoy lay to their left, while the edge of the Bois de Barri was dimly and mistily visible to their right. Once again a cannonade was directed at them, fire which was increased by the light galloper guns which Saxe had deployed to the front of his own infantry. The British and Hanoverian soldiers stoically stood the shot and closed up the widening gaps in their ranks with admirable discipline as they moved forward to complete their deployment and make room for the second line to emerge from the village. Cumberland, having left Ingoldsby with encouraging words to move forward without further delay, now had seven of his own light guns deployed under Colonel Lewis to drive off the French gunners and relieve his infantry a little. In this they had at last some success against their opponents, and in these early exchanges the Duc de Grammont, commanding the Gardes Françaises (and so perversely prominent at Dettingen with his premature advance), was gravely wounded by a round-shot while in sociable conversation with his uncle, Marshal de Noailles. The young man was riding a white horse, and accordingly offered a good target for the allied gunners who took suitable advantage of it; his thigh was shattered, and after agonising suffering borne very bravely he died later that day. Saxe directed the Duc de Biron to replace him, and that the Gardes Françaises and Gardes Suisse should retire a short way out of the fire of the allied batteries. As it happened this movement allowed Cumberland's infantry to gain a toehold on the plain with some ease, when they shortly came to move forward.

An hour or so later, while Ligonier's second line infantry were still in the process of getting through Vezon and forming in battle order, the duke went yet again to speak to Ingoldsby, but what passed between the two men is not known, as the aides-de-camp discreetly withdrew out of earshot, presumably to spare Ingoldsby's blushes in what must have been a blunt interview. If coffee had been available it is unlikely to have been offered by Cumberland, but it is fair to assume, however, that the duke expressed his disappointment and impatience with some force. What is apparent is that nothing much then happened, and soon afterwards Ligonier, furious with the delay in silencing the fire from the battery at the redoubt d'Eu, sent an officer with a message to Ingoldsby: 'The general bids me tell you that he wonders you have not advanced; and it is his order that you advance and attack.' The brigadier general's telling response was 'I have received the duke's orders to advance in line with that line,' indicating Ligonier's own infantry as they were formed up.[9]

Any intention to try to silence the guns in the redoubt d'Eu, before a general advance was made, seemed to have been given up. It was remembered with some bitterness that 'By consent of all the British commanders it was Ingoldsby's misunderstandings of his orders and his failure to capture the redoubt d'Eu that lost the battle.'[10] However, it should also be remembered that Saxe had placed strong infantry reserves on that flank, even down towards the outlying village of Ramcroix, so it may be asked whether Ingoldsby actually had the strength to both take and then hold the place, and perhaps he already had this doubt. If that were so, however, then he should have made the fact plain and seems not to have done so. A key element in Cumberland's rather unimaginative plan for the battle had nonetheless been set to one side, almost without much thought, and the consequences would have to be dealt with as best they could.

While Ingoldsby hesitated and paced to and fro outside the Bois de Barri, and Ligonier fretted with impatience as his infantry formed up in front of Vezon, the attack by the Dutch troops on the left of the allied line had begun. The long lines of blue coats and glistening bayonets, picked out in the faintly misty sunny morning, caught the anxious attention of

Saxe and his commanders, who assessed quickly whether Waldeck's advance against the right of their position would be matched, simultaneously, with an attack by the Anglo-Hanoverian infantry massing against their left. Still, their dispositions had been made with the best of care, little more could be done just then, and the outcome had to be awaited. According to a French report, the Dutch attack went in at about 9.00am, somewhat later than intended.[11] The burnt-out village of Bourgeon had been secured the previous evening, so the advance was relatively simple, and Waldeck's three cavalry brigades, commanded by Prince Ludwig von Hessen-Phillipstahl, had screened the initial advance of the two columns of infantry very well, although engaged with disturbingly heavy fire from the French batteries, particularly that sited at the windmill on the far bank of the Scheldt. All the same, the prince seemed to have carried out a rather perfunctory reconnaissance of the French positions around the villages of Fontenoy and Antoing, and what artillery preparation was undertaken by the Dutch batteries was soon found to have been not that effective.

Rather little has been written about the artillery activity prior to the allied attack, a most essential preliminary for the likelihood of success against a strongly entrenched opponent. Despite this, we can see that both Waldeck's and Cumberland's gunners were heavily engaged and doing their best to beat down the French batteries at this early stage. Major Richard Davenport remembered that 'Our cannons fired very briskly on their batteries, which appeared to be silenced and the troops marching up to their entrenchments in good order and with a strong appearance of victory.'[13] A ten-gun battery, established by Waldeck near Bourgeon, certainly kept the defenders in the village of Fontenoy under a well directed fire all the while. Appearances can be deceptive, and the French gunners may well have given up on the unproductive artillery duel (there was lingering concern over an adequate supply of ammunition), and just kept their powder dry while awaiting the expected allied attack, when better practice could be made.

As the Dutch cavalry moved aside to allow the infantry forward, the long, well regulated lines of soldiers suddenly came under a more intense and sustained artillery bombardment from the redoubts between the two villages. General von Cronstrom, the veteran Swedish soldier in Dutch service (and someone not on the best of terms with Waldeck), had the command of the troops during the attack on these redoubts. His eight battalions of infantry moved steadily forward, but in the misty morning they tended towards their left, despite the urging of their brigade commanders, and in so doing opened a gap in the Dutch attack from where

Waldeck was moving with twelve battalions towards Fontenoy village itself. Soon alerted to this potentially dangerous dispersal of effort, the prince brought forward four dismounted squadrons of dragoons from the Schlippenbach Regiment to restore the proper integrity of the line. The horse handlers went to the rear, and these useful men fixed their bayonets, picked up their dressing with admirable *sang-froid* and joined the Dutch advance, the side-drummers tapping the cadence of the step as they went boldly forward.

Waldeck's attack on Fontenoy and the adjacent redoubts, had it succeeded, would have enabled Cumberland to move to the right past the village without being caught in a French cross-fire. Cronstrom's attack, however, promised much more, as once the way forward through the redoubts was cleared, the massed Dutch cavalry, well closed up as they were, would be able to sweep through the gap created, drive off the French dragoons and gain the open plain behind the village, at the same time as Cumberland's attack with his British and Hanoverian infantry went in. Saxe had his squadrons of cavalry at hand, of course, and would have deployed them in response, but Cumberland's own cavalry and his army reserve would have been uncommitted as yet. The marshal would be left without further immediate reserves, and obliged to call on those he had grouped to his left – this would be a fatally time-consuming business; the dual allied stroke with Waldeck and Cronstrom on the left and Cumberland on the right would potentially be a battle-winning combination.

But so much for good intentions, for despite the slight cover afforded them by the now rapidly evaporating mist, the advance of Waldeck's infantry was hit hard by well directed French artillery fire, both from the front and the flanks. Assailed by a storm of canister and round-shot, officers and men in the leading ranks fell with a terrible rapidity, and the shot-riven battalions were unable to make any progress – the soldiers toiling forward into the fire, their heads bowed as if walking into a hailstorm, soon had little choice but to fall back to reform their battered ranks. Some particularly hard-hit units reportedly retired in disorder, having to take advantage of the smouldering ruins of some nearby cottages which had been burned on Saxe's orders the previous day. To their left the second column of Dutch infantry under Cronstrom's command, backed by several further squadrons of cavalry, advanced boldly with the Condé road to their left and the Bourgeon stream to the right, but they too were met with heavy artillery fire from the sixteen guns emplaced in the three redoubts constructed between Antoine and Fontenoy. The Dutch effort here also faltered and broke under the weight of fire, and it was soon very clear that the troops, for all their evident gallantry and severe losses in this opening engagement, had nothing to show for their trouble in making frontal attacks with too little preparation on a well entrenched enemy. Reports were soon circulated that Waldeck's and Cronstrom's regiments were actually routed, but these were an exaggeration; certainly their troops had been smartly repulsed, but in the main they maintained their order when retiring, and now needed to find a place to reform away from the French fire: Given the ferocity of their reception, they could sensibly do little else for the moment, while their officers regrouped and reordered their shaken soldiers ready for a fresh effort.

In falling back to conform with the infantry the Dutch squadrons remained within range of the French gunners, and these continued to batter them with no risk of retaliation. That the prince's troops were dispirited at the fierceness of their repulse was perhaps no surprise, and one of their cavalry regiments even made its way smartly off the battlefield and well out of the fight for the day. Their colonel would have to explain this conduct at a later point, but apparently did so successfully, as he escaped censure and it was not clear what effort Waldeck had made to bring them back into action. Most of the Dutch squadrons, however, remained firm. As it was, by about 10.00am the French had neatly seen off this first major attack on their position, although the lavish expenditure in ammunition by their now smoke-grimed gunners, in particular canister-shot fired at too great a range to be most effective, was already raising concerns for Saxe and his generals.

The Duke of Cumberland soon learned of the failure of the first Dutch effort on the left of the army and resolved that, despite the setback, the redoubt d'Eu should be carried without further delay, in order that the advance of the allied right wing could proceed unhindered. At about 11.00am he sent a message to Colonel von Borschlanger to take his Hanoverian battalion into the woods and seize the position regardless of cost. With Königsegg's agreement, he also ordered the British and Hanoverian infantry to prepare to move and simultaneously advance in the centre. The troops had been standing under intermittent French fire for some hours, enduring the ordeal with commendable calm, and with only their own field batteries able to respond. This they had done with vigour, but had still not beaten down the French batteries to any noticeable degree. Cumberland was, of course, attacking with his flanks not yet secure and under enfilade fire, but the only alternative open to him was to withdraw from the field, and he saw no reason for this course of action at this point in the day. A hard blow delivered along the most direct line might still pay a handsome dividend, while any attempt to re-order the advance so as to cut past the outer edge of the thickets of the Bois de Barri, and so outflank Saxe's position, would now be too time-consuming and complicated to really contemplate. Furthermore, in that event, the two wings of the allied army would have to diverge even more than they already had, and any such move, had it even been practical, would further dilute hopes for any chance of success.

Cumberland sent a request to Waldeck to renew his attack on the left, and the Dutch troops were now stiffened by the transferring of the 12th Foot (Duroure's) and Colonel Munro's (Murray's) Black Watch from Ingoldsby's brigade on the right to assault Fontenoy village itself. Von Borschlanger's Hanoverian battalions were moved to the left to lend support to this attack, although it remains unclear to what extent they were actually involved, before being told to take up a position with Ligonier and his infantry. Reports that they took part in the attack on the village are difficult to verify, and an eye-witness wrote: 'The left Wing [Waldeck], favoured by the fire of our batteries, and supported by two *English battalions* [author's italics] which his royal highness sent to favour the attack on Fontenoy.'[13] Colonel Scipio Duroure was given the command of this hastily gathered force, and he resolutely took up the challenge so suddenly presented, but such a move can hardly have bolstered the already flagging attempts to clear the French infantry from the Bois de Barri. Even so, a clear effort was being made to put additional pressure on to a key point in the centre of the French position, but such a late re-ordering of the composition of the allied attack on the right indicates that the arrangements had not been well thought out at the onset of the action.

Flexibility and the ability to react to circumstances were admirable attributes for any commander, but a whiff of confusion amongst the allied commanders was evident. If Duroure was successful against Fontenoy, the French reaction was likely to be prompt and violent, and what reserves were in place to reinforce the colonel in the village, apart from the Hanoverians who would soon enough be ordered back to form part of Cumberland's grand advance, were not too clear. It might be thought in any case that Munro and his nimble highlanders would have been better employed in driving the troublesome *Grassins* out of the edge of the wood. Meanwhile, as regards the likely chances of success, 'The French artillery was well posted at the redoubt and in Fontenoy, and vigorously served.'[14] However, at Königsegg's suggestion a British four-gun battery of howitzers was moved forward to engage the defenders of the village, and to give some additional cover to Duroure's advance.

At this critical moment, with more than an element of confused thinking apparent in Cumberland's plan, Ingoldsby was wounded by a stray French musket ball. He plainly could not continue in command of the now reduced brigade on the right flank, and so was helped to the rear, and this task devolved on the Hanoverian Major General Ludwig von Zastrow. He, apparently not aware of (or perhaps disregarding as impractical) Cumberland's latest instructions regarding the troublesome redoubt in the wood-line, ordered the 13th Foot (Pulteney's) to join in the grand advance in the centre. This, of course, tied in with the duke's last instructions to Ingoldsby to regulate his advance by that of the infantry of the right wing. Munro's highlanders, meanwhile, had moved swiftly down the sunken lane behind the massed allied infantry. They needed no urging in their newly given task and they covered the ground with admirable speed – their prompt and forthright attack erupting on to the defenders of Fontenoy surprised the French commanders, who up to this point had been content with the steady progress of their part in the escalating battle. 'They rushed upon us with more violence than ever sea did when driven by a tempest.'[15] The tactics used by the highlanders undoubtedly came as something of a shock to the French, as it was recalled that:

> Sir Robert [Munro] acceding to the usage of his countrymen ordered the whole regiment to clap to the ground on receiving the French fire, and as soon as it was discharged, to spring up, and move close to the enemy, when they were to pour in their fire upon them.'[16]

Colonel Munro remained standing throughout the French fusillade, however, less from a desire to encourage his men with his valour than from his own corpulence making it no easy matter to clap himself to the ground and then regain his feet with any semblance of dignity unless assisted to do so. Having broken into the barricaded defences of the village, the highlanders engaged in a sharp hand-to-hand combat with the defending soldiers of the Dauphin regiment, and a battery of French guns was overrun. Those gunners who did not smartly make off were bayoneted alongside their pieces. The Comte de Chabonnes had been summoned by Saxe to replace the mortally wounded Grammont, so the command of the French troops in Fontenoy had been briefly passed to the Duc de Biron, and he led the du Roi regiment to the aid of the garrison. His personal bravery under fire set a fine example to his men, who rallied and fought back with great vigour against Duroure's attack, which had briefly threatened to unhinge the whole French line of defence at its most vulnerable point.

Maria-Theresa, Empress of Austria, Queen of Hungary and Bohemia.

Maurice de Saxe, Marshal of France.

William Augustus, Duke of Cumberland.

King Louis XV of France.

Lieutenant General Sir John Ligonier.

British infantry advancing, c.1745. A still from the excellent Stanley Kubrick film *Barry Lyndon* (1975) (*Courtesy of Warner Bros. Studios*)

French artillery in action, c.1745.

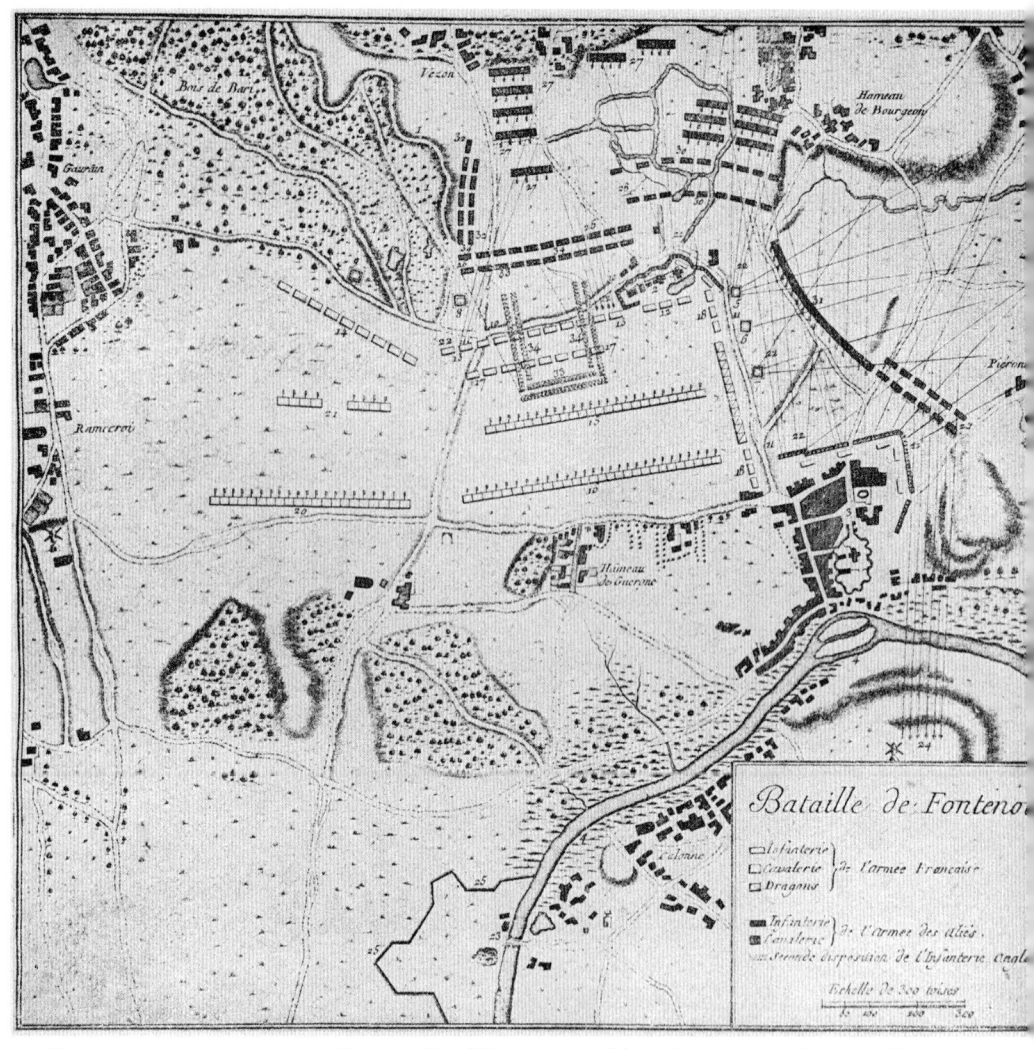

A French contemporary map of the battle of Fontenoy. Although some details are indistinct, the three-sided column of Cumberland's infantry can be seen breaking into the French position.

siege of Tournai, 1745 (previously thought to represent the 1709 siege by Marlborough).

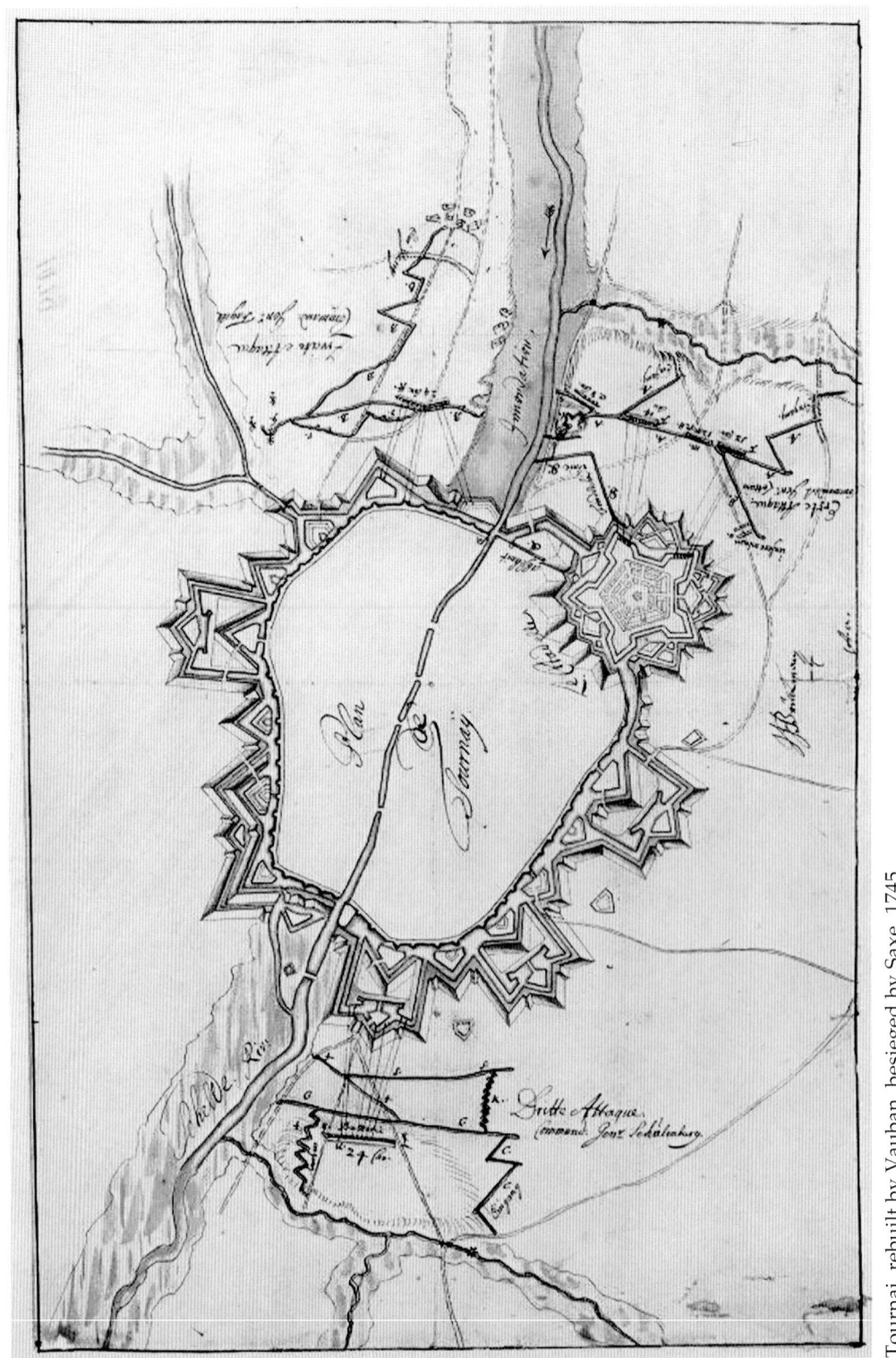

Tournai, rebuilt by Vauban, besieged by Saxe, 1745.

For all their valour, the highlanders soon had to withdraw, largely because Waldeck's second attack, with troops drawn from the Gardes te Voet, Ayla, Constant-Renecque and Sturler regiments, had again met a ferocious hail of round-shot and canister, and found no more success than the first attempt. 'The Dutch quite gave way, and Sir Robert Munro thought proper that we should retire.'[17] Cronstrom's regiments to the left, in particular, were also seen to hold back, and Waldeck remonstrated with him for the lack of progress, ordering Lieutenant General von Schomberg-Lippe to take over the command, but the result was just the same – the French position was just too strong to be forced, even at prohibitively heavy cost. Overall, it could be seen that Cumberland had, in fact, simply reinforced failure with the redeployment of the Black Watch and the 12th Foot, when they might have been used to better effect on his right flank. All the same, as so often on a battlefield, there were still opportunities for a little personal profit, and the rascally veteran Sergeant MacLeod recalled killing one of the defenders of the village, a Colonel Montard, and lifting both his pocket watch and his purse, well stocked as it was with gold ducats.[18] MacLeod was then accosted by an Irish officer in the French service who was also engaged in a degree of private enterprise and attempted to relieve him of his booty. In the same manner the Irishman had to be struck down by the Highlander's broadsword, so that MacLeod could safely get back to his comrades with the gratifying haul – whether he shared his booty is not clear.

The casualties suffered by Duroure's men in their gallant attack on the village were severe, with the colonel mortally wounded by a round-shot and carried from the field, and six other officers from his own regiment amongst those killed. Only Captain Rainsford of the 12th Foot remained standing, and able to gather his men back from the ferocious fighting around the gardens and cottages of the villages, to withdraw as best they could in the face of French pressure. A part of the village and at least one battery had briefly been in British hands, and the place was the kingpin of the whole French position that day; had Colonel Duroure gone in with sufficient resources, and had enough reserves been ready and at hand for him to call on, as his French opponents could, then the whole of Saxe's army might have been split in two just as Cumberland's main attack went in on the allied right. The duke had, in effect, fallen between two stools: he had weakened the already faltering effort to clear the French out of the Bois de Barri, but not put sufficient strength into the attack on Fontenoy to make it really count. That the renewed Dutch attack had stalled once more, perhaps inevitably given their experience earlier in the morning, simply demonstrated the stark inability so far of the allies to disrupt Saxe's well thought-out plan of defence.

The time was just before mid-day, and Saxe's right flank had certainly held firm under pressure. Antoing village on his right flank remained packed with troops, and was clearly under little threat, so instructions were sent to move the Piemont regiment towards the redoubts closer to Fontenoy, but this does not seem to have happened, the message apparently getting lost in the turmoil of the battle. Although having with some difficulty mounted his horse for the first time that day, the marshal responded coolly to cries of congratulations at what had been achieved. These sentiments seemed at best to be premature, as Cumberland's main effort had not yet been seen, and Saxe remarked to those officers standing around him that they still had to meet the English. At the same time, though, instructions were sent to the troops guarding the bridges over the Scheldt at Calonnes that anyone making off from the firing line and attempting to cross to safety was to be mustered and brought back to the ranks at point of bayonet if necessary. It seemed that, although holding firm so far, the French army was more than a little shaken.

Meanwhile, the Duke of Cumberland had led his British and Hanoverian infantry forward from their forming-up point in front of Vezon, and onto the slope leading to the open plain between Fontenoy and the edge of the Bois de Barri. In this he committed a significant error, not in ordering the advance of the infantry, for much might still be achieved, but by actually accompanying them on horseback with his staff. He ceased to be the commander-in-chief directing the battle and in effect took charge of a subdivision of the army, a role that could certainly have been safely entrusted to Ligonier. Cumberland also lost the ability to communicate either with Waldeck on the other side of the village of Fontenoy, or with the Earl of Crawfurd, now the commander of his cavalry. Both Ligonier and Königsegg apparently protested at his decision to go in with the attack but to no avail, and the duke and his retinue of aides and staff officers rode forward.

Some 16,000 infantry, with drums tapping and colours flying bravely, took part in this imposing advance, supported by the seven 3-pounders, dragged with such effort over the wet grass and uneven ground. (Some reports say twelve guns, although the presence of a second, reserve, battery is likely to account for this.) Despite the protests of his staff that he should take up a more sheltered position, the duke was prominent and close to the front rank in his conspicuously laced coat, astride his favourite grey horse. 'When our lines were drawn up in good order, with the cavalry behind them, H.R.H. put himself at their head and gave orders to march directly on the enemy.'[19] Personal bravery and setting a fine example are admirable, but they also have their time and place.

At once the allied infantry again became caught in a crossfire of French artillery from both flanks; casualties amongst the leading ranks mounted, but the gaps were closed up with disciplined promptness, the soldiers dressing their ranks to the right, and the advance was not slowed to any appreciable extent despite the toll taken. The official report on the battle, published six days later on 17 May, added that 'Prince Waldeck moved at the same time to attack Fontenoy, which the left wing did but faintly.'[20] This, of course, had coincided with Duroure's attack and, given the earlier repulses of the Dutch attack, this reported lack of vigour of the second attempt was perhaps not a surprise, and it is not clear what expectations Cumberland had at this point of really vigorous support to his left. Nor is it easy to see what information he was receiving about the success or otherwise of the Dutch effort there. At least it could be said that by at least threatening a further advance, and thus tying down the French units in that part of the field, Waldeck was making it difficult for Saxe to re-deploy those troops to meet the more severe threat now visibly building in the gap between Fontenoy and the edge of the Bois de Barri. Cumberland was hopeful of success all the same, and to add to the marshal's difficulties at this point, his head of artillery, the very capable Chevalier du Brocard, was struck down and killed by a British round-shot. This was a sore loss as he was a skilled gunner, and Saxe had already warned him not to take too many risks, advice that he knew would not be heeded, and he commented sadly to an aide that du Brocard was just going to get himself killed.

The front rank of the allied infantry at first comprised the 1st English Foot Guards at the post of honour on the right, then consecutively the 3rd (Scots) Foot Guards, the 2nd English Foot Guards, then the 1st, 21st, 31st, 8th, 25th, 33rd and 19th Foot. In the second line were the 3rd, 23rd, 32nd, 11th, 28th, 34th and 20th and the 13th Foot detached from Ingoldsby's brigade. These were supported by the Hanoverian regiments of Sporken, Zastrow, von Borschlanger, Du Oberz and Campen, drawn in once more from their threatening demonstration against Fontenoy. 'The English came on in two very broad lines,' it was remembered by an admiring French officer, 'that slow pace for which they were famous.'[20] Cumberland appeared to have just the one aim from now on: to thrust his British and Hanoverian infantry into the left-centre of the French position, and then, having by-passed the strongpoint of the village of Fontenoy, to wheel to the left and, by rolling up the line, like a wet blanket as it were, to break open his opponent's position. Frederick II of Prussia afterwards said that this was all that was required to achieve a momentous victory, but he, of course, was not there to try to do such a thing. That much by way of brutal tactics on the battlefield was plain enough, and could work, but of course all depended upon the resilience and reactions of the duke's opponents.

The British and Hanoverian infantry moved steadily across 800 yards or so to the damp and slippery grassy slope, still under a brisk cannonade from French guns on either flank. The Hanoverians soon found that they had insufficient room to maintain their correct formation, and fell back slightly to form a third line in the column as it advanced. The slight undulations in the ground gave some shelter as the soldiers marched steadily on, the ground littered with their dead and wounded as they passed. Then, of a sudden, the leading troops were confronted at the crest of the gradual slope by the regular lines of the four battalions of Gardes Françaises and two more of Gardes Suisse, drawn up in fine battle array, with the Aubeterre and de Courten regiments in support, although standing rather closer to Fontenoy. Across the front of the French infantry line ran a sunken lane, a 'ravine' as some described it, eroded by years of use by farm carts and of a type common to the area. The sudden appearance of their opponent's leading ranks, out of what was in effect dead ground, together with their light field guns, came as something of a shock to the French troops. British and French regiments of guards now faced each other at close range, a moment of some martial drama, with many of the officers on both sides recognising old acquaintances in the others' ranks. Lord Charles Hay, serving as a captain with the 1st English Foot Guards and a man with clearly a nice sense of occasion, gallantly shouted a toast to the health of his French counterparts with a flourish of his hip flask. That this might contain nothing more exciting than watered brandy, topped up from a stream the previous evening, does not detract from the charm of the often-related tale.[21]

Hay called out a taunting challenge to the French officers, that he hoped they should stand their ground this day, unlike at Dettingen when they had fled. He then called for three cheers from his own men and these were hoarsely but heartily given, the men threateningly shaking their muskets above them as they did so. The Comte d'Anterroches called to his own men to respond, which they did with rather less verve, but they then brought their muskets to the shoulder. On the order, although some men anticipated the actual command, the entire French front rank fired a volley into the leading British battalions at a range of about 70 yards. The effect upon the British front rank, while not slight, was nowhere near as severe as would had been hoped – men fell, but were quickly replaced by those stepping forward from the second and third ranks in accordance with the well practised drill for such occasions.

This French attempt at disciplined firing by an entire rank was an outmoded technique, well known by the mid-eighteenth century to be less effective than the controlled platoon firing adopted by many armies since Marlborough's days. Within a few years the French would also formally adopt the method, although some regimental officers had already tried to instruct their men in the drill. Saxe had wanted to avoid such a toe-to-toe contest, which he felt sure his men would lose, and in this assumption he was quite correct. The French, as so often was the case, had fired high, at too great a distance, and to poor effect. The response of the British guards, the red-coated men taking a step forward and with muskets brought to the shoulder on tap of drum, was much more telling. 'The order came to fire, and they did fire, two men loading for one.'[2] Firing their muskets by groups of platoons, as they had been endlessly taught and drilled, the British infantry stepped through the drifting smoke until they were at close range to the French. Their musketry rippled in scorching fashion from right to left, the NCOs and officers taking care that the muzzles of the men's muskets were lowered. It had long been observed that: 'The manner of our firing was different from theirs; the French fired all by rank, which can never do equal execution with our platoon-firing, especially when six platoons were firing together. This is undoubtedly the best method.'[3]

The effect on the French soldiers facing the Foot Guards was simply devastating; with their foremost officers and men shot down and the ranks broken, the fine battalions of Gardes Françaises and Suisses went reeling back in confusion to find their supports, having alone lost over 400 killed and wounded in the single opening exchange.[34] The Comte d'Anterroches was wounded by two musket balls, although he survived the day, just about, but the senior French officers who fell in this torrent of close-range musketry included the Marquis de Clissom, Monseigneur de Ligney and Monseigneur de la Paye. Colonel Courten was also killed as he brought his regiment forward to the Garde's support, and his men had to fall back to conform with the general flight of their comrades, but they still lost nearly 300 of their number to the telling fire of Cumberland's infantry.

Major Richard Davenport, who saw the spectacle, wrote rather derisively afterwards to his brother that 'The French Foot Guards ran away at the first fire, as at Dettingen.'[25] It should be mentioned that a captain in the Crillon regiment wrote that the Gardes fell back with only little loss, but if that were so, then their conduct in fleeing was all the more to be condemned. In any case, a broken formation is broken and not a lot can save it immediately – the French infantry had undoubtedly been bested in the first test in the open, just as Saxe had expected they would in such circumstances, but then he had not perhaps anticipated Cumberland's bold, almost bull-headed, advance in quite the way that it took place. 'The English', a French observer wrote, 'then commenced a running fire by divisions. They advanced as if performing a part of their exercise; the Majors levelling the soldiers' muskets with their canes to make their discharge more sure.'[26] Dillon's Irish infantry moved forward to bolster the French line but they were not supported, and for the time being had to fall back. The most eagerly looked-for support for those broken French infantry battalions were the squadrons of cavalry massed some 400–500 yards to the rear, but they were rather too far distant to be of immediate use, and something approaching a panicked flight ensued, with the French foot-soldiers in the centre of the army desperate to escape the relentless and well disciplined lash of British musketry. 'There was', the Marquis d'Argenson wrote, 'one dreadful hour in which we expected nothing less than a renewal of the affair at Dettingen; our Frenchmen being awed by the steadiness of the English, *and by their rolling fire which is really infernal*' [Author's italics].[37]

Despite this success in the opening encounter, the galling fire from the redoubt d'Eu and the *Grassins* in the copses to the right of the Foot Guards did cause some confusion amongst the British battalions. Still, order was recovered quickly and as the lines of infantry fixed bayonets and pressed forward, urged onwards by Cumberland and Ligonier, the effect of the damaging French cross-fire gradually lessened, and with this diminished hindrance the vital left-centre of Saxe's position was carried and to all appearances was in British and Hanoverian hands. The resolution of the duke, and the calm discipline of his infantry, under a terrible French fire, seemed after all to be about to carry the day.

Saxe's best infantry battalions had collapsed and fled before his eyes and those of the now fidgeting royal party, some of the fleeing soldiers actually elbowing their way through the ranks of the cavalry who watched their flight in dismay and astonishment; it seemed that the French were close to facing a catastrophe. The marshal hurried across the field to the king who, unlike his now thoroughly alarmed courtiers, remained commendably calm. Despite the urging of Marshal Noailles that he should withdraw with the dauphin to the far side of the Scheldt, Louis replied, 'No, I am going to stay where I am.'⁵⁸ He almost certainly understood what the effect would be on the morale of the French army if it were known that while they were in the thick of the battle, their king was making off to a place of greater safety. Saxe was able to offer some hasty reassurance, pointing out that reserves were nearby and, despite the clear gravity of the present situation, it remained to be seen whether the allies had enough strength in hand and as yet uncommitted to make the most of the success they had so far gained. The king apparently had no doubt, as he watched the almost invalid Saxe leave his side to hurry about the battlefield, that he would do what was necessary. Much would depend on matters on the right of the French position between Fontenoy and Antoing, and whether the Dutch attack would be renewed with any vigour, if at all.

For all the marshal's admirable firmness, matters did look grim for the French at this point, with the centre of their position apparently broken open. The dense column of allied infantry, tipped with a hedge of glistening bayonets, moved remorselessly forward, inclining slightly away from the tormenting French fire from the wood-line, the soldiers loading and firing their muskets by divisions with great regularity to the steady tapping of side-drums, and in the process ruthlessly wrecking the ranks of the Aubeterre regiment which gallantly came forward and attempted to bar their progress. Saxe ordered forward the du Roi regiment to move against the flank of the column, but they too were driven back with savage loss by the 2nd English Foot Guards. In turn the Hainault, Royal, de Vaisseaux and Soissons regiments moved out from behind Fontenoy to try to close the gap and restore the French position but despite the desperate bravery of their officers, many of whom fell to the rolling British musketry, all these fine battalions were pushed aside with heavy casualties. The commander of the French infantry, the Marquis de Lutteaux, was gravely wounded by two musket balls but refused to leave the field and died from loss of blood while being tended by his own surgeon. In the meantime, it was remembered, 'The French troops gave way, and the enemy penetrated no less than 300 paces into their camp.'³⁹

All this time Saxe was committing his scant infantry reserves in order to hold Cumberland's advance from making ground, and if the Prince of Waldeck could only renew his assault with any vigour, then the allies might yet be successful. 'If the Dutch had but put themselves in movement and joined hands with the English, there would have been no resources, nay, no retreat, for the French army, nor in all probability, for the king and his son.'³⁰ In truth, Cumberland could hardly win the battle on his own, nor had he expected to, but such close cooperation between the two wings of the allied army was not now achievable, and in any case the Dutch had been stopped in their tracks by the solid French defence amongst the villages and redoubts on the right of the position. Now, the duke was not controlling the battle as a commander-in-chief – he had no overview of what was happening, or real contact with Waldeck, and no way to really judge matters on the far side of Fontenoy, nor was he able bring his own powerful personality into play in encouraging the Dutch commander to fresh efforts. In addition, as Cumberland moved forward, his ability to communicate with Crawfurd and his cavalry, and the now diminished army reserve, was progressively lessened.

The dreadful losses sustained by the French infantry were not in vain, for the British and Hanoverian infantry had also suffered badly (as had the Dutch on the left, of course), and for the moment their forward movement slowed and became held up in an advanced, constricted and exposed position, without immediate support. An English officer wrote home that:

> Then things had a very good appearance, and there was a fair prospect of a complete victory, for our infantry bore down all before it, and the enemy were driven three hundred paces beyond the fort [redoubt d'Eu] and the village [Fontenoy], and we were masters of the field of battle as far as their camp. But the left Wing, though favoured by the fire of our batteries, and supported by two English battalions [Duroure's and the Black Watch] which his royal highness sent to favour the attack on Fontenoy, not having succeeded in their attack, and the fort, as has been said before, not having been attacked at all, we found ourselves between cross-fires of small-arms and cannon, and were likewise exposed to that from the front, so that it was necessary to retire ... by the attention of H.R.H. [Cumberland] and the marshal [Königsegg] it was stopped.[31]

The duke determined to press forward and wring the most from the advantage gained at such cost – he was, however, only in command of those thousands of foot-soldiers immediately around him, the mass of British and Hanoverian infantry now grimly formed up with as yet little forward impetus, while caught in a re-doubled French crossfire under Saxe's direction.

It is always tempting to see these things happening in a neat sequence, with the result of the first incidents, for good or ill, having an immediate and direct effect on those that follow. This is of course an illusion, for while Waldeck was striving without success to force the redoubts on the French right, Duroure was breaking into Fontenoy village and Ingoldsby was making up his mind what to do about the Bois de Barri – the Duke of

Cumberland in expectation of these gentlemen being on the point of accomplishing their allotted tasks was moving forward with his infantry onto the plain between the village and the copses. Such a step made sense; he could hardly wait while everything else was accomplished and only then set off, having allowed his opponent leisure to recover his poise and reorder his dispositions in the meantime. Had Cumberland done just that, he would have been understandably criticised for it. The question must remain, though, whether or not those secondary tasks, of such importance to the overall success, were in fact capable of being achieved in the circumstances and with the resources available. Cumberland was on good terms with, and trusted, all three men, so his anticipation of their success, or failing that their timely notice of the fact, is not too surprising. This was taking far too much for granted, that is plain, and with the startling brilliance that hindsight permits, this is all so obvious to us, and yet, in the noise, smoke and tumult of that May morning, things were not nearly so clear to the duke and those around him.

Despite this, against all probabilities, and regardless of both Saxe's careful preparation and Cumberland's lack of creativity in laying his plans, the French army in position was straining under the pressure of the duke's remorseless attack. Whether the marshal could yet succeed in re-establishing order amongst his troops, and realigning his reserves to cope with the looming threat and by doing so hold firm, was far from certain.

Chapter 8

The Infernal Column

The further they penetrated the more they were exposed.[1]

The time was now about 12.30pm, and the early afternoon was warm. The allied infantry with Cumberland were massed in the constricted ground between Fontenoy on their left and the Bois de Barri outcrop to the right; they had been formed by Sir John Ligonier into a great three-sided rectangular column, rather narrower to its front than to the flanks, with the guns to the fore. 'Their infantry', a French officer wrote, 'had formed themselves into a kind of column of square battalions.'[2] Constrained by the narrowing gap into which they had been thrust, the Hanoverian battalions had already fallen back a short way to form a third line. The front 'face' of the column was formed by the Royal brigade (*see* Appendix 1), with the Guards brigade on the right 'face' looking towards the copses on the edge of the woods where Saxe's infantry reserves, hastily drawn from his left flank, were now gathering under the direction of von Löwendhal. The guards were supported by Howard's brigade, while the left 'face' of the column was composed of Onslow's brigade with Sowle's brigade in support. The duke and Field Marshal Königsegg, together with their mounted staff, were stationed in the centre of the column just in advance of von Zastrow's Hanoverians.

At the word of command, with a steady tapping of side-drums, a fresh advance began once more across the undulating grassy plain towards the scattered French infantry, trying to reform their broken ranks. This advance ran no serious risk of being encircled and perhaps cut off, for Saxe had no *masse of manoeuvre* to deploy to do so, as his own reserves were only then being hurried into place to save the army from Cumberland's remorseless attack. If the duke could maintain a real forward momentum, this would clear the path for the British and Hanoverian cavalry to move forward and deploy on the plain beyond the village of Fontenoy. For a brief moment, and despite the lack of success for Waldeck and his Dutch troops on the left, the initiative lay with Cumberland, with the outward appearance of his still having everything to play for.

With few cards left in his hand to show, but judging that the Dutch attack on the redoubts would not be renewed with any vigour, and that his hold on Fontenoy was once more secure, Saxe staked everything he had on holding Cumberland back. He committed his one major formed reserve, calling on his cavalry commanders to move forward and strike the advancing allied column. (Some reports say that Louis XV ordered the squadrons forward, but that seems unlikely, the king appreciating the risk of interfering in a battle while in progress.)

This initial French cavalry effort was, however, curiously disjointed and lacking in punch, as under the impetuous leadership of the redoubtable Comte d'Estrées only the first line mounted regiments of Fiennes, Royal Cravates, FitzJames and Clermont-Prince, sixteen squadrons in all – something approaching 2,500 troopers perhaps – rode forward to try to throw back the duke and his formidable infantry column. This was undeniably a grand martial spectacle with the thrilling calls of their trumpets and the ground throbbing beneath the hooves of the ranks of horses, but the other first line regiments from the Colonel General and Prince Camille brigades did not go forward, the order to do so being confused or misunderstood, and so the French blow was not as heavy as it might have been with a fully concentrated attack. Despite this, with admirable discipline d'Estrées' squadrons were kept well under control so as not to tire the horses too soon, and must have seemed unstoppable in their power and forward impetus. Surely the outcome of the day would depend upon the discipline and sturdiness of those foot-soldiers whose sadly depleted ranks were about to receive the massed charge of French horsemen.

As with so much in this battle, things were not quite what they seemed. Despite the awesome spectacle and all the fine show, cavalry by this time could hope to achieve little against unbroken infantry, well drilled as they were in the best way to receive their charge. This was especially so when those horsemen were faced with disciplined formations and a dangerous levelled hedge of British and Hanoverian bayonets. Colonel Lewis's gunners fired off their last charges of double-shotted canister, leaving knots of struggling screaming horses before them, and then ran for the shelter of the infantry column. At the given signal, to the thrilling shouted command of ''Ware cavalry', the front-rank men dropped to the knee, musket butt to the ground and bayonet uppermost, while the second and third ranks shouldered their muskets to deliver their deadly slashing volley at a range of about 50 yards. For all their dash and bravery, the French troopers were held back by a seemingly invisible hand as the fire of the allied infantry took its awful effect. Their horses were the largest and most obvious target, and wounded animals crashed and rolled to the ground in stricken heaps, inevitably impeding the progress of those in the following ranks, and the fierceness of the initial attack faded away in the noise and the smoke. The gallant and futile French attack incurred dreadful losses but the valour of the attempt was widely admired by friend and foe alike that day.

The smoke-grimed ranks of Cumberland's infantry column remained firm, their well directed volleys of musketry lashed the troopers unmercifully, as the remainder of the French first line cavalry – the Royal Rousillon, the Carabiniers du Roi, Prince-Camille, Colonel-General and Brancas regiments – came forward to join in the attack. Despite the most strenuous efforts of those able to urge their horses close enough to reach out and slash with their long cavalry swords, they could not properly come to grips with opponents secure beyond the line of deadly bayonets. The French were forced to rely on discharging their carbines and horse pistols at the ranks of infantry, but in such a brutal exchange their fire was ineffective. Those troopers who were not shot down or unhorsed turned away from the flashing wall of musketry, trying in the rapidly building smoke to regain and reform their ranks for a fresh effort.

The repulse of the French cavalry was a severe blow, but the effort to hold Cumberland back had to go on and, urged on by d'Estrées, who had already received several musket balls through the tails of his coat, the twenty French second line squadrons – those of the Noailles, Penthièvre, Chabrillant, Royal Etranger, Brionne and de Pons regiments – moved forward in their turn to try to overwhelm the allied foot-soldiers, but their reception was the bloody same, with the added difficulty that the ground around the allied infantry column was now littered with the awful debris of the first cavalry attack. At least three more times the French horsemen came bravely on, but their efforts were increasingly desperate and ill-coordinated – the Carabiniers du Roi alone lost twenty-seven officers killed and wounded in their attacks, a fair indication of the ferocity of the fighting around the column. A French officer remembered that, 'It was like charging two flaming fortresses rather than a column of infantry.'[3] Saxe, who was always reluctant to waste the lives of his men, ruefully wrote later that, 'It was essential to distract their attention by repeated cavalry charges which were, it is true, unable to produce a decisive effect, but gave us time to organise the general attack on which all depended.'[4]

Another desperate attack was attempted, and a few troopers from the Noailles regiment even managed to force their horses into the ranks of the 2nd English Foot Guards, but were all quickly either shot or bayoneted – their dashing commander, the Marquis de Lignacourt, was amongst those killed, and the French regiment lost a standard to a Hanoverian soldier. The battered French squadrons, all but played out now, had once more to rally and fall back to recover their order, before the four squadrons of the Royal Rousillon regiment gallantly came on yet again one last time. Their tired horses were now unable to make more than a walking pace forward, and they just got in the way of the soldiers of the Irish brigade as they attempted to deploy. The ground was thickly strewn with dead and dying troopers and their horses, a sad and sickening spectacle, but their fine effort had not been in vain, for at such considerable cost the cavalry had, albeit briefly, halted Cumberland's advance and gained a breathing space for the army at a crucial moment. Their task accomplished, but with depleted ranks, the bloody and weary troopers and their exhausted horses fell back from the fight for the time being.

It would be well to reflect here that there could be no lengthy exchanges of musketry on the battlefield at this time, whether Cumberland's soldiers were facing French infantry or cavalry. His soldiers carried into action only twenty-eight rounds per man (some reports say just twenty-four), and even in the hasty fumbling of a hectic battlefield a trained soldier could expect to fire off three rounds in the space of a minute, or at worst two rounds as fouled barrels, encrusted with powder residue, made ramming a slower process. In this way, the ammunition carried by each man would soon be exhausted if the rate of fire was not carefully controlled. In the time-honoured way of old soldiers, a few spare rounds might well be tucked away into the folds of a tricorne hat or coat pocket, but there were no relays of perspiring runners following the column with armfuls of fresh cartridges for use. The allied infantry had, of course, already expended some of their ammunition beating down the French Gardes and those other infantry regiments that moved to their support, so their pouches must have been fairly light as the French horsemen approached. Even though the soldiers could stoop to rifle the pockets and pouches of their killed and wounded comrades, to retrieve additional ammunition for use, and even pilfer those of their fallen opponents (the French musket ball being smaller than that used by the British and Hanoverians meant that it could, *in extremis*, be employed), such fresh supply would be limited and uncertain. So, despite stirring accounts of the devastation caused by the allied fire at this time, the likelihood is that the repulse of the French cavalry had as much to do with the steadiness of the soldiers in the column and the massed bayonets that they presented, as it did with the ferocity of the musketry produced. The difficulty was acknowledged, and within fifteen years each British soldier would carry sixty rounds into action.

Having driven off the French cavalry, Cumberland's infantry trudged resolutely on once more, in many cases having to step over the low rampart of dead and stricken men and horses that all but encircled them. The 2nd English Foot Guards were directed by the Earl of Albemarle to turn half left, the flanking battalions conforming to the move, so that the column gradually edged away from the Bois de Barri as if to finally envelop the village of Fontenoy. Saxe was alert to the movement, so potentially dangerous to his dispositions, and directed infantry from the Vaisseaux and Normandie regiments, hitherto guarding the left of the army but drawn in towards the centre where the threat was most acute, to move against the right flank of the column. This hurried effort, overseen by von Löwendhal, was in vain and once more the French ranks wilted under the weight of the British and Hanoverian attack, while a fresh attempt by the wounded Comte de Danois, who led the du Roi regiment against the other flank, also failed.

The French army was hanging on, just, when a message came to Saxe that his artillerymen in Fontenoy were reduced to firing blank cartridges as their stock of round-shot and canister was exhausted. Word was again sent to the royal party that it was no longer safe to remain, and that they should prepare to withdraw to the far bank of the Scheldt; in effect, they faced defeat and only some miscalculation or inaction on the part of their opponents could save the army. Saxe was not pleased when he heard that such a message was sent, but in any case the king was still resolute in his confidence in the old marshal, and determined to remain where he was – if he would not go, of course, his increasingly nervous party must stay where they were, although presumably occasionally glancing over their shoulders to the bridges over the Scheldt.

The fog of war, often commented on, obscures many things that are so clear to the observer who does not have to contend with the mist, smoke and confusion of a teeming battlefield. Such a dire state of affairs that faced Saxe was, of course, not known to Cumberland and Königsegg, mired as they were in the savage close-quarter fighting that still raged around their slowly advancing column. In this, the dreadful losses suffered by the French, cavalry and infantry alike, was no worthless sacrifice; the point was that the critical moment in the battle, on which all hopes or fears of success and failure hung, had passed by almost unnoticed on both sides of the field. The Comte D'Espagnac recalled that:

> As long as the enemy had not taken Fontenoy or the redoubt [in the woods], *its successes in the centre were of no advantage to them* [Author's

italics], since they did not have any support. The more they marched forward, the more they exposed themselves to being taken on the flank.[5]

Crucial factors were plainly in play, for Cumberland, 'brave and bloody', was in the centre of his shot-torn troops and unable to issue firm instructions to his cavalry commander, the Earl of Crawfurd, to move into action. Nor could he urgently request the Prince of Waldeck to renew, at whatever hazards might be, his attacks against the French centre and right, possession of which would have caught them neatly in what could become a pincer movement. Allowing that Waldeck was unlikely to have followed any such suggestion, given the bloody experience of his troops earlier that day, the fact was that Cumberland as the commanding general was out of position and out of contact with his principal colleague, and not really in control of the battle or able to grasp what so nearly might have been a notable victory.

Before long, as the onward progress of his infantry slowed, the futility of pushing further onwards without support was increasingly apparent, and the duke at last rode to the rear of the column and sent a staff officer with orders for Crawfurd to bring the British and Hanoverian cavalry forward. This was done with no delay, but the earl's own advance was hampered by some Dutch squadrons who were in the process of moving to a quieter spot, and only the Blues, the 8th Horse (Black), and the 1st (Royal) and 2nd (Royal North British) Dragoons were able to advance with any purpose. Even then, their numbers were not enough to have had any real effect, however well employed, and the most promising moment for their involvement had already slipped by. As M. Gandilhon has commented, 'The presence of the Anglo-Hanoverian cavalry would no doubt have made the French defence more difficult if not impossible.'[6] The cavalry, that important uncommitted second echelon that might in the right circumstances have moved forward to drive Saxe and his disordered army to destruction, could not see a way to get past the solid and now almost inert mass of allied infantry. Cumberland's infantry were hedged around by French troops battered but resolute in their determination to halt any further advance into the heart of the position. Those British and Hanoverian battalions stood on the open ground which, despite the sodden nature of the ground and occasional sunken farm track, had been seen to be quite suitable for the employment of horsemen as Saxe in his desperation had proved while sacrificing his cavalry. The outcome of the battle had, it seemed, already been decided, as the marshal had just to hold on, while Cumberland, constrained by the terrain and unable to properly deploy his cavalry, had no fresh recourse open.

It is a rare battle that shows no examples of missed chances, and one of the most tantalising of those at Fontenoy was this inability of Cumberland to get his cavalry into action. The ground on the allied left was rather constricted for Waldeck's squadrons to be used effectively, even if the French defences had been beaten down. However, some of those same Dutch troopers had scouted the ground beyond the Bois de Barri the previous evening, and there had been a thought that General Campbell could move his British and Hanoverian squadrons along that same route, the road leading from Leuze-en-Hainault to Tournai. This was hardly a promising option when Saxe was not yet committed to a general action around the village of Fontenoy and could shift powerful forces to his left to counter such a move. It did, though, perhaps hold out the chance for a neat cavalry movement to take the French army in the flank once the action began, and just at the moment that the marshal was stripping his reserves from that very spot to hold Cumberland's infantry advance back. As it was, no such attempt could be made, perhaps because Campbell was struck down so early on in the morning, and his perfectly capable replacement, Crawfurd, was not fully aware of the opportunity it offered. Hindsight shows us these missed chances, but at any rate it was the case that the commander of neither army was now really controlling the battle; it had taken on an implacable character of its own – the outcome would result from a mix of circumstances that arguably were not controlled all that firmly by either Cumberland or Saxe.

The force behind Cumberland's bold advance steadily ebbed away, and Captain Hercules Isnard of the Vaisseaux regiment had the presence of mind, despite being wounded, to have his men drag over a battery of four field guns to fire canister into the close-packed allied ranks. Saxe had ridden over to the Normandie and Vaisseaux regiments, and rallied their broken ranks and sent them back into action alongside the battered remnants of the Gardes Françaises and Gardes Suisse. He also called for von Löwendhal to bring on the Irish brigade, almost his last formed reserve, to move into the attack on the allied column, and this they did with admirable determination. These relatively fresh regiments moved forward with great dash to the strains on fife and drum of the old Stuart anthem 'The White Cockade'. The numbers of native 'Irish' soldiers present by then may have been relatively small, with the ranks of these renowned regiments filled out with German, Scots and even French recruits, but their fine reputation as fighting soldiers persisted.

The scorching British musketry tore through the leading ranks of the regiments of Clare and Dillon, and things quickly became a hand-to-hand, toe-to-toe, contest with the bayonet, with Colonel James Dillon lying amongst the dead. The Carabiniers du Roi also renewed their attack and in the drifting smoke mistook the red coats of their Irish comrades, and lashed about them with their long swords in the confusion until the error was realised. No matter, for all the enthusiasm and valour of the Irish regiments they too were forced back, heavy losses having been inflicted on both sides; Sergeant Wheelock of Bulkely's regiment claimed to have captured a British colour from the 2nd English Foot Guards, but Cumberland's report after the day of battle stoutly maintained that no 'colours, standards or kettledrums' were lost.[7] The duke had his faults, but he had a tendency to strict regard for the truth, and so the bold Irishman's claim remained thereafter in some dispute. The elite mounted squadrons of the Maison de Roi, the Gendarmes, Chevaux-Légers, Mousquetières, Grenadiers à Cheval and the Garde du Corps now came forward to add their weight to the counter- effort, a last chance attempt to employ cavalry to disrupt Cumberland's troops. They were no more successful than their comrades had been earlier in the afternoon, and fell back, although the dauphin tried, before being firmly dissuaded by an aide, to accompany them in their advance.

The repeated cavalry attacks had been gallant but futile, but the dogged fighting abilities of the tired French and Irish infantry, when put to this test, atoned to a considerable degree for their lack of steadiness earlier that day. Saxe's best battalions had at first fallen to pieces on the plain next to Fontenoy, but they had recovered both composure and order at terrible cost; he alone now had the ability to manoeuvre, even if it were only in a limited way, and try to accomplish the destruction of the Anglo-Hanoverian infantry column. Despite all they had endured, the French infantry had reformed a fighting line of sorts, and their cavalry, although badly depleted in numbers and mounted now on very tired horses, could be seen to be regrouping for yet another fresh effort under the command of the Comte de Montesson.

It was plain that Cumberland's grimy and formidable men had been fought to a hard-won standstill, and the duke had the sense to realise it – there was nothing to be done but to extricate his army from what was rapidly becoming a very tight spot. Reluctantly, he gave the order to retire and the bloody ranks, sorely diminished by their losses, held their discipline very well while breaking contact in the heat of an action, a move that in less steady hands could have turned into a rout. In fact, the men of the 3rd Foot (Howard's, the Buffs), commanded by Lieutenant Colonel George Howard, were at this point still advancing gamely into the heart of the French camp – so near had Cumberland come to success. The battalion had to be recalled from almost certain destruction by Sir John Ligonier with the urgent words, 'Colonel, cease beating your drums and face about, and retire as quickly as you can.'[8]

There is no more testing military manoeuvre than to disengage in the face of an active enemy, and the allied withdrawal was successfully undertaken in the most difficult circumstances. Saxe wrote in grudging admiration, 'Such things we have seen, but pride forbids that we should speak of them, for we know well, that it is not in our power to imitate [emulate] them.'[10] The battlefield was wreathed still in drifting smoke, and in both armies officers hoarsely shouted orders and sergeants bustled their remaining men into what passed for orderly ranks ready for the expected onset of fresh fighting. This might even be a fresh drive forward by Cumberland perhaps, for few, if any, of the commanders that day were too sure just what had happened, and what might lay immediately ahead. It was now about 2.30pm. We, of course, now know that the allied thrust was spent and could not be revived and renewed, meaning that a withdrawal from the field in good order was necessary – and although Saxe could not be sure of it yet, he would soon learn that, after all that had happened, he would soon be acclaimed as the victor of that awful day.

Crawfurd's squadrons of cavalry, still fairly fresh, moved forward to cover the allied withdrawal, the Blues performing particularly well after coming under renewed French artillery fire. The 34th Foot (Cholmondeley's) was also noted for its particular steadiness during this hazardous phase in the battle, and an eye-witness wrote of their conduct:

> With the French artillery ploughing through the ranks and the squadrons of French horse riding around it, the regiment, with cool soldierlike courage and discipline, covered the retreat of their comrades so effectually as to allow no trophies to the enemy.[9]

The regiment was by no mean an exception, and the steady withdrawal from contact by Cumberland's infantry attracted admiration from observers in both armies.

Within the space of about twenty minutes of the order being given, Cumberland's slow and careful retirement from the field was in steady progress; his troops could rightly claim not to have been beaten but they were not able to stay where they were. To do so would be to court catastrophe, but it was plain that the British guns that had gone in with the column could not be hauled off, and they had to be left as trophies for the French. This was perhaps inevitable, as they had been dragged by hand into position during the advance, and the gun teams left near Vezon had meanwhile taken themselves off the battlefield. The loss of such pieces was a matter of sore regret, no matter how inevitable, but a French officer remembered that to their front stood the six field guns, and there was no option but to charge them as they fired still at close range. In only a few minutes the final salvoes of canister killed or wounded, it was estimated, sixteen officers and 250 men, but the French infantry overran the guns in triumph all the same.

The allied soldiers made their way doggedly back, brushing off the grasping but weary clutches of their French opponents, and Saxe's troops increasingly realised that they had on their hands an unexpected victory. Although they might have hoped to turn their opponents' withdrawal into a rout, this was not possible. All the same, the result was clear: 'The soldiers threw their hats in the air, shouting "Long live the king – victory is gained".'[11] The torn-up ground over which the two armies had grappled together with such ferocity was littered with long and sombre lines of fallen and broken men in their red, light grey and blue uniforms, eloquent testimony to their valour. 'Our brave and not to be excelled forces are retiring', a young British cavalry officer wrote, 'in as much order as they advanced and we wish for no more than that the enemy would advance from behind their batteries.'[12] Perhaps so, but he also noted that he had not expected to survive the day as he and his troopers covered the withdrawal of the infantry.

In actual fact, Cumberland's army was able to march away without much difficulty or interference: 'The battalions fronting the enemy every hundred paces, that there was not the least attempt made by the enemy to disturb us ... The cannon lost was left behind for want of horses, the contractors having run off with them.'[13] Not all Cumberland's officers by any means felt the need to retire, however, and the Earl of Crawfurd wrote of his annoyance at hearing 'a damned drum beating a retreat, ordered by whom I never could learn.'[14] Still, commanding the cavalry to the rear of Cumberland's infantry column, he probably had not the best view of what had taken place, and what was and was not able to be achieved by this point in the day.

Despite the losses to his army, and the trying circumstances of the withdrawal from contact with an active if weary opponent, Cumberland was able to reform his troops in good order behind the village of Vezon, gathering in Waldeck's regiments and Königsegg's few Austrians as he did so. Given the battering that the French army had just received, the duke judged that his opponent's energy too was spent, and in this he was proved right. As the afternoon and evening wore on, there was an unchallenged, if rather dejected, march by the allied army to the fortress of Ath just 13 miles away. Much of the army's equipment was also got away (other than the guns left on the field, and some kit that the ever-troublesome *Grassins*, expert foragers as they were, managed to seize). With little further difficulty Ath was reached by the troops early the following morning. That so much was achieved, and at relatively little additional cost after such a trying ordeal, speaks highly for the discipline and good order of Cumberland, Waldeck, Königsegg and their all-but-exhausted men.

Saxe, for all his clear success in the battle, was soon to be criticised for not mounting a vigorous pursuit of the allied army as it marched away – nothing much in fact was attempted that might have turned the withdrawal from contact into something more serious. The marshal halted his troops a few hundred yards or so from the edge of the plain, still close to Fontenoy village, and seemed to think of little more for the moment than restoring the order of his own army. The reasons for this lack of action are perhaps clear: the French troops were fought out and could do no more that day; much had been gained, and Saxe was content with that and preferred not to push his men to do more and take risks after all that had been achieved. The main reason for this was evident, and he frankly recalled that 'We had had enough.'[15]

The marshal, of course, was by now in a state of near-total physical exhaustion, tormented by thirst and having to be helped from his saddle – he personally could attempt to do little more that day. The covering force of allied cavalry was a strong deterrent to making too close a pursuit, although in one of the late skirmishes on the outskirts of Vezon Field Marshal Königsegg was thrown from his horse and only escaped capture by clinging to the pommel of a passing trooper's saddle.[16] Nonetheless, the allied army, if battered and sore, was certainly not broken, and the troops were probably in no worse shape than their opponents, so Saxe's caution was well warranted, although not all his regiments had been heavily engaged, and might have been sent in to make a more determined pursuit. Von Löwendhal and d'Estrées, aggressive and highly competent, were both on hand and could surely have been given command of such a task, but it was not done, illustrating the state of the French army after its trials that day.

Saxe had fought at Fontenoy to prevent Cumberland from lifting the siege of Tournai. He had also, it seems likely, deliberately sought to draw the allies forward and into a direct confrontation on a battleground of his own choosing, where the mistakes of Dettingen would not be repeated and a smart repulse could be delivered. There was also a distinct limit to what the marshal could expect his army to do, and he had the sense to see this. In the whole endeavour he had undoubtedly succeeded, and the operations against the garrison in Tournai could now proceed without hindrance. Therefore, Saxe had clearly achieved his aim, and mauled the allied army in the process, albeit in a steady rather than brilliant fashion and at a staggeringly heavy cost paid by his own troops. Those men were now very tired, so apart from cautiously moving some units towards Vezon to form a protective screen for his army, he attempted nothing more that day. After so much effort this is not that surprising, although a commander not so wearied by ill-health might surely have done more.

Louis XV, unsurprisingly, was jubilant at the repulse of the allied attack – the army had not been defeated, that counted most – they still held the field of battle and had captured guns to show for it, a sure sign of success. Louis XV was the first French king to be present on a successful field of battle for many, many decades, and it was a great moment. 'Everything', he declared with slightly overblown enthusiasm, 'comes from God and Maurice de Saxe.'[17] The king rode around the battlefield, thickly littered as it was with the dead and broken men and horses of the two armies, offering thanks and congratulations to his smoke-grimed soldiers, together with the grant of a field commission for Sergeant Wheelock of the Irish Brigade, who plainly, if nothing more, told a good tale. The sergeant did not retain the commission for long and sold it soon afterwards, as was his right.[19]

That day, 11 May 1745, had been a harsh test for both armies, with losses that were by any yardstick severe, when judged against the likely benefit for either commander in the event of success. Cumberland, Königsegg and Waldeck had fielded 50,000 troops (although not all had taken a very active part in the fighting) and their army's casualty roll for the day was some 7,300 killed, wounded or missing, of whom commendably few, reported as just 288, were apparently taken as unwounded prisoners.[19] This figure is a little too precise to perhaps be overly relied on. Amongst the wounded was the 'Stepney Amazon' Phoebe Hassell, a redoubtable female soldier masquerading as a man, who was wounded with a bayonet slash to the forearm. The heaviest loss, as might be expected, occurred in the ranks of the British and Hanoverian infantry, at some 5,700 killed or wounded – Königsegg's Austrian squadrons and *Freikorps* companies had been hardly engaged at all and had fewer than 100 casualties. The 23rd Foot (*Royal Welch Fusiliers*) lost twenty-two officers and 300 other ranks as their reported casualties, while the 12th Foot (Duroure's) saw nineteen of their twenty-one officers fall out of a total of 321 killed or wounded in the desperate fighting for possession of Fontenoy. Amongst the losses to the allied cavalry, the 2nd (Royal North British) Dragoons notably lost James Campbell, colonel of the regiment, together with one of their treasured mitre caps, a distinction awarded after Ramillies in 1706, which was afterwards displayed as a trophy in the Musée de l'Armée in Paris.

On the other side of the field, for Saxe and his king, the grisly toll of killed or wounded in the 56,000 strong army he had deployed for the battle was remarkably similar to that suffered by the allies at 7,450 – although this figure includes an estimate only for the undoubtedly heavy losses amongst some of the squadrons of cavalry that dashed themselves at such cost against Cumberland's infantry. Once again, individual units suffered quite differently, depending upon their fortunes on the day – the casualties amongst the Gardes Françaises and Suisses have already been mentioned, while the Aubeterre regiment lost 328 men out of fewer than 600 who stood to that morning. The nimble and efficient Arquebusiers de Grassin, who caused Richard Ingoldsby so much trouble in the Bois de Barri, had 241 casualties out of a total of just 820 present in those copses. By contrast, the Touraine, Auvergne and Piemont regiments were hardly engaged all day, and had only slight losses as a result.

The king, having warmly congratulated the weary Saxe on the performance of his troops, turned to his son, who was understandably also elated at the success achieved; gesturing to the battlefield, he commented that the blood of their enemies was also the blood of men, and he should not forget it. As after Dettingen, commendable efforts were made by the French to tend to the wounded of both armies in makeshift dressing stations and hospitals initially around Tournai, and subsequently, after a bone-jolting cart journey over poor roads, in Mauberge, Valenciennes and Le Quesnoy in northern France. Despite some rough and ready treatment, many of the wounded survived appalling wounds, but Cumberland was later moved to protest to Saxe that the allied wounded left on the field suffered some neglect. This was largely due to a misunderstanding of what, with the best of intentions, had to be a somewhat haphazard affair. However, allied surgeons and their assistants were certainly accosted as they moved about the field, and their medical chests rifled before Saxe put a stop to it. The French medical teams, and those troops detailed to recover the wounded, would naturally be inclined to give first attention to their own fallen comrades, but they did their best for their stricken opponents all the same. Burial parties were hard at work to clear away from the fields around Fontenoy the almost 5,000 dead soldiers, not to mention the hundreds of slain horses who lay alongside them.

For all his errors in judgement and limitations when reading (or misreading) the battle, Cumberland had displayed conspicuous courage during the fighting; his horse was struck three times by French musket balls and he received a glancing blow to his elbow. His firm handling of the infantry column, wedged between Fontenoy and the outcrop of the Bois de Barri at the moment when the battle turned in French favour and catastrophe beckoned, commanded wide admiration. Still, it could not be denied that the woods to the allied right should have been cleared as a necessary preliminary to any attack, and the duke neglected to ensure that this was done. He did not insist that Richard Ingoldsby got on with the task when it was given him, nor, on seeing Ingoldsby's hesitation, whether warranted or otherwise, did he move to replace that officer with someone more determined. Ingoldsby would face a court-martial for his negligence in due course, but the main fault on that score on the day lay with the duke, in his failure, or inability, to sufficiently grip the battle at an early stage. The wounded brigadier general, who had plainly failed in the task given, attracted much of the blame for the lack of success on the day; he would endure public disgrace and be obliged to give up his commission and leave the army. (*See* Appendix 2.)

Over all that, allied success had come tantalisingly close for a brief time, as Saxe's line bent and cracked under the pressure exerted by Cumberland, and Sir John Ligonier recalled that he thought the day was won at one point. As a French report related:

> I do not know whether many of our generals would have dared to push infantry into open ground in the teeth of a great body of cavalry, and imagine that they could maintain twelve or twenty battalions for many hours in the midst of a hostile army as the English did at Fontenoy. This without being once shaken by cavalry charges or once relaxing their discharge of musketry.[20]

The Duke of Cumberland's despatch to London on the day's events was a model of brevity and veracity, for that was his way, and the key passage read:

> I marched yesterday from the camp at Brussoel with the whole army about two in the morning, to attack that of the enemy near Tournai, which was posted between the Chaussée d'Ath and the Scheldt; but I am sorry to say it was not with the success I hoped for. My infantry was

formed in two lines before the enemy's camp between three and four; but as the horse that was to support them had some defiles to pass, they could not be in readiness so soon, so that the whole army did not move to the attack until about seven, and in this interval the infantry was exposed to a furious cannonade. The right wing, however, advanced with great resolution and gained ground of the enemy; but being continually galled by the fire of the batteries and redoubts on the flanks, and also of a very smart and continued discharge of small arms, and the left wing not advancing equally with them, they could not maintain the ground they had got, but were obliged to retire. They were twice rallied, but without effect, so it was judged necessary about one of the clock, that the army should retreat, and it was done with so good order and countenance that the enemy did not give us any disturbance.[21]

The duke was noticeably reserved in offering only mild criticism regarding Waldeck's inability to make progress on the allied left, and was also commendably silent on his own very brave conduct on the field with his men under heavy and prolonged artillery fire. Still, an aide added a distinctly admiring private note which was found attached to the despatch:

The duke would not allow anything to be said of him, in the relation made, but certainly nothing but his presence and example could have established that order with which the retreat was made. There was hardly any confusion ... He saw, and examined, and gave his orders with the utmost calmness and precision.[22]

George II, however, was clear that much of the cause of the failure of the attack could be laid at the door of the Prince of Waldeck and his apparent lack of enterprise in forcing the French lines between Fontenoy and Antoing. 'The King attributes the miscarriage of the attack upon the French lines at Tournai ... solely to the misbehaviour of the left wing.'[23]

However, the king was partial to a marked degree where the conduct of his son was concerned, and in no real position to judge with any certainty. Waldeck's lack of success in what might be viewed as an all-but-impossible task was certainly most convenient when finding ways to divert blame for the failure from Cumberland. The aims and the concerns of the Dutch in the campaign, though, were not necessarily the same as those of the British and Hanoverians; Waldeck was in sole command of his own troops, and solely responsible for them. He was not simply and unthinkingly subject to Cumberland's orders, but in receipt of clear instructions from The Hague as to how his regiments should be employed and to what risk they should, and importantly should not, be put. Historical shadows are long, and arguably these instructions did not countenance attempting at whatever cost, as was notoriously done at Malplaquet in 1709, to batter a way with inadequate preparation through fixed defences resolutely held by French troops who were plentifully supplied with artillery.[24] Even so, much of Cumberland's plan had relied upon Waldeck, and it is hard not to feel that he could have given more support than he did, perhaps with a more thorough preparation and prior reconnaissance ready for the assault by his infantry, no matter what challenges he faced.

On that same point, Field Marshal Königsegg, in his own despatch to Maria-Theresa and her husband in Vienna, said that the lack of success was due to the inability of Waldeck to press home his attack to good effect. He added, rather improbably, that only one Dutch battalion of infantry (not named) had made any progress in going forward to close grips with the French defenders. He must, however, have had to rely in this on reports by others, as he rode with Cumberland that morning and was in no position to actually see the Dutch infantry go in to the attack. Such second-hand reports tend to be unreliable, especially when all around were looking for someone else to blame. That Waldeck's attacks failed is undeniable, and had a consequent impact on what Cumberland attempted, but whether the task he was given was ever in the first place achievable is less clear. For all that, Saxe was constrained in his ability to move troops from his right, between Antoing and Fontenoy, to counter Cumberland's thrust, and in this we can see his concern for the pressure, both real and potential, that Waldeck's attacks, together with Colonel Duroure's effort against that village, delivered. Antoing, never under threat, remained packed with French infantry throughout the day. It should also be remembered that the Dutch regiments, and their German and Swiss-recruited comrades, whose performance was afterwards so derided by those who were not there to see them go into action against the French batteries, suffered some 1,500 casualties in their attacks. If they failed in their given task, then arguably it was not for want of trying.

As it was, there might have been a great deal of truth in the bystander's comment that in respect of Tournai 'there was no other chance of relieving the siege'.[25] That chance was always rather slender, but to have defeated Saxe at Fontenoy would not in itself have saved the fortress, as long as the marshal could still operate with his army in the field; his concerns about their ability to manoeuvre have already been mentioned, but his opponents laboured under a similar handicap. Sieges tended to have an almost indomitable dynamic of their own, and while the covering army, in whatever condition, could hold off or hamper a relieving force for a time, the siege would be able to go on to the inevitable point of submission by the garrison.

This begs the question whether the tempting prize of relieving the garrison in the fortress actually warranted the cost of giving battle against a numerically superior opponent, moreover a veteran campaigner who had been allowed the opportunity to entrench a position of considerable strength. The alternatives open to the allies – to try to manoeuvre the French out of position, or to threaten a French fortress of equal importance to Saxe and so lure him and his army away – were promising missed chances that have already been commented on. Oddly, a defeat for Saxe on 11 May 1745 would not of itself have saved Tournai unless Cumberland and his fellow commanders had shown a desire, hitherto absent, for a subsequent campaign of manoeuvre in order to force the French army still further away from its close investment of the fortress. The Scheldt river, so potentially perilous to the French had things gone wrong once the action began, would have also served as a shield behind which they could probably have gone on with the operations against the fortress.[26]

With the awful total of over 15,000 dead and mangled men divided into broadly equal proportions between the two contending armies at Fontenoy, it might be tempting to ask whether the outcome was actually a draw with the honours more or less even. Clearly not, as the two army commanders had fought with the same intention, although from diametrically opposed angles. Saxe sought to drive the allied army off, inflict on his opponents a sharp blow, and then get on with the siege of Tournai, while Cumberland fought to drive the French away from the fortress, save the place, and deliver a sharp blow of his own in the process. In pursuit of these aims the French commander was plainly successful and Cumberland was not. Still, to term Fontenoy as a great victory for the elderly marshal seems to exaggerate the fact, for he fought a distinctly limited action and manoeuvred on the field without finesse and only then to bolster his sagging line, for no greater reason. 'The margin of victory had been narrow.'[27] Also, Saxe failed entirely to follow up the allied withdrawal and take advantage of a promising opportunity to make the most of what he had so bloodily achieved. 'We had had enough that day' – telling words from the veteran warrior, who was ailing, it is true, but he had subordinates, men of skill, around him who could have taken up the task if he had so ordered things, or perhaps thought the risk worth taking. For Cumberland, of course, the disappointment of his failure – for as army commander it was his and no other's – was severe; mistakes and miscalculation were evident, and a lack of experience once exposed is usually made to pay the due price, one paid on 11 May 1745 by the duke's indomitable men. All the same, he got his battered army off the field in good order, and in the circumstances of that day this was no mean feat, and should be properly recognised as such.

Hanging over any consideration of the day of battle at Fontenoy is the obvious puzzle of Ingoldsby and his failure to clear the woods on the allied right. His own explanation for this is given in Appendix 2, but what is not explained is why Cumberland, who plainly appreciated (a little belatedly) the importance of having the thickets cleared of French troops, and the battery in the redoubt d'Eu silenced, did not ensure that this was done. The duke, for all his shortcomings, had a forceful personality and was used to being heeded; he was on good terms with Ingoldsby and could surely have impressed him with the absolute necessity of what he had to do. If Cumberland was aware that the woods were not yet clear, why did he persist in an advance that would be made into an increasingly constricted space, and under enfilade artillery fire from either side, a danger that had been pointed out to him the previous evening? This begs the question of whether the duke was under a misapprehension, and in fact thought that the clearing operation on his right had progressed further than it had; the late instruction to Ingoldsby to keep pace with the main infantry advance to his left indicates that this may have been so. No excuse, of course, for a field commander must be held responsible for his failings and shortcomings, but this may, at least in part, provide an explanation to what took place.

It was generally acknowledged that Cumberland's behaviour under fire had been admirable – this was no simple sycophancy, but there were also some comments on the general lack of firm direction during the battle. The duke, though, felt that success had been tantalisingly close at one elusive point, and he wrote to his sister on 22 May: 'All the account I can give is that the Allies have been within a trifle of destroying the whole French army, and taking King, cannon and baggage. The whole right wing did their duty.'[28] This private correspondence, with no intention of distribution to a wider audience, smacks of veracity, reflecting a general feeling among the duke's officers on what had almost been in their hands. The Prussian king, Frederick II, on reading a report of the battle, pulled a wry face, shrugged, and said that a half-swing to the right or to the left by Cumberland would have rolled up the French army in position and driven it into the Scheldt. For Louis XV, of course, the reaction to the success of the day was one of unrestrained relief: his soldiers had stood firm in his presence and the muddle and disgrace of Dettingen two years earlier was expunged. In essence, the jubilant report of the battle, published in Paris on 26 May 1745, included the telling comment, 'Our victory may be said to be complete; but it cannot be denied that the Allies behaved extremely well.'[29]

Chapter 9

Luscious Sweets of Success, Bitter Fruits of Failure

Nothing shall be wanting to make the best use of our diminutive army.[1]

After the sharp repulse and heavy losses suffered by their army at Fontenoy, Cumberland and his fellow commanders could do little more to raise the French siege of Tournai, unless the garrison held out while the field army recovered its poise and was able to try again. This was not likely to happen soon; although the withdrawal from the field on 11 May had been well handled and in the broadest sense successful, there was understandably an atmosphere of deep disappointment after so much unavailing effort and cost. Recriminations for failure were inevitable, as was a certain seeking for scapegoats, and Captain Watts of the 2nd (King's) Regiment of Horse was charged with misconduct in the face of the enemy during the allied withdrawal: 'The squadrons came galloping back in great disorder, and the foremost of them was Captain Watts.'[2] The gallant captain was able to demonstrate that he was swept away by a sudden flight of a handful of horsemen at some point, despite his own efforts to stand fast, and was accordingly acquitted of misconduct. The episode does, of course, cast a measure of doubt on accounts of the complete good order in which Cumberland got his army off the field of battle. Some accounts do ascribe this lack of steadiness to the conduct of the Dutch and Austrian soldiers on the allied left and centre, but this might be doubted as there was general agreement that, overall, the movement was well done. It was also acknowledged that many men had conducted themselves very well, and a soldier in the Black Watch, who was under sentence of a flogging for allowing a French prisoner to slip away, was pardoned by the duke after attention was drawn to his otherwise excellent conduct.

Having faced such disappointment, and with an army so reduced in numbers that replacements and reinforcements were needed, Cumberland found that it was not tenable to remain at Ath in such close proximity to

Saxe, who might yet spring into fresh action. For five days the troops lay in camp, almost literally licking their wounds, while returns for the dead and missing were prepared and reports made. Good order was insisted on, and the bereaved wives of the fallen were sent away to make their uncertain way to their homes (unless those enterprising ladies found a new husband in the meantime, of course). Several French deserters who had been quietly engaged as servants by senior officers were also sent away, and a suspected spy, named Patrick Crowe, was hanged on what appeared to be rather slim evidence.

On 15 May Cumberland had to deploy a few squadrons of dragoons to sweep the environs of the camp and drive off troublesome French *Grassins* who were trying to harass the sentries. The next day the allied army withdrew in different directions; the Dutch marched to Liège to draw on the supply depots established there, and effectively took themselves out of the active campaign for the time being by diverting troops once more to man their fortresses. Cumberland went with the British and Hanoverians to Lessines on the river Dender, where he received fresh troops from the garrisons in Oudenarde and Ghent. Efforts to restore allied strength in the Low Countries did bear fruit, and Austrian and Hessian regiments, fortified with cash subsidies from London, soon arrived to more than make good the losses suffered at Fontenoy. However, the initiative in the campaign, for the time being, lay firmly with Saxe. The marshal was constrained, too, and had chosen not to pursue the allies as they marched away, at least in part because the fortress of Tournai still had to be taken and the garrison, although understandably despairing of early relief, were commendably active in what had become rather challenging circumstances.

Ten days after the battle Richard Davenport wrote: 'We have the mortification to hear the French continually firing upon Tournai, without any possibility of succouring it.' Something, it was hoped, might yet be done for he added: 'The Governor, it is said, behaves with great resolution and is resolved to hold out to the utmost extremity.'[3] Such optimism was misplaced, as Saxe's covering army was still in place, naturally elated at their recent success, and the allies were in no state to challenge them for the present. Nor, due to long neglect and indolence by past governors of the place, were the munitions and supplies in the fortress sufficient for the garrison to hold out for much longer, however resolute they may have felt. With little hope of relief, the governor gave up the town on 23 May 1745, and sensibly capitulated the citadel on 20 June rather than face a storm by the French 'sword in hand'. Saxe entered the *Grande Place* of Tournai to great acclaim as victor, having previously done so as a junior officer in company with Marlborough and Eugene in the late summer of 1709. Despite this undeniable success, the place had held out against a formal siege for fifty-six days (counting from the initial investment of the town) – a commendable effort in the circumstances and tying the French down in the process; Marshal Vauban with his keen appreciation of the true value of formal defences would have approved. Most accounts of the battle of Fontenoy pay little attention to the garrison's admirable performance in restricting the freedom of Saxe and his army for considerably longer than expected, and the fact that little advantage of this effort was taken by Cumberland, Waldeck and Königsegg does not detract from the good work of the ill-equipped Dutch and Swiss garrison.

Following the capitulation of the citadel of Tournai, Saxe could put into the field larger numbers now that there was no longer a need for the besieging force to remain in trenches. He promptly sent his columns marching northwards towards Ghent, deep in allied territory, and Count von Löwendahl arrived before the unsuspecting town on 11 July, an allied attempt to intercept his progress having been forthrightly thrust to one side in a fierce little affair at Melle two days earlier. A report of the action written by Colonel Pechell of the 31st Foot (Beauclerk's) tells how the 1st Foot (the Royal Scots) 'Captured an enemy battery and held it for a time under a murderous fire, but the other regiments could not make headway, and though the Royals fought their way through to Ghent half the force fell back to Alost.'[4] Lieutenant General von Moltke had been caught at Melle by a substantial French force under the command of the Duc de Chayla, and his outnumbered troops were badly mauled before they could get away. Brigadier General Thomas Bligh reported to Cumberland that:

> The enemy were coming down in full march about three miles from Ghent where they attacked us on each side from houses and a battery of cannon from the right. Our losses are very great having fought for a long time ... I am afraid the general [von Moltke] is either killed or taken prisoner.[5]

In fact von Moltke made his escape, but the allied troops had to fall back and Ghent could not be reinforced, perhaps fortunately as the soldiers involved would just have become prisoners of the French before too long.

With great dash, von Löwendahl's troops stormed the meagre defences of Ghent, and the place was in his hands within a matter of hours. Bruges fell to a detachment commanded by the Marquis de Souvre a few days later, without the need to fire a single shot. By 22 July von Löwendahl was also in firm possession of Oudenarde. The allied position in the Low Countries had fallen to pieces in the face of a dynamic French campaign. The performance of the allied garrison in Ath (another of Vauban's masterpieces) was a bright spot, however, and they staunchly held out against a siege conducted by Saxe himself, and only submitted early in October after a very gallant defence. The troops in the fortress deserved special merit for their stout conduct, and this was widely acknowledged.

Stirring events were taking place all the while to the east, where on 4 June 1745 Frederick II defeated an Austrian and Saxon army at Hohenfreidberg in Silesia. The Prussians went on to advance into Bohemia but, faced with Maria-Theresa's obstinate stance and stiffening resistance, the king concluded a peace with Vienna at the Congress of Hanover late in August. This would not last very long, of course, but Frederick confirmed his support for the candidature of Archduke Francis-Stephen for the imperial crown. This election duly took place on 13 September, and the empire had a Habsburg ruler (at least by marriage) once more. The plans laid by Emperor Charles VI so many years before seemed at long last to have come to fruition, but there was an unresolved war to be fought all the same.

Cumberland was all this time active in rebuilding both the fighting strength and the fighting spirit of the allied army; that this was a pressing necessity is shown by reports that Saxe was replacing his losses at Fontenoy more rapidly than the duke. Not all French units were back to anything like full strength after their ordeal at Fontenoy, but the allied army had the same problem over manpower. This had been made even worse by the insistence of the Dutch that they reinforce their fortress garrisons at the expense of the field army – such a policy offered false security, not unlike a drowning man clinging to the anchor of a sinking ship for safety. The most certain security for those fortresses would have been to have a powerful and active army operating in the open, and this was clearly lacking. Cumberland did, however, take the precaution to reinforce the garrison in Ostend, so important to the flow of troops and supplies to and from southern England and the Low Countries. Fresh troops were also sent by London, but the full import of the reported Jacobite adventure had not at that point been realised; it was noticed also that the quality of those men sent as reinforcements was not impressive. The additional troops in Ostend were in place in good time, though, as a spirited French attempt to surprise the place was made on 9 August 1745.

Two days earlier, fourteen merchantmen had entered the harbour with guns and stores to augment the garrison, and this was not a moment too soon. Von Löwendahl attacked and quickly took the outwork known as Fort Plassendael, and was able to emplace heavy guns on the adjacent sand-dunes to ward off those British and Dutch warships that tried to assist the allied garrison. Cumberland, having joined forces with Waldeck once more, established his headquarters at Vilvorde, intending to shield Antwerp from attack. 'Should we lose Antwerp', he wrote, 'we should be unable to subsist ourselves or keep communications with Holland.'[6] Meanwhile, the Dutch commander covered the approaches to Brussels. Morale in the allied army was noticeably fragile with an increased rate of desertion, for which the most severe penalties were imposed. 'Daniel White', it was reported, 'tried for endeavouring to seduce men to desert, to receive 1,000 lashes at the head of every brigade of foot.'[7] Saxe, meanwhile, was at Alost, accompanied still by Louis XV and his elegant entourage, and he moved against the small allied garrison in Dendermonde, thwarting a belated attempt to reinforce the place on the same day that von Löwendahl arrived before Ostend.

> H.R.H. attempted to throw a detachment in to Dendermonde but was disappointed. 300 men from each army embarked in boats from Antwerp, but about St Amand they found detachments of the enemy, and the river there being narrow, the tide slack and wind contrary, there was no contending and as many as could came back. The major who commanded the Dutch, a worthy, gallant officer, was killed.[8]

The French drained the water out of the defensive works and began a bombardment of the garrison, who, outnumbered and outgunned and with inadequate defences, quickly capitulated. The guns captured were immediately sent by Saxe to add to the pressure on Ostend; the harbour itself was soon under French fire, preventing any further reinforcement for the allied garrison, whose Austrian commander, the Comte de Chanclos, was commanding ill-trained men whose morale was understandably rather poor. With no hope of relief, the garrison surrendered, and Nieupoort also fell into French hands. Saxe's troops now commanded the Channel shore, and the direct link between London and Hanover, so dear to George II, was directly threatened.

Arrangements were in hand for an exchange of those prisoners, both French and allied, taken in the campaign so far, a practice not unusual at the time as this would both augment the fighting strength of armies, and also relieve each commander of the task of having to house and feed, after a fashion, their captives. Saxe's letter of 13 August to Cumberland on the subject was laced with courteous, even affectionate, terms, for such was the custom of the age between active opponents out on campaign:

> I have much pleasure, monseigneur, in repaying the courtesy and goodness with which your Royal Highness has deigned to honour me in your last letter. I am so fully sensible of these favours as I am eager to seek an opportunity of convincing you of my wish to deserve them.[9]

For all these niceties, the campaign was pressing on, and the next step for the marshal was to move and attempt to seize Brussels. Despite his ill-health, the rather controversial plan was to campaign through the cold winter months when his opponents would expect all armies to have gone into warm quarters. Many of the French generals were sceptical of the chances for success, especially as four main waterways – the rivers Scheldt, Dender and Senne, and the Vilvoorde canal – would have to be negotiated and safely crossed during the approach march. If any of these obstacles had been held in strength by his opponents, then Saxe's whole plan would surely have fallen to pieces. Despite such reservations, the allies' attentions were elsewhere that winter, not least in northern England and Scotland where the Jacobites were a growing threat. In mid-January 1746 the French army began to move quietly northwards on the roads leading to Halle, Malines, Louvain and Vilvoorde, all of which were occupied without serious difficulty. By the last day in the month the outskirts of Brussels came in sight of the marching columns; French cavalry patrols clashed that night with Dutch outposts, and the city was quickly invested. Not for the first time in the year's campaign, the allied commanders had been caught unawares.

The garrison in Brussels, under the command of the very capable Austrian Count Kauntiz, comprised some 12,000 men, and they were well supplied with guns and provisions. The defences were not in good order, but the count could expect relief from Dutch troops encamped at Antwerp before too long, and the weather soon turned bitterly cold, increasing the hardships of the 22,000-strong French army as it shivered in encampments in the surrounding frost-covered fields. Seen in a calm light, the position that Saxe had achieved with his surprise move appeared not too promising, as Kauntiz showed no sign of submitting and his artillery was active in bombarding the investing French troops. The setting-up of proper siege batteries proved particularly difficult in the now sodden, now frozen fields, and all the while the weather continued to worsen. Saxe attempted to flatter and bluff his opponent into surrender, writing on

11 February that 'I am aware of the respect due to a large and brave garrison, and would be delighted to accord it all the honours of war. But Brussels is an untenable city; any army which attempts to save it risks certain destruction.'[10] The allusion to the allied defeat at Fontenoy is clear – what had been served out to Cumberland the previous May could be provided again if the opportunity arose. There was also a degree of menace in Saxe's outwardly polite message, as he went on: 'The factor that causes me the most uneasiness is the high spirit of my men ... They are fully conscious of their superiority.' In effect, the count was being warned to submit or face a storm by troops, whose behaviour could not be controlled once they were in the city.

Count Kauntiz was an able commander, and not so easily browbeaten, and he delayed a decision until 20 February, when, seeing the French completing their preparations for an assault, he capitulated on good terms. Saxe's success was, without doubt, remarkable and the haul of paroled prisoners and booty taken at Brussels included eight cavalry squadrons, seventeen infantry battalions, all Kauntiz's artillery, and no fewer than twenty senior Austrian and Dutch officers. The personal baggage of the Prince of Waldeck and the now absent Duke of Cumberland was seized, but courteously returned by Saxe to its owners. The loss to the French in this startlingly successful operation was slight, at just some 900 killed or wounded,[11] and Louis XV was once more suitably warm in his congratulations:

> Your abilities and experience have overcome innumerable obstacles; the rigours of winter, the problems of transport, the response of a large garrison, and the propinquity of a relieving army. Your unshakeable resolution has been an inspiration.[12]

The king was particularly delighted that Saxe was able to send to Versailles no fewer than fifty-two captured colours and standards, together with the *Oriflamme* banner lost by King Francis I at the dreadful defeat at the hands of Spanish troops at Pavia in February 1525. This was a French success on a truly significant scale, and demonstrated in the starkest fashion that the initiative in the Low Countries still lay firmly with the marshal.

Rather less delighted at this point was Frederick II of Prussia, who still pursued his argument with both Austria and Saxony over the vexed question of Silesia, recovery of which Maria-Theresa was determined to obtain. A rash attempt to thrust at Frankfurt-on-Oder by an Austrian and Saxon army was foiled in November 1745, with the Saxon troops defeated at Hennersdorf. The Prussian response was rapid, with the king's armies converging on Leipzig, and then marching towards Dresden, where the Austrians hoped to regroup with their allies; on 15 December 1745 the Saxons were beaten yet again, at Kesseldorf. The Austrians had little alternative but to fall back into Bohemia, and Dresden was occupied by Frederick. On Christmas Day the Prussian king got his reward with a treaty agreed with both Austria and Saxony, which left him in possession of Silesia. The significance of this episode was immense, as Prussia in the process became the pre-eminent German power, a fact that would grow ever more apparent in the coming decades, while Austria by comparison, in losing Silesia, was noticeably diminished in its ability to exert influence in German affairs, and would become less and less influential as time went on. Hitherto little regarded events in Scotland had, in the meantime, firmly captured the attention of the king and Parliament in London, and for the time being campaigning in Europe would have less than their full attention.

PART III
HARD ROADS TOWARDS PEACE

Chapter 10

The Jacobite Distraction

I am surprised to see this romantic expedition revived again.[1]

On 13 August 1745 the Duke of Cumberland received news that the Young Jacobite 'Pretender', Prince Charles Edward Stuart, had landed in Scotland from a French frigate, the *Du Teilloy*. The prince had raised the standard against George II and what he regarded as illegitimate (in fact Hanoverian) rule in London. The young man, of course, was acting on behalf of his father, the son of James II, who had gone into exile in France in 1688. Charles Edward did not at all regard this action as a revolt or rebellion, as he believed that he was coming to reclaim what was right, but perhaps inevitably there were many who did not share this view. His own adherents, many of them ambitious and with a fortune to make, may have quietly shared the same opinion, but were determined to chance all no matter what might come of it.

Word of the expedition setting off from France soon got out, and the Duke of Newcastle wrote to the duke from London: 'Your Royal Highness will have heard that all accounts in France agree that the Pretender's son embarked at Nantes on the 15th past, N.S. and, as is confidently given out, for Scotland.'[2] This whole adventure was intended by the French, and certainly had that effect, to distract the British from their campaign in the Low Countries, while expending little effort or treasure in doing so. Tentative plans were made, though, for a landing by French troops in southern England to support the Young Pretender, but the arrangements all seemed a little hazy and ill formed.

Such an attempt at a 'Rising', as these episodes had become known (1715 and 1719 had seen similar occasions, marked in each case by extraordinary incompetence), was long expected and General Sir John Cope, commander-in-chief in Edinburgh, had been tasked by the government to prepare the defences in the north. Support for the Stuart cause, once the prince actually landed on Scottish soil, steadily grew but his arrival in the Western Isles was by no means widely welcomed, as many could foresee the trouble that would result.

Cope warned the government of growing unrest in the Highlands, and suggested that the clan Campbell, who could be relied upon to oppose the Jacobites in whatever was attempted, be re-armed. 'It is a pity', the Duke of Argyll wrote to London on 11 August, 'that we should be in so much danger from the Jacobites in the Highlands, when the government has certainly a great majority in the country on its side.'[3] Such warnings were not heeded in either Edinburgh or London, but Cope did send the 6th Foot (Guise's) to garrison the newly built government strongholds at Fort Augustus, Fort William and Fort George. The prince's freedom of action in hoping to raise the clans *en masse* in his support was hampered in the process, but by 29 August, as the Jacobite threat grew, Cope and his outnumbered troops had fallen back to the security of Inverness.

With Cope effectively brushed to one side, the Young Pretender set his gradually growing 'Highland' army marching south, passing Dunkeld, Perth and Stirling with little interference. On 16 September Edinburgh came in sight, and the following day a Jacobite advance party gained entrance into the city by subterfuge. The castle, towering over the city, was securely held by troops commanded by the 86-year-old Lieutenant General Sir Joshua Guest (yet another veteran of Marlborough's wars), and he had no intention of submitting to any impudent summons to hand over his charge. Guest made it clear that any attempt to take the castle by force would be met with a prompt bombardment of the city, regardless of the consequences to the populace.

The initiative for the time being seemed to lie with the prince, even though his welcome amongst the cautious citizens of Edinburgh had been subdued. Still, time was pressing, as General Cope had marched his troops to Aberdeen and embarked them on ships sent from Leith for the purpose, and was busily shipping them southwards. Landing with his infantry at Dunbar to the south-east of Edinburgh, Cope joined forces with two regiments of dragoons, and confronted the Jacobites at Prestonpans on 20 September 1745. There the government forces were soundly defeated, and the inexperienced soldiers, daunted by the energy of the highlanders' attack, proved no match for their headlong charge with broadsword and Lochaber axe in hand. 'The infantry in the first line were miserably massacred by the rebels. Such as threw down their Arms and begged for Quarters upon their knees, were inhumanely mangled.'[4] The dragoons, newly raised and inexperienced, but all the same men who might have made themselves very useful, as the clansmen had no experience of or liking for facing mounted opponents, made off as soon and as quickly as they could manage. The whole affair was all over in little more than twenty minutes, but it is significant that the reports of the brutal treatment of the wounded soldiers by the victors were widely talked about, and equally widely believed to be true. As so often, the tales grew with the telling.

George II and his ministers in London, having taken a rather dismissive view of the Jacobite adventure north of the border up to that point, were now alarmed, and Cumberland was instructed to bring ten battalions of British infantry to England from the Low Countries. Their transports arrived at the Thames estuary a few days before the fighting took place at Prestonpans, while two battalions sailed with the duke direct to Newcastle, arriving there a couple of weeks later, and two more battalions were summoned from garrison duty in Ireland. In addition, several thousand Dutch troops, recently released on parole after the fall of Tournai on the understanding that they would not serve again in the Low Countries, were landed at Newcastle, and the assistance of Hessian troops was also obtained.

A quite substantial government force was in this way gathered in north-eastern England, but the Young Pretender took a route south passing to the west of the Pennines. Carlisle was reached on 9 November, and the march went on south into Cumberland, Westmoreland and Lancashire. Preston was reached without difficulty, while government commanders tried to organise their lagging campaign to counter the confident Jacobite advance. Local reaction to the approach of the Jacobite army was still lukewarm (as it had been in much of the Scottish lowlands), although some volunteers for the prince's cause were raised in Manchester. Significantly, there was no evidence of a popular rising in favour of the Jacobite cause, amongst either the gentlefolk or the populace generally.

Much of the prince's plan had been based on firm assurances he had received of a warm welcome in both Scotland and England, and also Wales, but this was not so. Undeterred, at least to outward appearance, by the lack of popular support or real interest, the Young Pretender marched southwards and reached Derby on 4 December 1745. The army had achieved a great deal, and met little real resistance since the fight at Prestonpans, while the road south to London beckoned and appeared to be open. This was a cruel illusion, for government forces were gathering to bar the route, and there was no practical means to harness French support in the teeth of the squadrons of the Royal Navy prowling the waters of the English Channel. Assurances from Louis XV had in fact proved of little worth once British attention had been deflected from Flanders, and hopes of support from English gentry and people had not materialised –

both outcomes could have been foreseen, perhaps. Then there was the Duke of Cumberland, dangerous but not yet engaged and in the field, with a strengthening army which, as it mustered, was more numerous than the Jacobites, the highlanders and their few adherents.

At an acrimonious council of war in Derby on Thursday, 5 December 1745 the decision was taken to withdraw to Scotland to refresh, rest, re-equip and recruit the Jacobite army. The discussion understandably grew heated, and Charles Edward was disappointed at the outcome, but the decision taken to march back to the north stood. As soon as this development was known, General Wade was instructed to take his troops across the Pennines into Lancashire, to cut off the route the Jacobites would take, but he moved too slowly to do so. The decision to withdraw to Scotland was also reported in France, where preparations had indeed been made to attempt an armed landing in southern England to coincide with the arrival in London of the Jacobite army. That plan was now abandoned, but in any case it is hard to see how it would have proceeded unless the French gained control of the Channel. The young prince was resentful at the decision that he felt had been forced on him and declared that he would summon no more councils of war and would make his own decisions from now on. He would have to have more councils, that much was inevitable, given the strong-willed men he led, and his cause might have prospered more if he had paid closer attention to the advice he received. In fact, with the Highland clans at best able to muster only some 20,000 fighting men in total, and with not all the clans by any means supporting him (most prominent amongst the government supporters being the Campbells), the prince had needed to rely upon a rising of Jacobite loyalists both in the Scottish lowlands and in England, and this had not happened. That being so, the decision to withdraw from Derby, while tantalising as one of the much-discussed 'what ifs' of history, was unavoidable, while the whimsical myth of Jacobite popularity was exposed for what it was.

Cumberland's attention was diverted for a time by a false report of an imminent French invasion of southern England, but this passed and on 18 December 1745 his troops clashed with the Jacobite rear-guard at Clifton Moor in Lancashire. Nothing succeeds like success and the contrary is also true – the villagers and townspeople who had been coolly curious to see the Jacobite army on the march south were more hostile on their return. The Young Pretender and his army fell back past Carlisle and re-entered Scotland; unwisely, he left a small garrison in place, mostly comprising English volunteers – those who had not already seen clearly how the wind blew and quietly deserted. Carlisle did not hold out for long, and after a short bombardment the Jacobite garrison surrendered on 30 December, explicitly without the promise of good terms, for which apparent omission Cumberland was afterwards rather strangely criticised.

Any claim that such men, clearly considered to be rebels by the government forces, might have had upon mercy at this time was not too clear; there was a sharp price to be paid for armed rebellion, of which all were surely well aware, however noble their cause might be thought. Sentiment in government circles, and amongst many of the citizenry, was strong against the Jacobites and the trouble being caused, and a general feeling was evident that stern measures must be taken. There were also exaggerated accounts of occasional acts of misconduct in what had largely been a well behaved Jacobite army, whose discipline even amongst the disheartening circumstances of what many regarded to be a retreat northwards, had held up well.

The prince's army regrouped at Glasgow and, after levying a fine of £10,000 sterling on the unsympathetic citizenry there, marched on to Stirling, cautiously followed by government forces under the temporary command of Lieutenant General Henry Hawley. Charles Edward was now reinforced by a modest number of regular French and Irish troops belatedly sent by Louis XV, in addition to some fresh recruits from amongst those Scots who hitherto had tended to hang back; other regular troops sent from France were waylaid on the high seas by the Royal Navy. A siege of the government-held Stirling castle was begun, but Hawley approached with a force of 8,500 troops, many of them veterans of the Flanders campaigns who would, it was hoped, better stand against the highlanders than had happened previously. A general action was fought at Falkirk on 12 January 1746, with the Jacobites doing well once again and driving Hawley's men back in disorder. Just as at Prestonpans, reports of highlanders butchering wounded men as they lay were circulated and widely believed, no matter how truthful or otherwise the tales might have been. Despite this undoubted success, no real pursuit of the government troops was attempted. The siege of Stirling castle was renewed, but once more without result, as the Jacobites lacked the equipment, heavy guns and expertise – and probably also the temperament – to take forward such a formal operation. All the while, precious time was trickling past and the initiative was slipping away from Charles Edward, for the government campaign, lagging for so long, was now taking firmer shape.

The Duke of Cumberland resumed command of the troops in the north on 30 January, and reprieved dozens of soldiers Hawley had planned to shoot or hang for their cowardice and occasional desertion at Falkirk. The duke now marched his army northwards once more and the siege of Stirling castle was abandoned by the Jacobites, who fell back to Perth after spiking their guns and blowing up the powder magazine. A growing trickle of desertions from the Jacobite ranks was partly the cause of this apparent timidity on the part of an army that had smartly trounced its opponents so recently; Cumberland sought to encourage this trend, with instructions sent out to harry those Highlands districts in rebellion. Harsh orders perhaps, but they were hard times, and this ruthless course had wide general support, and nor was the Young Pretender averse to similar measures.

There were certainly limits on what should and should not be done, and incidents of ill-discipline amongst Cumberland's troops were punished, with two soldiers being hanged for looting near Aberdeen, which the army reached without difficulty in early March. That some misdeeds would go undetected and the miscreants escape justice was inevitable, but it is perhaps only fair to comment that the Jacobites were by no means blameless in such pillaging endeavours. The Duke of Atholl, prominent amongst the prince's supporters, directed that his highlanders should burn and destroy the houses and goods of those who refused to join him. This mirrors Cumberland's orders closely, while the prince's own stern instructions on 4 March to burn the houses of all those who ignored his summons are clear as to what was to be done to encourage enlistment into his by now shrinking army. These were hard times indeed for those who wished not to get involved in such affairs, and the conclusion that both armies were guilty of excesses, either sanctioned or otherwise, seems to be a reasonable assessment of their general conduct.

The Jacobites fell back again; Charles Edward was increasingly short of money and prominent backers and active support was faltering, while his army's strength ebbed away as his fighting men in growing numbers sought their own homes in the Highlands. In early April a rather feeble attempt to seize Fort William was abandoned, and any chance of moving to attack Cumberland – and perhaps repeat on a grander scale the success at Falkirk – was frustrated by a lack of supplies with which to sustain the army. On 8 April 1746 Cumberland marched north from Aberdeen, the duke now being anxious to settle things with a firm victory in open battle rather than to have matters fade away into the hills without real conclusion. The fear was real that such a course was open to the Jacobites, with perhaps a renewed advance by the prince in the summer, involving

Cumberland and his army in a lengthy campaign while matters in the Low Countries languished.

As it was, four days after leaving Aberdeen the duke was at the river Spey, and rather to his surprise the army crossed without trouble. By 14 April Cumberland's advanced guard, after some light skirmishing with Jacobite outposts, had reached Nairn. His health was drunk by his soldiers the next day, on the notable occasion of his 25th birthday, ordered as a day of rest, with brandy being provided at his own expense for each man. Not surprisingly, the men cheered him as he rode past, and the duke doffed his hat in response. 'Perhaps the talk across the copper kettles that night was of the dead ground at Fontenoy, twelve months before.'[5]

The Jacobite army was now dispersed over the locality to find forage and food, but despite the difficulties everything remained to play for – a resounding success in battle against the government army would soon set all to right, and Charles Edward would be able to take his campaign southwards once more. The prince chose to concentrate his forces on Drumossie Moor near Culloden House, there to make his stand; his choice was not really approved of by his senior officers, who thought that the ground near Dalcross Castle would be more promising for the best tactical employment of the nimble highlanders. A Jacobite council of war decided first of all to attempt a night march with an encirclement of Cumberland's army by two columns, and a dawn attack while they still lay in camp – a difficult operation certainly, but one that offered the hope of a fine reward. The hungry men began their move in the evening of 15th April, but the leading column under Lord George Murray went astray near Kilravock House in the dark and mist, and by dawn on the 16th only some 5 miles had been covered rather than the 9 intended. The march had also been observed by Cumberland's outposts and surprise was no longer possible, so the operation had to be abandoned. The prince could have fallen back on Inverness to gather in his still absent foragers and feed his men with what little was available, but instead it was decided to regroup with those men he had to hand, and stand and fight on the open moor.

Cumberland advanced the 10 miles from Nairn on Wednesday, 16 April 1746 with some 7,800 men, well closed up and on the alert for any sudden attack. Charles Edward arrayed his own tired army, reduced by stragglers during the abortive night march to little more than 5,000 strong, with the wind and rain blowing cold into their faces. An unfortunate argument broke out amongst the Jacobite commanders over the question of who was to have the post of honour on the right of the line. By long custom this would be held by the clan MacDonald, but the prince had agreed that George Murray's Atholl men should have the honour, a decision that did nothing for the harmony that should have existed within the ranks of the Jacobite army at such a moment. In any case, the troops on both sides had little to be cheerful about – the highlanders were hungry and disgruntled, while their opponents had yet to face the headlong charge that had carried the day at Prestonpans and Falkirk. 'It was a very bad day', wrote Edward Linn, one of Cumberland's soldiers, 'for wind and rain, but thank god it was straight upon our backs.'[6]

However, the government infantry might have been encouraged by a new bayonet drill to which they had been introduced. It had been noticed in previous engagements that the highlander was clearly at his best in the charge, typically firing his musket at range, then closing to fire off his pistols, if carried, and then rushing in to close quarters with the small targe (or shield) and fearsome broadsword. The highlander would catch the soldier's bayonet on the targe and thrust it upwards and out of the way, laying the soldier open to a killing stroke with the sword. This ferocious close-quarter fighting tactic had been very effective, and to counter it each soldier was instructed to ignore the highlander immediately to his front – no easy task and calling for strong nerves – and to thrust instead with the bayonet to the right, under the raised sword arm of the highlander attacking his comrade to that side. Given the bunching effect of the Highlanders' headlong charge, the forward impetus and sheer verve of which was part of the tactical value, the line of soldiery would almost always overlap that of their opponents and so each man would be sure to have his comrade to his left covering him. This called for a high degree of discipline and cool-headedness in difficult circumstances, but was a tellingly effective innovation, as would be seen.

The Jacobite artillery opened fire at about one o'clock, but the guns were badly served and the measured reply from Cumberland's gunners, under the command of Colonel Belford, was to much better effect, their round-shot soon causing dozens of casualties in the Jacobite front line. After some frustrating delay and confused orders, the impatient highlanders charged. On the right their headlong rush had some initial success, despite the sharp fire they endured, and hand-to-hand fighting began, with bayonets, musket butts, Lochaber axes and claymores plied with vigour. The highlanders' attack was not well supported by those on the left, and was firmly repulsed by the government troops who stood their ground and effectively used the new drill they had learned. The newly re-armed Campbell levies, placed in the enclosures on the left of Cumberland's line, and with clearly no liking for the Jacobites, also poured their musketry fire with great effect into their flank as they came on.

In less than thirty minutes the Jacobite army was beaten, unable to penetrate the government line in significant numbers, and fell back in confusion and disorder with many of their leaders amongst the killed and wounded. They were covered to a limited degree by their few mounted troops, and the French and Irish regulars present; Charles Edward Stuart left his men to fend for themselves and fled the field with a few attendants (or was led away protesting loudly, depending on the account given); in effect, he was now a fugitive with a handsome price on his head. The prince's men, also now fugitives, were pursued by Cumberland's dragoons and many were cut down as they fled. Such a ruthless pursuit was, and long remained, a common feature of a defeat in the field, with the victors clinching their success as opportunity arose and preventing their opponents from rallying.

Smiling broadly, as might be expected, the duke rode along the line of smoke-grimed and blood-spattered soldiers, acknowledging their cheers, their waving hats and chants of 'Billy, Billy' and 'Flanders, Flanders' pointing clearly to where they thought their next campaign trail should be. Cumberland thanked them warmly for their efforts, while a staff officer was sent spurring southwards to take ship to London with the good news of victory. Pitched battles always have a grim aftermath, and some, but by no means all, of the wounded Jacobites were despatched with the bayonet as they lay helpless on the field as Cumberland's men moved forward – any spirit of mercy towards those regarded as rebels was not evident, and the memory of the highlanders' own conduct in the aftermath of both Prestonpans and Falkirk undoubtedly had a role in this grim work. Whether true or not, the reports had been believed and that was the crucial point.

Accounts of the losses sustained at Culloden vary, as might be expected, especially as there is no reliable precise estimate of the actual numbers of Jacobites present on the day. However, there seems general agreement that Cumberland's army lost 309 killed or wounded (with one man rather inexplicably listed as missing), while it is recorded that 2,000 Jacobites were interred in the mass 'clan' graves that still mark the battlefield; the figure is suspect, of course, and far too precise to be taken at face value. Some 222 French and Irish soldiers were taken prisoner, and as regulars in uniform they were given good terms; much less kindly handled were about 320 highlanders and those captured under arms but wearing civilian dress, who were regarded as rebels. The haul of abandoned booty secured by the victors was impressive, listed as 22 cannon, 2,500 muskets, twenty-seven barrels of powder, and 1,019 round-shot; without much doubt the '45 as a serious matter was over and done with.

Months of hazardous wandering through the Highlands lay ahead for Charles Edward, as romantic legend tells us. Sometimes dressed as a girl, living in squalid shelters and tormented by gnats and midges, he perhaps understandably often relied too heavily on the bottle for solace. Some turned a shoulder to him in his flight, partly through indifference or perhaps fear of government reprisals, but despite a very handsome reward of £30,000 sterling offered for his capture, dead or alive, he was not once betrayed. At last the young prince boarded a French ship in Loch Nanagh, and he safely but miserably reached France on 20 September 1746.

Central to this account is the conduct of the Duke of Cumberland, and the degree to which he has been vilified, then and later, often by those who had a Jacobite axe to grind. Lurid and hard to credit stories of deliberate and calculated atrocity were given out and widely believed, but they are, in the main, difficult to substantiate. While government troops were scouring the countryside to round up fugitive Jacobites, instances of ill-discipline were almost inevitable, as the districts through which the troops now moved were regarded as enemy territory and in consequence warranted little consideration. That many areas of the Highlands had not risen in support of the prince was not clear to local commanders. Cumberland was active in enforcing tough measures against those troops caught in such acts of looting or ill-treatment, and severe sentences of flogging were not uncommon, even if they were usually remitted to a lesser severity in practice. It might also be well to again mention and to remember that at that time those regarded as rebels, in Great Britain and elsewhere, could expect little mercy unless the victor chose to offer it. One highland officer in the Young Pretender's army even commented on some of the more lurid tales of atrocity that he had never heard of the rebels being killed in cold blood. This is perhaps overstating the case, and the victors were certainly ruthless in their behaviour, but it was also believed among Cumberland's men that the Jacobites had their own orders to give no quarter in victory and, as with the memory of their own reported ill-treatment of the wounded, this would certainly have coloured the attitude of the government soldiers after Culloden.

Measures were taken to harry those who had fled to the Highlands: that much was prudent from the point of view of the government, and to be expected. Once again, hard times call for hard measures, and reports certainly circulated of excesses and brutality by troops, but there is a strong sense that the tales grew in the telling. In fact, those Jacobites who willingly gave up their arms and returned to their homes were in many cases pardoned – a lot did so, but quite a number of others remained at large, armed and unrepentant, and defiant of lawful authority. In those cases it would be surprising if they had not been harried and met with stringent measures when apprehended. No more could the senior figures in the Rising easily escape justice, unless they fled abroad to await the time when pardons might be doled out by a government tired of the whole affair. Other notables found their way to a reckoning on the scaffold on Tower Hill in London, and could surely have expected little else. In many cases, however, a marked degree of leniency was shown to the prince's followers, as with the young Simon Fraser, who led his father's clansmen in the rising but was pardoned after conviction for treason. He then raised a regiment for government service in 1757, fought under Wolfe at the Plains of Abraham in Canada, and prospered sufficiently to become a major general in 1771.

Of course, to beat a smaller army of ill-equipped and hungry rebels, and to harry the survivors sufficiently (and perhaps more than sufficiently) so that there should be no recovery, did not begin to mark Cumberland as a great commander. Still, had he failed in the task his own fate that day may be assumed to have been an unhappy one. Greater leniency and clemency could have been shown over the whole affair – of course that is so, but whether the measures taken were extreme, by the standards of the day, is less obvious. Whether he behaved well or ill in this whole sad matter, Cumberland was, quite understandably, the nation's hero of the hour, and widely lauded as such on both sides of the border. The French strategy, without too much effort or expense, to divert Great Britain's gaze and military effort from affairs on the continent had worked very well, but this escapade was now thoroughly at an end. The duke's attention could, after a decent pause for rest for himself and his veterans, be devoted to a wider stage: a stage in the Low Countries that in recent months had been left open for Marshal Saxe.

Chapter 11

The Treaty of Aix-la-Chapelle

Now tell us all about the war, and what they fought each other for . . .[1]

The Treaty of Fusen in September 1745 saw the election as emperor of Maria-Theresa's husband, Archduke Francis-Stephen, and this would seem to have settled the key question that hung over the war of the succession. All the same, there had been too much unfinished business, particularly in Silesia, for a peace to come about all that quickly. While tragic events were unfolding in northern England and Scotland, the war stumbled on and in the Low Countries the campaign for the summer of 1746 was once again distinctly lacking in sparkle, being largely confined to sieges of some not unimportant fortresses. Louis XV and many of his courtiers were in Brussels, once more to comfortably enjoy vicariously the rigours of campaigning, and their presence proved a distraction for Saxe, so that he was very content to see them all return to Versailles in June. 'The courtiers', Frederick II of Prussia remembered, 'rent the camp with intrigues and generally thwarted the marshal's intentions. So numerous a court required 10,000 daily rations of fodder for their horses.'[2] Since the provision of adequate fodder for the thousands of horses that accompanied any army was an enduring headache for commanders, this was no meagre consideration. Significantly, Antwerp, and Valenciennes and Mons were all taken by the French by August, and attention switched to the great arsenal at Namur, still held by the allies. With that fortress in their hands, the French could fall on Liège and Maastricht and truly start to lay the borders of Holland open to the threat of invasion.

Just as with Tournai the previous year, the allies could not lightly give up Namur, and their army, commanded in Cumberland's absence by Sir John Ligonier and the Prince of Waldeck, took up a position to cover the fortress; Saxe, for once, appeared hesitant in his intentions. One problem the marshal had to contend with was the appointment of men to positions of command, despite having less than complete faith in them to do their jobs properly; he wrote, 'I have detailed 40,000 men for the investing of

Mons, and the siege is to be conducted by M. le Prince de Conti. Almighty bless him!'[3] Saxe's lack of enthusiasm for the appointment is clear, but the fortress was nonetheless secured on 10 July and Valenciennes was then captured by the prince.

Meanwhile, Prince Charles of Lorraine had assembled a powerful Austrian force on the Rhine, but although the allied armies managed to combine forces, their supply lines were threadbare and the commanders, Waldeck and Prince Charles, appeared unsure how to counter Saxe's moves. After some manoeuvring for position, a French threat to take Huy on the river Meuse neatly unbalanced the allied arrangements, and Namur tamely fell to the marshal's troops on 19 September. Saxe wrote to Louis XV:

> I have held Prince Charles who is encamped within cannon-shot of this position; indeed we are separated by a stream [from us]. However, I do not believe he will attack me, and think I have effected a good deal in forcing him to abandon Namur to us without committing myself to a battle, whose issue is always doubtful when one cannot rely on the discipline of one's troops ... They do not show well in manoeuvring on open ground.[4]

Waldeck and Prince Charles, with Ligonier and his British detachment, moved into place to cover the approaches to Liège. The two armies faced each other in poor autumn weather at Rocoux on the Tongres road to the north-west of Liège. The right wing of the army comprised Prince Charles with 45,000 Austrians, while the left wing was formed by Waldeck with 25,000 Dutch under command. Ligonier held the centre of the allied position with 24,000 British, Hanoverian and Hessian troops. The position was a good one, and the small villages were put into a state of defence, but the allies were trying to cover too long a frontage with too few troops, and Saxe noticed this defect.

In the early afternoon of 11 October 1746 the marshal attacked the allied army in position, and the Comte d'Estrées carried the small village of Ans, which lay almost on the outskirts of Liège. The allied left was under pressure, and Saxe drove hard against the centre, the villages of Rocoux, Liers and Veroux, all held by Ligonier's twelve battalions. Despite a stout defence, the position was carried by French infantry, albeit with heavy losses, by 4.30pm. Prince Charles could not shift his troops to Ligonier's aid, due both to the poor intervening ground and the menacing presence of a powerful French force that he could see gathering to his front. There was little that the allied commanders could do but retire in whatever order they could manage, and despite the handicap of having to cross the river Meuse while getting off the field, this was safely achieved. The allies lost some 4,500 men that day, while the casualties in Saxe's army were listed as 3,518. Just as after Fontenoy, the French commander did not pursue the allied forces with any vigour, an apparent neglect in part because of a lack of adequate supply for the army. Saxe had been noticeable for his almost reckless bravery under fire during the engagement, but he remained far from well. Ligonier seemed to feel that he could have received more immediate support, writing rather waspishly the next day that 'This affair, to give it the right name, cannot be called a battle, for I question whether a third of the army was engaged.'[5] Whether or not this was really so, winter was coming on, and the armies went off to find their quarters.

As is often the case with a war that had become fought for its own sake, the time for a negotiated conclusion to affairs was near. Fresh approaches were made by Louis XV's ministers to conclude terms for a peace, on the main basis of a restitution to their rightful owners of all fortresses and lands occupied during the struggle. Given such remarkable French success in the Low Countries, this might have been viewed as a handsome and welcome offer, and was naturally attractive to the Dutch, whose own territory was by now under such threat. Despite lingering concerns for the security of Hanover, this was less appealing to the British, and larger subsidies were voted by Parliament in London to sustain Maria-Theresa and her army. On a far wider stage the British also had no intention of lightly giving up their territorial gains made in French Canada, most particularly at Cape Breton, or on the Indian sub-continent, and without a carefully negotiated settlement France had little hope for their recovery.

So the tired conflict went on, the fighting having come perilously close to the Dutch border; accordingly, the flagging military effort of the States-General, now under the direction of the Stadholder, William IV, Prince of Orange, was reinvigorated. The Duke of Cumberland, fresh from his success against the Young Pretender and back in the Low Countries once more, undertook the training and preparation of Dutch forces in preparation for the coming campaign in 1747. The encampment ground near Breda was poorly chosen, though, and the morale and well-being of the army suffered accordingly. The French could once more field greater numbers in the Austrian Netherlands than the allies, having stripped other armies of men to bolster Saxe's strength, but Cumberland now had a contingent of excellent Bavarian troops under his command. Moving swiftly, Saxe sent troops in late April to seize a number of small and poorly defended Dutch fortresses near Antwerp and in the province of Zeeland, movements that Cumberland failed to prevent, having to manoeuvre to cover the approaches to Maastricht. The latent threat to southern Holland remained, and the duke faced a dilemma, but he judged correctly that Maastricht was really Saxe's principal goal in the campaign; the loss of the fortress would entirely rupture the allied dispositions in the region. After trying but failing to isolate and destroy a French detachment under the Duc de Clermont near Tongres, Cumberland was faced by the combined French army on 30 June. Two days later battle was joined at Lauffeldt, some 2 miles to the west of the outlying defences of Maastricht.

The British and Hessian troops held the left and centre of the position adopted, with the Dutch, Hanoverians and Bavarians to their right, while Austrian troops anchored the far right flank of the army. Sir John Ligonier commanded the allied cavalry, in rear of the infantry and astride the road leading to Maastricht from Tongres. The villages of Wilre on the left and Lauffeldt and Wilfringen in the centre were at first occupied by British and Hanoverians, then evacuated on Cumberland's orders and prepared to be fired, and then occupied again, leaving little time to properly prepare them for defence. Saxe deployed his army on the Heights of Heerdern, with d'Estrée's powerful corps of cavalry on his right, de Broglie alongside and de Clermont in the centre with the bulk of the infantry. The mixed cavalry and infantry of Clermont-Tonnère formed on the left of the army. Marshal Saxe was perplexed by the apparent indecisiveness of the allied movements in and out of the villages, which clearly had to be held firmly at all events, and formed the opinion that Cumberland might, after all, be about to decline to give battle and retire. 'For more than two hours the marshal believed that the enemy was manoeuvring to recross the Meuse.'[6]

The battle opened that misty morning with de Clermont's infantry advancing to clear Lauffeldt, only to be thrown back by ferocious musketry from the defenders, who made good use of the cottages and gardens for protection. Ligonier moved a battery forward, which took the French infantry under enfilade fire, and completed their repulse with terrible losses. The fighting escalated quickly along the whole line, but Saxe pushed more troops into the assault on Lauffeldt and Wilfringen. He was desperate to take advantage of what he still thought was an opponent on the point of withdrawing, and who might be hustled to destruction in the act of trying to get across the river Meuse. In fact, the allies were standing their ground and fighting very well. The Marquis de Salière's infantry were sent in to attack Wilfringen, but the defenders, under the command of Landgrave Frederick II of Hesse, fought back with great courage, losing both villages at one point but promptly regaining them at the point of the bayonet. An officer recalled that the British soldiers had:

> Carried into the field twenty-four rounds a man. Afterwards they had a supply of eight rounds a man more. After this was spent they made use of all the ammunition amongst the dead and wounded, both of their own and of the enemy's. When no further supply could be had, they formed themselves immediately to receive the enemy upon the bayonet.[7]

The bloody contest went on for a gruelling four hours, but Saxe's grim determination to seize the villages was matched by the dogged resolve of the Hessian and British soldiers to deny him. Battalion after battalion was fed in to the contest by the marshal; the losses were appalling, but with the king once more at his side Saxe was intent on carrying the day. The Comte d'Aubeterre, prominent on the day of victory at Fontenoy, was amongst the senior French officers shot down at the allied barricades, alongside many of the men he led.

Cumberland also reinforced the infantry holding his centre, bringing nine Austrian battalions of infantry over from the right flank where they could see and do nothing. The gunners in both armies were pouring in round-shot and canister, and the du Roi regiment suffered particularly badly with its commander, the Comte de Bavière (half-brother to the late Emperor Charles VII), amongst those killed. At last, after a supreme and costly effort, de Salière gained a firm foothold in Lauffeldt, and the allied grip on Wilfringen began to loosen. Saxe now sent forward d'Estrées with his massed cavalry, but they were met with a spirited counter-charge by Ligonier's squadrons, and the respite enabled Cumberland to withdraw his infantry from the field in good order.

The losses that day were frightful: 'Never was anything more horrible seen. The plain and villages all round were covered with dead and wounded men.'[8] Saxe had been successful, watched by his king once more, but his 'victory' was only achieved at the cost of 14,000 French casualties – more than twice the number suffered by his beaten opponent. Sir John Ligonier, commanding the allied cavalry, valiantly provided the rear-guard for Cumberland's army as it marched away, and he was amongst those taken prisoner, falling into the hands of two French dragoons. Ligonier was taken to be introduced to Louis XV, who graciously received him at the end of the day: 'Well, general, we will have the pleasure of your company at supper tonight.'[9] The king was astonished to learn that Ligonier was French-born, and had been forced into exile with his family due to their adherence to their Huguenot beliefs by his own great-grandfather,

Louis XIV. Ligonier was released on parole, and having gone to the allied camp to settle his affairs, returned to temporary and comfortable captivity with the French as agreed. Such instances of courtesy are heartening, but for Saxe, his reputation as a great commander would always have the shadow of the bloodily mishandled day at Lauffeldt hanging over it.

Maastricht remained firmly in allied hands despite the setback for Cumberland on 2 July. Saxe wrote, 'We made so many mistakes that we had to draw back,'[9] and instead he changed tack and sent troops northwards to threaten Bergen-op-Zoom on the river Scheldt. The Dutch garrison was well equipped and provisioned, and the van Coehorn-designed defences of the town were formidable (if a little dilapidated), so that preparation had to be made by the French for a formal siege. Both Saxe and Cumberland were obliged to send additional troops, while the attention of the French was distracted by the defeat of one of their armies far to the south in Piedmont. As the colder months of autumn came gradually on, the fumbling siege of Bergen progressed slowly until on 16 September the fortress was stormed; the garrison was massacred and the town disgracefully sacked by von Löwendhal's troops, who ran wild and out of their officers' control. The affair caused widespread revulsion across Europe, and Louis XV expressed his horror at the tales of gross outrages committed. Yet for all that, Cumberland still covered Maastricht, so key to the plans for the allied campaign, and adroitly foiled every attempt by Saxe to manoeuvre him away from the fortress.

Europe was tired of war, and moves towards a peaceful settlement were still in progress, spurred on by the entry into hostilities of Russia to support Maria-Theresa and her allies. In the spring of 1748 Saxe achieved a final coup, feinting towards Breda and Tilburg, and drawing his opponent's attention away, while quickly marching his main army to invest Maastricht. This strategic shift was a fine exploit, and this time the allies were taken by surprise and were badly out of position, so that by 15 April the fortress was encircled by the French and thousands of impressed labourers had begun to dig siege trenches. The work continued and a bombardment of the defences began, even though just two weeks later preliminary articles for a peace were on the conference table at Aix-la-Chapelle, where the thunder of the French siege guns at Maastricht could be clearly heard. The 10,000-strong Dutch and Austrian garrison in the fortress fought gamely under the leadership of Prince von Aremberg, mounting at least one spirited sortie to spike the French guns and ruin the entrenchments, and on 4 May Saxe learned that peace terms had at last been agreed. Ignoring this inconvenient impediment, he continued with preparations for an assault, and six days later Aremberg, with the consent of both the Dutch Stadtholder and Cumberland, submitted on good terms, and was permitted to march out with his men, their guns, colours and baggage intact, on the road to s'Hertogenbosch.

Peace, imperfect but welcome, settled over western Europe with the Treaty of Aix-la-Chapelle – Cape Breton and Louisburg were reluctantly given up to France by Great Britain, for the time being at any rate, since the frontier disputes between the two countries in North America were far from settled. Nonetheless, after so much hard-won military success gained by Saxe and his soldiers in the Low Countries, it was galling for the French, army and people alike, that the peace terms ratified on 18 October 1748 saw the demolition once again of the defences of the port of Dunkirk, and returned the entire Austrian Netherlands to Maria-Theresa and her husband. 'After the first moments of joy that peace had been concluded, they were filled with consternation at the poor conditions which France had obtained.'[10] Saxe was understandably vocal amongst those who thought that too much had needlessly been given away, writing before the terms of the treaty had been ratified:

> I think we ought to make some sacrifices to keep such a province as Flanders, which gives us magnificent points, millions of subjects, and an easily defended frontier ... I see that the king of Prussia has got all that he wants, and is to retain Silesia, and I only wish I could imitate him.[11]

True enough, for all the effort, expense, anguish and bloodshed of the years of war, not a great deal had been settled, other than having Maria-Theresa's husband secure on the imperial throne. She, however, was not satisfied with what had been accomplished, particularly as Prussia retained Silesia, and quietly but persistently, as was her way, she resolutely looked for redress. The burgeoning rivalry between Great Britain and France, both anxious to establish an overseas empire, not least in North America and on the Indian sub-continent, where the port of Madras was relinquished to British traders, and the nagging sense that too much had been ceded by Louis XV already, would lead soon enough to renewed war on a wider scale than before. Marshal Saxe, however, would not live to see it.

It could be said truthfully that while Great Britain had been generally very fortunate on the high seas, and in building up an empire, it was Louis XV who had been most successful on land. One Dutch writer commented:

> that France had conquered so much of the debateable lands (the southern Netherlands) was due to British failures as well as those of

Britain's allies, and certainly more to British than to Dutch obstinacy. Nothing is more natural, therefore, than that England, unable to help its ally directly, surrendered a colonial conquest [Cape Breton] in order to save them from a situation she had done much to create.[13]

The British had the financial strength to enable the employment of large numbers of foreign troops to carry out their campaigns, to which could be harnessed the resources of Hanover, but the realisation was dawning in London that the best way to counter French ambitions and influence was to deny them easy access to the world's oceans, and not to grapple with her armies on land. To this end, the old antagonism between London and Madrid, largely over trade (although the tricky question of the British occupation of Gibraltar always simmered away), was resolved in 1750 by courtesy of some neat diplomatic footwork by both sides, so that with renewed conflict Spain would adopt a neutral stance, despite the assurances of support that had been given to France. This new-found amity between London and Madrid would not last long, but it was useful all the same.

As there was so much unfinished business left from the war for the imperial throne, it seemed that renewed conflict was both inevitable and widely anticipated. Eight years after the treaty terms agreed at Aix-la-Chapelle hostilities broke out once more – the principal antagonists being, unsurprisingly, Austria and Prussia, for Maria-Theresa was still intent on recovering Silesia. Alliances had shifted considerably and although the outbreak of the French and Indian War in North America had already made Great Britain and France enemies once more in 1754, Prussia had an alliance with the British and now faced the combined armies of France and Austria, hitherto traditional opponents on the battlefield. In August 1756 Frederick II attacked Saxony, and the following January Vienna declared war on Prussia. This led to Prussian troops invading Bohemia and defeating an Austrian army at the battle of Prague in May 1757. The next month, however, the Austrians got their revenge when beating the Prussians at Kolin, causing Frederick to withdraw in some haste.

In November 1757 the Prussians succeeded in defeating a combined French and Saxon army at Rossbach, and went on to beat Maria-Theresa's troops in bitterly cold weather at Leuthen in December. Meanwhile, the Duke of Cumberland had been defeated by the French at Hazenbrouk and was obliged to agree the Convention of Kloster Zeven. June 1758 saw the French fail in battle at Krefeld, while Frederick II beat the Russians at Zorndorf two months later, although the Austrians achieved a quite surprising victory over a Prussian army at Hochkirk in October. In August 1759 Frederick had his revenge at Kunersdorf, although the same month saw the British and Hanoverians triumph over the French at Minden, while the Royal Navy defeated a French invasion fleet off Lagos in Portugal. In the wider world the British had taken possession from Spain of Havana in Cuba and Manila in the Philippines, and won the battle of Plassey in southern India. General Jeffrey Amherst's brilliant campaign ruthlessly cleared out the French garrisons in North America and Canada, and Montreal in Québec was captured in September 1759, while victory at Wandewash in India in January 1760 cemented British control over much of the sub-continent. Berlin was briefly occupied by Russian troops, but Frederick II again defeated the Austrians at Targau in November.

The year 1761 saw mixed fortunes, with victories for the British at Pondicherry in India and for the French at Vellinghausen in Westphalia. George II died and his grandson George III, on taking the throne, urged that British aid to Prussia should cease. The Prussians then defeated Maria-Theresa's army at Burkersdorf in July 1762 and at Reichenbach the following month. The war staggered to an end with the Treaties of Fontainebleau (1762) and Paris (1763); Cuba and the Philippines were returned to Spain, but the British held on to their gains in North America and Canada, and in India; the French never recovered their position on either continent. Lastly, the Treaty of Hubertesburg in February brought hostilities to an end between Austria, Prussia and Saxony, leaving Frederick II in possession of Silesia after all. What had begun as a dynastic quarrel, and had spilled out over much of western Europe for some twenty-two years, with occasional brief and uncertain pauses, had at last come to a long overdue and welcome end.

Appendix 1

Orders of Battle of the Armies at Fontenoy

The French Army

Commander-in-Chief: Marshal Maurice Saxe (Louis XV present but not actively commanding)

Household Cavalry

Gardes du Corps (companies drawn from the Régiments de Charost, Villeroy, d'Harcourt and Noailles)
Gendarmes de la Garde (1 squadron)
Chevau-Légers de la Garde (1 squadron) (Note: this was not a light cavalry unit, despite the title, which was originally just an indication that the troopers did not wear armour.)
Mousquetaires (2 companies)
Grenadiers à Cheval (1 squadron)

Gendarmerie de France (made up of composite squadrons)

Gendarmes Dauphin and d'Orleans (1 squadron)
Gendarmes de la Reine and de Berry (1 squadron)
Gendarmes du Dauphin and Chevau-Légers d'Orleans (1 squadron)
Gendarmes Ecossais and de Bourgogne (1 squadron)
Gendarmes Anglais and Chevau-Légers de Bourgogne (1 squadron)
Gendarmes Bourguignon and d'Aquitaine (1 squadron)
Gendarmes de Flandres and Chevau-Léger de Aquitaine
Chevau-Légers de la Reine and de Berry

Horse

Carabiniers du Roi (10 squadrons)
Colonel-General Brigade – Régiment de Colonel-General (4 squadrons) and Régiment de Brancas (4 squadrons)
Clermont-Prince Brigade – Régiment de Clermont-Prince (4 squadrons) and Régiment de Fitz-James (4 squadrons)
Royal-Cravates Brigade – Régiments de Royal-Cravates (4 squadrons) and Régiment de Fiennes (4 squadrons)

Prince-Camille Brigade – Régiment de Prince Camille (4 squadrons) and Régiment de Royal Rousillon (4 squadrons)
Noailles Brigade – Régiment de Noailles (4 squadrons) and Régiment de Penthièvre (4 squadrons)
Chabrillant Brigade – Régiment de Chabrillant (2 squadrons) and Régiment de Royal-Etranger (2 squadrons)
Brionne Brigade – Régiment de Brionne (4 squadrons) and Régiment de Pons (4 squadrons)
Régiment de Berry (4 squadrons)
Dragons Maitre de Camp Général (4 squadrons)
Dragons Royal (4 squadrons)
Dragons Bauffremont (5 squadrons)
Beausobre Hussars (4 squadrons – detached to cover approaches to Tournai)
Lynden Hussars (4 squadrons – detached to cover approaches to Tournai)

Artillery Train
8 × 12-pounders
6 × 8-pounders
36 × 4-pounders (long)
30 × 4-pounders ('Swedish' light pattern)

Foot
Brigade de Grassin – Arquebusiers à pied, and Arquebusiers à cheval
Brigade d'Auvergne – Régiment d'Auvergne (3 battalions) and Régiment de Nivernois (1 battalion)
Brigade de Touraine – Régiment de Touraine (3 battalions)
Brigade d'Eu – Régiment d'Eu (2 battalions), Régiment de Royal Corse (1 battalion) and Regiment de Angoumois (1 battalion)
Brigade de Normandie – Régiment de Normandie (4 battalions)
Brigade de Royal-Vasseau – Régiment de Royal Vassaux (3 battalions) and Régiment de Traisnel (1 battalion)
Brigade de Gardes – Gardes Françaises (4 battalions) and Suisse (2 battalions)
Brigade du Roi – Régiment du Roi (4 battalions)
Brigade des Irlandais – Régiments de Bulkely, Clare, Rooth, Dillon, Lally and Berwick (each 1 battalion)
Brigade d'Aubeterre – Régiment d'Aubeterre (1 battalion) and Régiment de Courten (3 battalions)

Brigade de Dauphin – Régiment de Dauphin (3 battalions) and Régiment de Beauvois (1 battalion)
Brigade de Bettens – Régiment de Bettens (2 battalions) and Régiment de Diesbach (1 battalion)
Brigade de Crillon – Régiment de Crillon (3 battalions)
Brigade de Piemont – Régiment de Piemont (3 battalions) and Régiment de Royal La Marine (1 battalion)
Brigade de la Couronne – Régiment de la Couronne (3 battalions) and Régiment de Soisonais (1 battalion)
Brigade Royal – Régiment Royal (3 battalions) and Régiment de Hainault (1 battalion)

The Allied Army
British and Hanoverian (Right Wing)
Commander-in-Chief: William Augustus, Duke of Cumberland

British Horse
1st Line
  Rothe's Brigade – 3rd (King's Own) Dragoons (3 squadrons),
    7th (Queens Own) Dragoons (3 squadrons)
  Bland's Brigade – 3rd Troop Horse Guards, 4th (Scots) Troop Horse Guards, 2nd (Scots) Troop Horse Grenadiers, The Blues
    (1st Regiment of Horse – 3 squadrons)
2nd Line
  St Clair's Brigade – 2nd (King's) Regiment of Horse (3 squadrons),
    8th (Black) Regiment of Horse (2 squadrons)
  Onslow's Brigade – Campbell's 2nd (Royal North British) Dragoons (3 squadrons), Stair's 6th (Inniskilling) Dragoons (3 squadrons)

British Artillery Train
10 × 6-pounders
10 × 3-pounders
4 × 8-inch howitzers
36 × 2-pounders

British Foot (all 1 battalion)
The Foot Guards – 1st English, 2nd English (subsequently the Coldstream), 3rd Scots
The Royal Brigade – 1st Foot (Royal Scots), 12th Foot (Duroure's), 21st Foot (Argyll's), 31st Foot (Beauclerk's – *aka* Handsyde's)

Onslow's Brigade – 8th Foot (Onslow's), 19th Foot (Howard's), 25th Foot (Rothes'), 33rd Foot (Johnson's)
Howard's Brigade – 3rd Foot (Howard's, the Buffs), 13th Foot (Pulteney's), 23rd Foot (Huske's, the Royal Welch), 32nd Foot (Skelton's)
Sowle's Brigade – 11th Foot (Sowle's), 20th Foot (Bligh's), 28th Foot (Bragg's), 34th Foot (Cholmondely's)

Hanoverian Horse
Launay's Brigade – d'Acerre Regiment (2 squadrons), Leibgarde (4 squadrons)
Montigny's Brigade – Dachenhausen Regiment (2 squadrons), Montigny Regiment (2 squadrons), Aldersleben Dragoons (4 squadrons)

Hanoverian Artillery Train
12 × 3-pounders

Hanoverian Foot (each 1 battalion)
Böselanger Brigade – Böselanger Regiment, Oberg Regiment, Campe Regiment
Zastrow Brigade – Zastrow Regiment, Spörcken Regiment

Dutch (Left Wing)
Commander: The Prince of Waldeck

Horse
Vrybergen Brigade – Buys Regiment (1 squadron), Sandouville Regiment (3 squadrons), Rechteren-Overjissel Regiment (3 squadrons)
Schagen Brigade – Hopp Regiment (3 squadrons), Carabiniers (1 squadron), Nassau-Ouwerkerke Regiment (1 squadron), Garde Dragoniers (5 squadrons)
Van Oyen Brigade – Schack Regiment (3 squadrons), Lijnen Regiment (3 squadrons), Gnkel Regiment (3 squadrons)
Van Schlippenbach Brigade – Hessen-Homburg Regiment (3 squadrons), Nassau Dragoons (4 squadrons)

Artillery Train
6 × 6-pounders
20 × 3-pounders
4 × 8-inch howitzers

Foot

Sturler Brigade – Cronstrom Regiment, Bentinck Regiment, Salis (Swiss) Regiment

Elias Brigade – Oranje Vriesland Regiment, Orange Stade en Lande Regiment, Buddenbroek Regiment, Rijssel Grenadiers

Salis Brigade – Ayla Regiment, Schaumburg-Lippe Regiment, Gardes te Voet

Efferen Brigade – Dorth Regiment, Constant-Rebecque (Swiss) Regiment

Burmania Brigade – Sturler (Swiss) Regiment, Broekhuizen Regiment

Halkett Brigade – Smissaert Regiment, Bronkhorst Regiment

Austrian

Commanders: Field-Marshal von Königsegg/General von Moltke

Károly Hussars (2 squadrons)
Belézney Hussars (2 squadrons)
Ligne Dragoons (2 squadrons)
Styrum Dragoons (2 squadrons)
Freikompagnie Bouvier
Freikompagnie Pertuiseaux

Army Reserve (with von Moltke)
7th (Queen's Own) Dragoons (3 squadrons)
Schlippenbach Dragoons (7 squadrons)
Murray's Highlanders (The Black Watch)
Waldeck Regiment (1 battalion)

Appendix 2

The Deposition of Brigadier General Richard Ingoldsby

The Deposition of Brigadier General Richard Ingoldsby, in relation to his conduct in the late action at FONTENOY. Published with permission.[1]

The Brigadier represents, that on the day of the battle, being 30th April O.S. his royal highness sent for him early in the morning, and told him he was to attack six pieces of the enemy's cannon situated in the wood, and that Captain Forbes, aide de camp, to Lieutenant-General Campbell, would shew him the place, who carried him to the orchard where the Highlanders [Munro's] were posted, and shewed him the wood; some of the officers of the Highlanders informed him, that the enemy had cannon at the point of it. On the brigadier's return, he acquainted the duke, he had been shewn the place, not thinking it was possible, for the person, that was sent on that purpose, to mistake his royal highness's intentions. The brigadier also told his major of brigade what was to be done.

The Duke further ordered the brigadier, if he took the cannon, to turn them upon the enemy; if he could not turn them, to nail them, for which purpose, some gunners were ordered and four battalions, viz. Duroure's, Pulteney's, Lord Semple's, and a Hanoverian regiment [von Borschlanger's]; which latter he was to take off from the post that lay some distance from the road, and obliged the brigadier to halt till that regiment joined him

In obedience to the above orders, the brigadier marched beyond the village [Vezon] into a hollow way, where he halted within a hundred yards of the wood, in order to reconnoitre; and from the banks of which he observed the enemy had a strong detachment in the wood, and at that juncture were marching several parties towards it; particularly one which lay down flat in the corn, about forty yards from the flank of the wood, and others which marched and joined some squadrons on a hill near it.

The brigadier finding the enemy thus advantageously situated sent Major Bernard to the duke, to acquaint his royal highness that he thought some pieces of cannon would absolutely be requisite to flank the enemy, while he marched to the attack, which the duke readily complied with and immediately ordered three six-pounders.

Soon after the brigadier sent Capt. Crawfurd of major-general Pulteney's regiment, to acquaint the duke with what he had observed, during which time the brigadier called the commanding officers together, acquainted them with what he was to do, and consulted with them the properest way to attack; it was resolved to draw up upon the right of the hollow way, where there appeared no difficulty to hinder our march, and likewise having it in our power to flank the enemy as we marched.

When the brigadier was putting this disposition in execution, Capt. Crawfurd returned and immediately after the duke came up. The brigadier then acquainted his royal highness with the observations he had made, the cannon then arrived and on the left of the hollow way.

His royal highness then ordered the brigadier to form on the left of the hollow way, the cannon to advance and fire, and the battalions to march and support them. And further ordered the brigadier to keep in a direct line with that part of the army, that was on the left, which orders were immediately executed. The brigadier apprehends as his royal highness altered his disposition, and gave him fresh orders, which orders were punctually obeyed, that he cannot be liable to a censure for disobedience of orders.

His royal highness some time after returned and ordered Lord Semple's regiment to the attack on the village [Fontenoy], which was the whole day afterwards separated from the brigadier's command. Whilst the brigadier was marching at the head of Duroure's regiment, in pursuance to the duke's last orders, he received a message from General Ligonier by his aide de camp Capt. [Jeffrey] Amherst, enquiring the reason why he had not attacked according to the orders given early in the morning; the brigadier answered that his royal highness had since ordered him to march and keep in a line with the left of the army. [Note: this reference to the left of the army must in fact refer to the advance of the right wing, on Ingoldsby's left-hand side, as he could have had no way of knowing the progress or otherwise of the left wing on the far side of Fontenoy.]

Some time after, the brigadier still marching at the head of Duroure's regiment, Capt. Napier acquainted him, that Major General von Zastrow was in command of that part of the line, but the brigadier never received any orders from him, neither did he see him.

The brigadier continued at the head of Duroure's regiment, within 150 paces of a redoubt [d'Eu], from which he was exposed to a continual fire, from the beginning of the action, which the loss of that regiment will make appear, and in the attack the brigadier had the misfortune to receive a wound, which obliged him to be carried off.

[Signed] RICHARD INGOLDSBY

The Case of General Ingoldsby. Sentence of the Court Martial held at Diegham, July the 15th 1745, N.S. and continued by several adjournments to the 18th.[2]

The court considering, that the not executing the order (which was to attack a redoubt or battery in the action near Fontenoy) did not proceed from want of courage in Brigadier Ingoldsby, but from a failure in judgement; they are therefore unanimously of opinion, THAT the said Brigadier Ingoldsby shall only be suspended during the pleasure of his Royal Highness the duke.

Editorial comment that accompanied the notice

The Duke approved the sentence and suspended the Brigadier for three months; and the court martial having expressly absolved him in point of courage, he thought the work was over and that when the term of suspension was expired he should be reinstated in his command and have his commission of major-general (which had been already made out, and signed by the king) delivered to him: but to his great surprise on his return to England he soon found himself exposed to a second condemnation, without so much as the pretence of a second fault, or the form of a second trial; for his majority in the guards was taken from him, without any consideration for it: and he had orders to sell his company [in the Foot Guards] which he had bought upwards of thirty years ago, for five hundred pound less than he was offered by several gentlemen for it: so that he is now in a worse condition in point of fortune, than when he entered into the army forty-three years ago: to say nothing of the time he has spent, and the blood he has lost in the service: and under these pressures has no other consolation, but the consolation of having done his duty irreproachably and that every officer in the army, as well as those under his command at Fontenoy, must do him justice.

Author's comments

The notion that Ingoldsby was made a scapegoat for the failure on 11 May 1745, and was held up to divert criticism from the Duke of Cumberland's handling of the battle is inescapable. The brigadier general may well have shown a lack of drive and initiative, but he had a good reputation as a veteran soldier and commander and, as the court martial found, he did not lack courage. The action to clear the woods was rushed, with little prior preparation or reconnaissance having been made the previous evening and during the night, and the orders given were both imprecise and contradictory. It is hard to see, for example, how Ingoldsby could both clear the woods ahead of Cumberland's attack to free his right flank from French interference, *and* keep in line with that same advance to his left at one and the same time. Colonel Robert Munro, who led the Black Watch with such valour on the day, wrote in Ingoldsby's defence that he had 'Given his orders as became an officer who understood his business, and was capable to execute it.'[3] However, Ingoldsby's assertion that he led Duroure's regiment into the wood is contradicted, but not challenged by the court-martial, by the fact that they were detached to attack Fontenoy village. There is a timing difference that is unexplained. The resulting loss of this officer's reputation might seem unjust, while the financial loss of his rank in the Foot Guards (no money value attaching to ranks above that of major) was severe. The distinguished historian Sir John Fortescue put the whole affair rather well in his first volume of the *History of the British Army*:[4] 'By consent of all the British command it was Ingoldsby's misunderstanding of his orders and his failure to capture the redoubt d'Eu that lost the battle … He was however acquitted of all but an error of judgement, and indeed there was no question of cowardice.' In plain fact, a man of Ingoldsby's long experience should not have failed to grasp the essential nature of his task; this must have been clear to him despite the contradictory orders he was given, and by application of a modicum of initiative he should have got on with what he was tasked to achieve. For all the suspicion that a scapegoat for the failure on the day was apparently sought and found, the fact that the brigadier general's reputation and future career were irreparably harmed appears to have had at least an element of justice to it.

Appendix 3

British Casualties at Fontenoy

The following lists are taken from the return contained in the *Gentleman's Magazine*, Vol. XV, 1745, pp. 247–9. Those listed as missing may well have rejoined the colours later, or been counted as prisoners in French hands when such returns were available. The meticulous accounting for lost horses on regimental strengths no doubt indicates an awareness of their value to the army. The original, slightly archaic, spelling of some of the ranks has been retained.

The Staff
Killed – Major General Ponsonby; Lieutenant General James Campbell.
Wounded – HRH The Duke of Cumberland; Sir Alexander Cockburn; William Keppel, Lord Albemarle; Major-General Howard; Brigadier General Sir Richard Ingoldsby; Lord Ancram; Lord Cathcart.
[Note: no non-commissioned aides, horse-holders or gallopers amongst the staff are mentioned as being casualties, so presumably they were contained in the regimental figures.]

3rd Troop Life Guards
Killed – 4 men and 10 horses.
Wounded – Lieutenant-Colonel Lamelonière; 14 men and 14 horses.

4th Troop Life Guards
Killed – 2 men and 4 horses.
Wounded – Captain Hilgrove; Cornet Burdet; 12 men and 3 horses.
Missing – 3 horses.

2nd Troop Horse Grenadier Guards
Killed – 4 men and 3 horses.
Wounded – Major Brerton; Captains Elliot, Burton, Thacker; 10 men and 7 horses.
Missing – 2 horses.

The Blues
Killed – 10 men and 79 horses.
Wounded – Lieutenant-Colonel Beake; Captains Lloyd, Migget; Captain and Quartermasters Hudson and Bat; 39 men and 62 horses.
Missing – 7 men and 9 horses.

2nd (King's) Regiment of Horse
Killed – 7 men and 20 horses.
Wounded – Lieutenant Brace; 4 men and 6 horses.
Missing – 1 horse.

8th (Black) Regiment of Horse
Killed – 2 men and 8 horses.
Wounded – Captain and Quartermaster Heath; 4 men and 6 horses.

1st (Royal) Dragoons
Killed – 14 men and 57 horses.
Wounded – Lieutenant-Colonel Naixon; Cornets Hartwell, Desmeret and Creighton; 31 men and 47 horses.
Missing – 1 horse.

2nd (Royal North British) Dragoons
Killed – 14 men and 25 horses.
Wounded – Cornet Glasgo; 11 men and 33 horses.
Missing – 1 serjeant.

3rd (King's) Regiment of Dragoons
Killed – 9 men and 28 horses.
Wounded – Captain Wade; Captain and Quartermaster Corbridge; 14 men and 34 horses.

6th (Inniskilling) Regiment of Dragoons
Killed – Captain and Quartermaster Baird; 3 men and 19 horses.
Wounded – 11 men and 7 horses.

7th (Queen's) Regiment of Dragoons
Killed – Cornet Potts; 10 men and 46 horses.
Wounded – Lieutenant-Colonel Erskine; Captain Ogilvy; Lieutenant Forbes; Cornet Maitland; Captain and Quartermaster Smith; 35 men and 47 horses.

The Artillery Train
Killed – Lieutenant Bennett; 1 serjeant, 1 gunner and 7 mattrosses.
Wounded – 1 Conductor; 2 serjeants; 1 corporal; 6 gunners and 13 mattrosses.
Missing – 2 gunners and 4 mattrosses.

1st Foot Guards
Killed – Captains Harvey, Berkeley and Brereton; Ensign Sir Alexander Cockburn; 3 serjeants and 82 men.

Wounded – Lieutenant Colonel Lord Charles Hay; Captains Hildelsey, Parker, Pearson and Bockland; Ensigns Nash and Vane; 9 serjeants and 133 men.

2nd Foot Guards
Killed – Ensigns Cathcart and Molesworth; two serjeants and 110 men.
Wounded – Colonels Needham, Corbett, Kellet, Moysten and Bertie; Captains Townshend and Cesar; Ensigns Burton and Vanbrugh; 4 serjeants and 112 men.

3rd (Scots) Foot Guards
Killed – Colonel Carpenter; Lieutenant-Colonel Douglas; Captain Ross; Ensign Murray; 3 serjeants and 102 men.
Wounded – Colonels Waldegrave and Frazier; Captains Laurie, Knevit and Maitland; Ensigns Haldane and Neil; 5 serjeants and 126 men.

1st (Royal Scots) Regiment of Foot
Killed – 2 serjeants and 85 men.
Wounded – Captain Thomson and Edmonston; Lieutenants Cockburn, Nairn, Elliot, Abernethy and Grant; Ensign Jones; 5 serjeants and 78 men.
Missing – 8 men.

3rd (Howard's) Regiment of Foot
Killed – Captain and Quartermaster Cummins; 1 serjeant and 10 men.
Wounded – Lieutenant Tanner; Ensign Paunceford; 32 men.
Missing – 8 men.

8th (Onslow's) Regiment of Foot
Killed – 16 men.
Wounded – Lieutenant-Colonel Keightley; Major Gray; Captains Dallons, Loftus and Ekins; Lieutenants Cook and Thomson; 2 serjeants and 81 men.
Missing – 1 serjeant and 30 men.

11th (Sowle's) Regiment of Foot
Killed – Captain Brawnc; Lieutenants Capel and Mowbray; Ensign Farrington; 49 men.
Wounded – Lieutenant-Colonel Tullikins; Major Montague; 6 serjeants and 106 men.
Missing – Lieutenant Hackshaw; 2 serjeants and 44 men.

12th (Duroure's) Regiment of Foot
Killed – Lieutenant-Colonel Whitmore; Captain Campbell; Lieutenants Bockland and Laine; Ensigns Cannon and Clifton; 5 serjeants and 148 men.

Wounded – Colonel Duroure (mw); Major Cosseley; Captains Rainsford and Robinson; Lieutenants Murray, Townsend, Millingten and Delgarne; Ensigns Dagers and Pearse; 7 serjeants and 142 men.
Missing – Captain De Casne; Lieutenants Goulston and Salt.

13th (Pulteney's) Regiment of Foot
Killed – Captain Queenchant; 2 serjeants and 35 men.
Wounded – Captain Nicholas; Ensigns Jones and Edhouse; 2 serjeants and 39 men.
Missing – 10 men.

19th (Howard's) Regiment of Foot
Killed – Lieutenant Legrand; Ensign Gibson; 17 men.
Wounded – Major Peritot; Captains Cockran and Douglas; Lieutenant Coots; Ensigns Cheap, Martin and Parterfeld; 1 serjeant and 69 men.

20th (Bligh's) Regiment of Foot
Killed – Lieutenant-Colonel Gee; 1 serjeant and 27 men.
Wounded – Captains Meyrac and Maxwell; Lieutenants Bouchitière and Vickers; Ensign Hartley; 1 serjeant and 34 men.

21st (Royal North British) Regiment of Foot
Killed – Lieutenants Campbell, Houston and Sargent; 1 serjeant and 2 men.
Wounded – Major Colvill; Captains Latau, Olivant and Knatchbull; Lieutenants Maxwell, Colville, Bullenden, McGacken and Townsend; 7 serjeants and 137 men.

23rd (Royal Welch Fusiliers) Regiment of Foot
Killed – Lieutenants Weaver, Pryce, Forster and Isaac; 4 serjeants and 191 men.
Wounded – Captains Hickman, Cary, Bernard and Drysdale; Lieutenants Izard, Awbry, Clarke, Eyre Roberts and Rolle; 6 serjeants and 71 men.
Missing – Major Lort; Captains Taylor, Sabine and Johnson; Lieutenants Berners, Grigge, Hawes and Lort; 5 serjeants and 34 men.

25th (Rothe's) Regiment of Foot
Killed – Ensign Bonnevillette; 2 serjeants and 52 men.
Wounded – Lieutenant-Colonel Kennedy; Major Dalrymple; Captains Ward and Lucas; Lieutenants Livingston and Hay; Ensigns Cockburn and James; 4 serjeants and 72 men.
Missing – 13 men.

Appendix 3: British Casualties at Fontenoy

28th (Bragg's) Regiment of Foot
Killed – Lieutenant Cliffe; two serjeants and fourteen men.
Wounded – Lord George Sackville; Captains Fitzgerald, Jocelyn and Holt; Lieutenants Wright, Edgeworth and Graydon; Ensigns Harman and Michelson; 65 men.
Missing – Captain Sailly; 1 serjeant and 44 men.

31st (Beauclerk's) Regiment of Foot
Killed – Lieutenant-Colonel Montague; Captains Baird and Pollock; Lieutenant Dalway; 4 serjeants and 125 men.
Wounded – Lieutenants Stafford and Porter; Ensigns Worsley, Brumley and Freeman; 6 serjeants and 130 men.
Missing – 12 men.

32nd (Skelton's) Regiment of Foot
Killed – Two serjeants and fourteen men.
Wounded – Lieutenants Lindsay, Mestin and Banks; Ensigns How and Prescott; 5 serjeants and 95 men.
Missing – Captain Farquhar and 17 men.

33rd (Johnson's) Regiment of Foot
Killed – Lieutenant-Colonel Clements; Lieutenant Greene, Colley and Houghton; Ensign Nesbit; 42 men.
Wounded – Major Mure; Captains Godfrey, Lacey, Eccles and Tighe; Lieutenants Gardiner, Burrough, Otway and Gore; Ensigns Rayner, Collis, Samson and Deseury; 4 serjeants and 84 men.
Missing – 2 serjeants and 28 men.

34th (Cholmondeley's) Regiment of Foot
Killed – 1 serjeant and 17 men.
Wounded – Lieutenants Cramer, Forest, Mure, Courtney and Hargroves; Ensigns Donallen and Stacey; 2 serjeants and 53 men.
Missing – 1 serjeant and 12 men.

Murray's Highlanders (The Black Watch)
Killed – Captain (John) Campbell; Ensign (Lacklan) Campbell; 30 men.
Wounded – Captain (Robert) Campbell; Ensigns (Rennald) Campbell, and (James) Campbell; 2 serjeants and 86 men.
Missing – 1 serjeant and 12 men.

Notes

Chapter 1: Problems with the *Pragmatica Sanctio*
1. Skrine, J., *Fontenoy, and Great Britain's Share in the War of the Austrian Succession*, 1906, p. 17.
2. Tabori, P., *Maria-Theresa*, 1969, p. 470. Tabori interestingly gives Maria-Theresa's year of birth as 1713, but this is presumably a misprint.
3. Duffy, C., *The Military Experience in the Age of Reason*, 1987, p. 320.
4. Tabori, *Maria-Theresa*, p. 42.
5. Ibid., p. 3.
6. Skrine, *Fontenoy, and Great Britain's Share*, p. 17.
7. Tabori, *Maria-Theresa*, p. 40.
8. Ibid., p. 78.
9. Reddaway, W., *Frederick the Great and the Rise of Prussia*, 1904, pp. 96–7.
10. Ibid., p. 80.
11. Ibid., p. 108.
12. Ibid., p. 91.
13. Tabori, *Maria-Theresa*, pp. 98–9.
14. Had the Prussians not been successful at the battle of Mollwitz, with Frederick II then forced to withdraw with his army from Silesia and cease making mischief, it is unlikely that the war would have expanded and escalated as rapidly as it did. In particular, the ability of the Austrians to defend their territory, had it been demonstrated in this way, would surely have made the French much less inclined to risk one of their field armies on behalf of the Bavarian Elector, in what eventually became a dismal adventure into Bohemia.
15. Geyl, P., *Holland and England during the War of the Austrian Succession*, 1926, pp. 18–19.
16. Reddaway, *Frederick the Great*, p. 123.
17. Tabori, *Maria-Theresa*, p. 209.
18. Duffy, C., *The Fortress in the Age of Vauban and Frederick the Great, 1660–1789*, 1985, p. 106.
19. Orr, M., *Dettingen 1743*, 1972, p. 59.
20. Skrine, *Fontenoy, and Great Britain's Share*, pp. 94–5.
21. Ibid., p. 97.
22. Ibid., p. 100.
23. Ibid., p. 113.
24. Ibid., p. 119.

Chapter 2: The Art of War in the Eighteenth Century
1. Gandilhon, D., *Fontenoy*, 2008, p. 13.
2. Nierinckx, P., *I Cannot Estimate the Damage* (JSAHR), 2015, p. 11.
3. White-Spunner, B., *Horse Guards*, 2008, pp. 209–11.

4. Guy, A. (ed.), *Colonel Samuel Bagshawe, and the Army of George II, 1731–1762*, 1990, pp. 16–17.
5. The 1st Duke of Marlborough used an ingenious system of 'running footmen', fit young aides in his personal service, who, clad in his own distinctive livery, would nimbly scour the battlefield and report to him on the progress, the ebb and flow, of the battle. Not being mounted, they were thought to attract less hostile attention than conspicuously mounted aides, and therefore were less likely to fall as casualties or be seized as prisoners. However, it does not appear that other commanding generals used this novel, and perhaps expensive, method of obtaining information, so perhaps the footmen were not as effective as is sometimes thought.
6. Chandler, D. (ed.), *The Memoirs of Captain Robert Parker*, 1969, p. 55.
7. Holmes, R., *Redcoat*, 2001, p. 32. A good flint, a well rammed charge, and a careful aim could often prove very effective in the hands of well trained soldiers.
8. Orr, *Dettingen*, p. 7.
9. Browning, R., *The War of the Austrian Succession*, 1993, p. 4.
10. Donaldson, J., *Recollections of the Eventful Life of a Soldier*, 1852, pp. 105–6.
11. White-Spunner, *Horse Guards*, p. 216.
12. Ibid., p. 203.
13. Fortescue, J., *The History of the British Army*, Vol. II, 1899, p. 142.

Chapter 3: The German Marshal – Maurice Saxe

1. White, J., *Marshal of France, the Life and Times of Maurice, Comte Saxe*, 1962, p. 101.
2. Ibid., p. 19.
3. Ibid., p. 26.
4. The battle of Malplaquet, 11 September 1709, was the fourth of the 1st Duke of Marlborough's renowned victories in open field over the armies of Louis XIV. The duke's opponent, the Duc de Villars, fought a doggedly skilful battle with inferior numbers but making the best of close and wooded country, hoping to prevent a siege of the French-held fortress of Mons. Although inflicting heavy casualties on the duke's army, the wounded French commander was forced from the field by the end of the day with the loss of thirty-five guns, and Mons fell six weeks later. Marlborough, whose losses at both Ramillies in 1706 and Oudenarde two years later were by comparison quite modest, attracted severe criticism for the casualties sustained at Malplaquet, although the Dutch were rather more forgiving than critics in London. That the allied casualties at Blenheim in 1704 had been severe, at some 13,000, and yet the occasion still could be counted to be a triumph, was conveniently forgotten by the duke's political opponents.
5. White, *Marshal of France*, p. 43.
6. Ibid., p. 110.
7. Ibid., p. 121.
8. Ibid., p. 142.
9. Ibid., p. 201.
10. Ibid., p. 247.

Chapter 4: Billy the Martial Boy – Cumberland, the last Captain General

1. Whitworth, R., *William Augustus, Duke of Cumberland*, 1993, p. 242.
2. Ibid., p. 23.

3. John Dalrymple, 2nd Earl of Stair, took the news to Queen Anne in London of the famous victory achieved by the Duke of Marlborough and Prince Eugene of Savoy over the French army under the command of the Duc de Vendôme at Oudenarde in July 1708. An active and effective campaigner at that time, he was elderly and frail by 1744 and past his best in the field.
4. Whitworth, *William Augustus*, p. 32.
5. Ibid., p. 120.
6. Ibid., p.132.
7. Ibid., p. 194.
8. Ibid., p. 195.
9. Reddaway, *Frederick the Great*, p. 208.
10. Skrine, *Fontenoy, and Great Britain's Share*, p. 352.
11. Ibid., p. 353.
12. Whitworth, *William Augustus*, p. 203.
13. Ibid., p. 208.
14. Nierinckx, *I Cannot Estimate the Damage*, p. 6.
15. Whitworth, *William Augustus*, p. 242.

Chapter 6: Tournai – the Great Fortress on the Scheldt

1. Whitworth, *William Augustus*, p. 97.
2. Skrine, *Fontenoy, and Great Britain's Share*, pp. 127–8.
3. White-Spunner, *Horse Guards*, p. 205.
4. Nosworthy, B., *The Anatomy of Victory, Battle Tactics, 1689–1763*, 1992, p. 208.
5. Skrine, *Fontenoy, and Great Britain's Share*, p. 123.
6. Ibid., p. 125.
7. Barrett, C., *The 7th (Queen's Own) Hussars as Dragoons during the Flanders Campaign*, 1914, p. 131.
8. Skrine, *Fontenoy, and Great Britain's Share*, p. 140.
9. Fuye, M., *Fontenoy, 1745*, 1945, p. 167.
10. Skrine, *Fontenoy, and Great Britain's Share*, p. 141.
11. White-Spunner, *Horse Guards*, p. 212.
12. Whitworth, *William Augustus*, p. 46.
13. Anon, *Gentleman's Magazine*, Vol. XV, 1745, p. 246.
14. See Skrine, *Fontenoy, and Great Britain's Share*, pp. 145–6, for an interesting analysis of the fighting strengths available to the two army commanders on 11 May 1745. Inevitably accounts differ as to precise numbers, but there is little doubt that Saxe had more men in play than Cumberland, even allowing for those troops detained in the siege works around Tournai. The theoretical possibility that the Dutch garrison might attempt to mount a sortie to support Cumberland had obviously not been discounted by Saxe.
15. Ibid., p. 144.
16. Ibid., p. 124.
17. Anon, *The Journal of the battle of Fontenoy*, 1745, p. 1.
18. *Gentleman's Magazine*, Ibid.
19. White, *Marshal of France*, p. 151.
20. Skrine, *Fontenoy, and Great Britain's Share*, p. 137.
21. Ibid., p. 153.

22. *Gentleman's Magazine*, Ibid.
23. The Arquesbusiers de Grassins were raised in 1744 by Colonel Simon-Claude de Grassin-Chatigny as a light infantry regiment well trained in sharpshooting. As with many such units, where personal initiative was called for they had an unwarranted reputation for ill-discipline, and performed very well at Fontenoy.
24. Fuye, *Fontenoy*, p. 170.
25. Ibid. See also Gandilhon, D, *Fontenoy*, appendix I, for a most useful list of the units actually engaged on the day of battle.
26. The Black Watch was formed in 1739, 1,000 men strong, from independent companies of highlanders loyal to the government, and was initially known as the Highland Regiment of Foot (Murray's). Lord John Murray was the brother of both the Duke of Atholl and the Jacobite-inclined Marquis of Tullibardine. The regiment's commander at Fontenoy, Lieutenant Colonel Sir Robert Munro, was killed at Falkirk in 1746, and the regiment was subsequently numbered 43rd in the line, but later became the 42nd Foot.

Chapter 7: A Breaking-in Battle

1. Grant, C., *The battle of Fontenoy*, 1975, front endpaper.
2. Fuye, *Fontenoy*, p. 176.
3. Skrine, *Fontenoy, and Great Britain's Share*, p. 159.
4. *Gentleman's Magazine*, p. 316.
5. Fuye, *Fontenoy*, p. 176.
6. Skrine, *Fontenoy, and Great Britain's Share*, p. 161.
7. Ibid.
8. *Gentleman's Magazine*, Ibid.
9. Skrine, *Fontenoy, and Great Britain's Share*, pp. 164–5.
10. Fortescue, *History of the British Army*, pp. 118–20. Also for interesting comments on the conduct of Richard Ingoldsby.
11. Anon., *The Journal of the battle of Fontenoy*, 1745, p. 3.
12. Frearson, W. (ed.), 'To Mr Davenport', the letters of Major Richard Davenport, 1742–1760 (SAHR), 1968, p. 55.
13. *Gentleman's Magazine*, Ibid.
14. Weaver, L., *The Story of the Royal Scots (the Lothian Regiment)*, 1915, p. 97.
15. Skrine, *Fontenoy, and Great Britain's Share*, p. 168.
16. Schofield, V., *The Highland Furies (the Black Watch)*, 2012, pp. 29–30. Colonel Munro's highland men, so recently recruited into government service, had been permitted to carry their own broadswords.
17. Skrine, *Fontenoy, and Great Britain's Share*, p. 169.
18. Schofield, *Highland Furies*, pp. 29–30.
19. Skrine, *Fontenoy, and Great Britain's Share*, p. 170.
20. Gandilhon, *Fontenoy*, pp. 55–6.
21. It was generally felt best to let an opponent fire first and thus waste their shot at too great a range to be really effective, before closing quickly and delivering a volley at a more effective range.
22. Weaver, *The Story of the Royal Scots*, p. 98.
23. Chandler, *Memoirs of Captain Robert Parker*, p. 89.
24. Gandilhon, *Fontenoy*, p. 58.

25. Frearson, *'To Mr Davenport'*, p. 55.
26. McKinnon, D., *The Origins and Services of the Coldstream Guards*, 1833, pp. 368–9.
27. Mc Laughlin, M., *The Wild Geese, the Irish Brigades in the service of France and Spain*, 1980, p. 13.
28. Skrine, *Fontenoy, and Great Britain's Share*, p. 175.
29. Hamilton, F., *History of the Grenadier Guards*, 1874, p. 122.
30. Skrine, *Fontenoy, and Great Britain's Share*, p. 178.
31. *Gentleman's Magazine*, p. 246. See also Skrine, *Fontenoy, and Great Britain's Share*, p. 176.

Chapter 8: The Infernal Column

1. Skrine, *Fontenoy, and Great Britain's Share*, p. 127.
2. Anon, *The Journal of the battle of Fontenoy*, 1745, p. 4.
3. Weaver, *The Story of the Royal Scots*, p. 98.
4. Skrine, *Fontenoy, and Great Britain's Share*, p. 177.
5. Gandilhon, *Fontenoy*, p. 66.
6. Ibid., pp. 78–9.
7. Skrine, *Fontenoy, and Great Britain's Share*, p. 185. Making it quite plain that this author had little doubt that the claim was an exaggeration.
8. Ibid., p. 183.
9. Sutherland, D., *Tried and Valiant, the History of the Border Regiment*, 1972, p. 30.
10. Hills, R., *The Royal Dragoons (1st Dragoons)*, 1972, p. 26.
11. Fuye, *Fontenoy*, p. 191.
12. Browne, P., *The Letters of Captain Philip Browne, 1737–1746*, 1926, p. 150.
13. *Gentleman's Magazine*, p. 3.
14. Knight, C., *Historical Record of the Buffs*, 1934, p. 48. M. Denis Gandilhon in his valuable account of the action, *Fontenoy*, p. 75, asserts that, 'In the middle of the eighteenth century it was not yet customary to carry on pursuing a defeated enemy.' This is a misapprehension, as the startlingly headlong pursuit by the Duke of Marlborough of the defeated French army after Ramillies in May 1706 amply and graphically demonstrated. His comments on the state of utter exhaustion of Marshal Saxe and his gallant soldiers are well chosen, however.
15. White, *Marshal of France*, p. 163.
16. Gandilhon, *Fontenoy*, p. 75.
17. Ibid.
18. See Skrine, *Fontenoy, and Great Britain's Share*, p. 185, for interesting comments on this point. That history has a tendency to repeat itself can be seen in the comment made in 1915 by Major Achille Burgoyne that 'The Convent of the Black Sisters at Ypres has been burnt, also the Convent of Les Dames Anglaises, *where hung the standards of the Irish Brigade who fought so well in the service of Louis XV at Fontenoy* [author's italics], as they did in the days of their fathers at Malplaquet.' Davison, C., *The Burgoyne Diaries*, 1985, p. 195.
19. Skrine, *Fontenoy, and Great Britain's Share*, p. 190.
20. Ibid., p. 200.
21. Ibid., p. 204.
22. Ibid., p. 205.
23. Ibid., p. 206.

24. Geyl, *Holland and England during the War of the Austrian Succession*, p. 49.
25. Skrine, *Fontenoy, and Great Britain's Share*, p. 203.
26. Such a close investment of a major fortress, even in the face of a superior army under the command of an experienced and skilled commander, could, if approached correctly, succeed to the point of forcing a submission of the garrison. This was seen to dramatic effect at the siege of Bouchain in 1711 when the Duke of Marlborough fended off the earnest attempts of Marshal Villars to save the place, even though the French commander was nearby and in day to day contact with the garrison.
27. Browning, R., *The War of the Austrian Succession*, 1993, p. 212.
28. Whitworth, *William Augustus*, p. 57.
29. McKinnon, *Coldstream Guards*, p. 372.

Chapter 9: Luscious Sweets of Success, Bitter Fruits of Failure
1. Skrine, *Fontenoy, and Great Britain's Share*, p. 237.
2. Ibid., p. 209.
3. Frearson, *'To Mr Davenport'*, p. 55.
4. Weaver, *The Story of the Royal Scots*, p. 100.
5. Pearse, H., *The History of the East Surrey Regiment*, 1916, p. 38.
6. Skrine, *Fontenoy, and Great Britain's Share*, p. 237.
7. Ibid., p. 254.
8. Ibid., p. 255.
9. Ibid., p. 257.
10. White, *Marshal of France*, p. 172.
11. Fuye, *Fontenoy*, p. 222.
12. White, *Marshal of France*, p. 173.

Chapter 10: The Jacobite Distraction
1. Skrine, *Fontenoy, and Great Britain's Share*, p. 258.
2. Ibid., p. 250.
3. MacLean, F., *Bonnie Prince Charlie*, 1988, p. 55.
4. Oates, J., *Sweet William or the Butcher?*, 2008, p. 42.
5. Prebble, J., *Culloden*, 1961, p. 13.
6. Oates, *Sweet William or the Butcher?*, p. 79.

Chapter 11: The Treaty of Aix-la-Chapelle
1. Grant, *The battle of Fontenoy*, front endpaper.
2. White, *Marshal of France*, p. 179.
3. Ibid.
4. Skrine, *Fontenoy, and Great Britain's Share*, pp. 309–10.
5. Ibid., p. 313.
6. White, *Marshal of France*, p. 212.
7. *Gentleman's Magazine*, Vol. XVII, 1747, p. 345.
8. Ibid., p. 218.
9. Ibid., p. 223.
10. Ibid., p. 225.
11. Skrine, *Fontenoy, and Great Britain's Share*, p. 247.
12. Geyl, *Holland and England during the War of the Austrian Succession*, p. 91.

Appendix 2: The Deposition of Brigadier General Richard Ingoldsby

1. *Gentleman's Magazine*, p. 316.
2. Ibid., Vol. XIX, 1749, p. 176.
3. Skrine, *Fontenoy, and Great Britain's Share*, p. 233.
4. Fortescue, *The History of the British Army*, pp. 119–20. Fortescue's sympathy for Ingoldsby is clear.

Bibliography

Anderson, M., *The War of the Austrian Succession*, 1995.
Anon.,
  Gentleman's Magazine, Vol. XV, 1745.
  The Journal of the battle of Fontenoy, published by order of His Most Christian Majesty (translated from the French), 1745.
  Gentleman's Magazine, Vol. XVII, 1747.
  Gentleman's Magazine, Vol. XIX, 1749.
  London Gazette, 12 March 1745.
  Army List, 1744–1747.
Atkinson, C. (ed.), *Gleanings from the Cathcart Mss* (*Journal of the Society for Army Historical Research* (JSAHR)), 1961.
Barrett, C., *The 7th (Queen's Own) Hussars, as Dragoons during the Flanders Campaign*, 1914.
Belaubre, J., *L'armee des Provinces-Unis des Pay-Bas pendant la guerre de succession d'Autriche* (Carnet de la Sabretache), 1995.
Bois, J., *Fontenoy, 1745*, 1996.
Bolitho, H., *The Galloping Third*, 1963.
Browning, R., *The War of the Austrian Succession*, 1993.
Brereton, J., *The History of the 4/7th Dragoon Guards*, 1982.
Browne, P., *The Letters of Captain Philip Browne, 1737–1746* (JSAHR), 1926.
Brunet, J., *Histoire de l'Artillerie*, 1842.
Burne, A., *Fontenoy* (Army Historical Review), 1938.
Cannon, R.,
  Historical Record of the Royal Regiment of Scots Dragoons (now 2nd or Royal North British, commonly called the Scots Greys), 1840.
  Historical Record of the 1st (Royal) Regiment of Foot, 1838.
  Historical Record of the 12th (Suffolk) Regiment of Foot, 1845.
  Historical Record of the 23rd (Royal Welch) Regiment of Foot, 1845.
  Historical Record of the 34th (Cumberland) Regiment of Foot, 1844.
Cart, A., *Uniformes des Régiments de Louis XV á nos jours*, 1945.
Chandler, D., *The Art of Warfare in the Age of Marlborough*, 1976.
  (ed.), *The Memoirs of Captain Robert Parker*, 1968.
Chartrand, R., *Louis XV's Army*, 4 vols, 1996.
Colin, J., *Les Campagnes de Maurice de Saxe*, 1906.
Dalton, C., *George I's Army*, 1912.
Dange, C., *Le Bataille de Fontenoy*, 1926.
Davison, C. (ed.), *The Burgoyne Diaries*, 1985.
Desbrière, E., *La Cavalerie de 1740 à 1789*, 1906.
Donaldson, J., *Recollections of the Eventful Life of a Soldier*, 1852.
Duffy, C., *The Fortress in the Age of Vauban and Frederick the Great, 1660–1789*, 1985.

Falkner, J.,
  Lieutenant-General Sir Joshua Guest (Oxford Dictionary of National Biography), 2004.
  Marshal Vauban, and the Defence of Louis XIV's France, 2012.
  The War of the Spanish Succession, 1701–1714, 2015.
Fortescue, J.,
  The History of the British Army, Vol. II, 1899.
  British Campaigns in Flanders, 1690–1794, 1918.
Frearson, W. (ed)., *'To Mr Davenport', the letters of Major Richard Davenport, 1742–1760* (SAHR Special Publication), 1968.
Frey, L., *The Treaties of the War of the Spanish Succession*, 1995.
Fuye, M., *Fontenoy, 1745*, 1945.
Gandilhon, D., *Fontenoy*, 2008.
Geyl, P., *Holland and England during the War of the Austrian Succession* (Journal of the Historical Association), 1926.
Gilbert, A., *Law and Honour among British Eighteenth-Century Army Officers* (Historical Journal), 1976.
Grant, C., *The battle of Fontenoy*, 1975.
Guy, A.,
  Oeconomy and Discipline: Officership and Administration in the British Army, 1714–1763, 1985.
  (ed.), *Colonel Samuel Bagshawe, and the Army of George II, 1731–1762*, 1990.
Hage, F., *La Guerre de Succession d'Autriche*, 2017.
Hamilton, F., *History of the Grenadier Guards*, 1874.
Hills, R., *The Royal Dragoons (1st Dragoons)*, 1975.
Holmes, R., *Redcoat, the British Soldier in the Age of Horse and Musket*, 2001.
Houlding, J., *Fit for Service, The Training of the British Army, 1715–1795*, 1981.
Hubert, E., *Les Garnisons de la barrière dans les Pays-Bas Autriche (1715–1782)*, 1901.
Hughes, B.,
  Firepower, Weapon effectiveness on the Battlefield, 1630–1850, 1974.
  Open Fire, Artillery Tactics from Marlborough to Wellington, 1981.
Ingrao, C., *The Habsburg Monarchy, 1618–1815*, 2000.
Kane, R., *A New System of Military Discipline*, 1745.
Knight, C., *Historical Record of the Buffs*, 1934.
Lee, A., *History of the 33rd (Duke of Wellington's) Regiment*, 1922.
Lee, S., *Sir Richard Ingoldsby* (Dictionary of National Biography), 2004.
Leslie, N., *The Succession of Colonels of the British Army, from 1669 to the present day* (SAHR Special Publication), 1974.
Letrun, L., *Dragoons 1669–1749*, 2014.
Louda, J, & Maclagan, M., *Lines of Succession*, 1981.
Lunt, J., *Scarlet Lancer*, 1964.
MacCarthy, D., *Le Bataille de Fontenoy, 11 mai 1745* (Revue de la Société des amis de Musée de l'armée, no. 38), 1979.
Maclean, F., *Bonnie Prince Charlie*, 1988.
MacLeod, D., *The Memoirs of the life and gallant exploits of the old Serjeant Donald Macleod*, 1791.
Marston, D., *The Seven Years' War*, 2001.
Maurice, F., *History of the Scots Guards*, 1934.

McKinnon, D., *The Origins and Services of the Coldstream Guards*, 1833.
McLaughlin, M., *The Wild Geese, the Irish Brigades of France and Spain*, 1980.
Mouillard, L, *Les Regiments sous Louis XV*, 1882.
Nierinckx, P., *I Cannot estimate the Damage* (JSAHR), 2015.
Nosworthy, B., *The Anatomy of Victory, Battle Tactics 1689–1763*, 1992.
Oates, J., *Sweet William or the Butcher?*, 2008.
Orr, M., *Dettingen 1743*, 1972.
Pajol, C., *Les Guerres sous Louis XV*, 1881.
Pearse, H., *The History of the East Surrey Regiment*, 1916.
Picard, E., *L'Artillerie Française at 18ième siècle*, 1906.
Pichat, H., *Les Campagnes de Marechal de Saxe, dans les Flandres*, 1909.
Prebble, J., *Culloden*, 1961.
Reddaway, W., *Frederick the Great, and the rise of Prussia*, 1904.
Reid, S., *King George's Army, 1740–93*, 3 vols, 1995–6.
Robinson, R., *The Bloody Eleventh, a History of the Devonshire Regiment*, Vol. I, 1988.
Rogers, H., *The British Army of the Eighteenth Century*, 1977.
Roider, K., *The Pragmatic Sanction*, 1972.
Royle, T., *Culloden*, 2016.
Russell, J., *John Ligonier, 1st Earl Ligonier*, 2012.
Sapin-Lignières, A., *Les Troupes Légères de l'Ancienne Regime*, 1979.
Schofield, V., *The Highland Furies (The Black Watch)*, 2012.
Schrijver, E., *Bergen op Zoom, Stronghold on the Scheldt* (History Today), 1976.
Screen, J., *An Account of the action at Melle, 9 July 1745* (JSAHR), 1995.
Skrine, J., *Fontenoy, and Great Britain's share in the War of the Austrian Succession, 1741–48*, 1906 (2012 reprint edition).
Susane, L., *Histoire de la Cavalerie*, 3 vols, 1874.
Sutherland, D., *Tried and Valiant, the History of the Border Regiment*, 1972.
Tabori, P., *Maria-Theresa*, 1969.
Townsend, G., *A Brief Narrative of the late Campaigns in Germany and Flanders*, 1751.
Tuety, L., *Les Officiers sous l'ancien regime*, 1908.
Venning, A., *Following the Drum*, 2005.
Weaver, L., *The Story of the Royal Scots (The Lothian Regiment)*, 1915.
Webb, E., *The History of the Twelfth Foot*, 1914.
Weygand, H., *Histoire de l'Armee Française*, 1938.
White, J., *Marshal of France: the Life and Times of Maurice, Comte Saxe*, 1962.
White-Spunner, B., *Horse Guards*, 2008.
Whitworth, R.,
  Field Marshal Lord Ligonier, 1958.
  William Augustus, Duke of Cumberland, 1993.
Wilson, A., *The Story of the Gun*, 1944.
Wilson, D., *The French Army in the War of the Austrian Succession*, 2014.
Wood, S., *In the Finest Tradition, the Royal Scots Dragoon Guards (Carabiniers and Greys)*, 1988.

Index

Aberdeen, 154, 158–9
Aix-le-Chapelle, treaty of, 37, 60–1, 165, 170–2
Albemarle, William, Earl, 96, 127
Allied Army, order of battle, 177–9
Amherst, Captain (subs. General) Sir Jeffrey, 173, 182
Ammunition supply, 34, 126–7, 169
Anterroches, Philippe Comte d', 116–17
Antoing village, 90–2, 98, 114, 138
Antwerp, 54, 147–8, 165, 167
Army of Observation, 62–3
Arras, 84
Ath, 54, 81, 85, 133, 143; siege of, 146
Atholl, Duke of, 158
Austrian (Southern) Netherlands, x, 11, 44, 54–5, 82, 167, 171
Austrian Succession, War of, 8–19, 72

Bagshawe, Samuel, 26
Barri, Bois de, tactical importance, 89–92; 95, 98, 106–7, 120, 123, 127, 129
Bavaria, ix, 167–8
Bayonet drill, 160
Bayreuth, Margrave of, 47
Belford, Colonel, 160
Belle-Isle, Louis-Charles-Auguste, Comte de, 13
Bergen op Zoom, 42, 55, 70, 170
Berwick, James FitzJames, Duke of, 50–1
Biren, Ernst, 51–2
Biron, Duc de, 107, 112
Black Watch, the, xiv, 90, 92, 101; attack on Fontenoy, 111; 143, 181, 184, 194
Bligh, Brigadier General Thomas, 145
Borschlanger, Colonel von, 110–11, 115, 181
Bourgeon village, 89, 108
Braddock, Major General Edward, 61

Brakel, Major General Joseph van, defence of Tournai, 83–4
British regiments, numbering, xiv, 96
Brocard, Chevalier Anton de, mortally wounded, 115
Broglie, Francois, duc de, Marshal of France, 12, 52–3, 168
Browne, Maximilien, Lieutenant General, 8
Bruges, 53, 80, 145
Brussels, 43, 54, 81, 87–8, 147–8, 165
Buchanan, Surgeon John, 39
Burkersdorf, battle of, 173
Byng, Admiral Sir John, 61

Calonne crossing, 83, 99, 105
Camp followers, 45
Campbell, clan, 156, 161
Campbell, General James, 96, 104; mortally wounded, 105; 129, 181
Canister shot, 37–8
Carabiniers du Roi, 125–6, 130
Carlisle, 155–7
Caroline of Ansbach, Queen consort, 58
Casualty toll at Fontenoy, 134–6, 185–9
Chabonnes, Comte de, 112
Chambonas, Marquis de, 93
Chambord chateau, 54–5
Charleroi, 81
Charles VI, Emperor of Austria, ix, 3–6, 8; death, 52; 67, 69, 146
Charles XII, King of Sweden, 27, 47
Charles-Albert, Elector of Bavaria, xv, 6–7, 11–12; crowned Emperor Charles VII, 13; 19; death of, 19, 59; 169
Charles Edward Stuart, the Young Pretender, 77; lands in Scotland, 151, 153; 155, 158; flight after Culloden, 162; 167

Charles (Birkenfeld), Prince of Lorraine, 18, 53, 166
Chotusitz, battle of, 13
Clermont, Comte de, 79–80; at Lauffeldt, 168
Clinton Moor, action at, 156
Convention of Neutrality, 11
Cope, General Sir John, 153–4
Courland, 49–51, 53
Courtrai, 17, 79
Crawfurd, John Lindsay, Earl of, 80, 90, 105, 114, 128, 131; regrets withdrawal, 132
Cremille, Louis-Hyacinth, Duc de, 80, 85
Cronstrom, General van, 108–10, 112–13
Crowe, Patrick, 144
Culloden, battle of, 35, 65, 159–62; treatment of wounded, 161; casualties, 161–2
Cumberland, William Augustus, Duke of, x, 15, 28, 30, 46, 55; birth and parentage, 57; naval service, 58–9; wounded at Dettingen, 59; appointed Captain General, 59; commands in the Low Countries, 78, 82; at battle of Lauffeldt, 60; ill-health, 61; commands Army of Observation, 62; agrees Convention of Kloster Zeven, 63–5, 172; resigns his appointments, 65; reputation, 67; later career and death, 66–7; 83, 87; preparations for battle at Fontenoy, 87, 95–6; intentions, 98–9; 101; orders to Ingoldsby, 103–4; 110; advances with infantry, 114–15; bravery under fire, 115; lack of command and control, xiii, 120–1, 128, 136; tactical dilemma, 121; orders withdrawal, 130–2, 143–4; despatch to London, 136; hears of Jacobite expedition, 153; commands in northern England, 156; refuses to offer good terms, 157; victory at Culloden, 161; conduct after the battle, 162; 167, 182–3

Dalcross castle, 159
Danois, Comte de, wounded, 127
Davenport, Major Richard, 80, 117, 144
Dendermonde, 147
Depp, Sergeant George, 37
Derby, 156
D'Estrées, Louis le Tellier, Duc de, Marshal of France, 62–3, 82, 124–5, 133; at Rocoux, 166
Dettingen, battle of, xi, xv, 15–16, 53–4, 59, 73, 79, 97, 106, 116–17, 135, 141
D'Eu, redoubt, 92–3, 102, 105–6, 110, 118, 139–40
D'Harcourt, Duc de, 82–3
Dillon, Colonel James, 118
Dort, Baron Johan Adolf, van, defence of Tournai, 83–4
Douai, 91
Dreux-Brézé, Achilles, Marquis de, 82; at siege of Tournai, 90–2
Drumossie Moor, 159
Dunkirk, 15, 77
Duroure, Colonel Scipio, attack on Fontenoy village, 111; mortally wounded, 113; 120, 138
Duroure's (12th) Regiment, 101, 111, 113, 134, 181–2

Edinburgh, 154
Elixheim, battle of (1705), 32
Elizabeth-Christina, Empress, 5, 6
Elizabeth Petrovna, Tzarina, 53
Espagnac, Comte d', 127–8
Eugene, Prince of Savoy, 7, 25, 27, 47, 71, 145

Falkirk, battle of, 157–61, 194
Fenelon, Louis-Armand, Comte de, 59
Ferdinand of Brunswick, Duke, 65
Fleury, Andre-Hercules, Cardinal, 8, 10
Fontainebleau, treaty of, 173
Fontenoy, battle of, x–xii, 19, 22, 30, 39, 45–6, 54, 67, 70; village, 89; tactical importance, 91; 92, 95, 98, 106, 111; bypassed by Cumberland, 115; 119, 120, 127, 140–1, 146; British casualties at, 186–9
Foot Guards, British, 35, 58, 65, 89, 96, 115–16, 125–7, 130, 167, 183–4
Fort Augustus, 154

Fort Dusquene, 61
Fort George, 154
Fort William, 154, 158
Francis-Stephen of Lorraine, Duke of Tuscany, 6–7, 9, 13, 146; elected as Emperor of Austria, 165
Fraser, Major General Simon, 163
Frederick, Prince of Wales, 58; death, 60
Frederick I, King in Prussia, 8, 10
Frederick II, King of Prussia, 8–13, 18, 25, 35, 55, 61, 64, 66, 116; opinion on allied opportunity at Fontenoy, 116, 131; 146, 149, 150, 165, 172
Frederick II, Landgrave of Hesse, 168
Frederick-Augustus, Elector of Saxony, King of Poland, 5, 11–12, 47, 50–1
Freikorps, Austrian, 87, 97, 134
French Army, order of battle, 175–7
Fusen, treaty of, 165

Gadebusch, battle of, 48
Garcia-Hernandez, battle of (1812), 32
Gardes de Cheval, 105
Gardes Francaises, 35, 106–7, 116–18, 126, 129, 135
Gardes Suisse, 107, 116, 129, 135
Gardes te Voet, 113
George I, King of Great Britain, 47; death, 57
George II, King of Great Britain, x, 8–9, 13–14; at Dettingen, battle of, 15–16; provokes France 16–17, 58–9; 57, 61–2; reaction to Kloster Zeven, 64; death, 66, 173; 77, 137, 153, 155
George III, King of Great Britain, 66–7, 72
Ghent, 53, 70, 80, 143, 145
Ghent–Bruges canal, 81
Glasgow, 157
Grammont, Duc de, 15; mortally wounded, 106
Grassin, Arquebusiers de, 31, 93, 103, 118, 135, 144, 194
Great Northern War (1701–1720), 24, 49
Greder (Saxe) Regiment, 49, 55
Guest, Lieutenant General Sir Joshua, 154

Habsburg dynasty and empire, ix, 3–4, 7, 26, 146
Hanover, 9, 11, 58, 62, 73, 78; Congress of, 146; 167, 172
Hassell, Phoebe, the 'Stepney Amazon', 134
Hastenbek, battle of, 62
Hawley, Lieutenant General Sir Henry, 157
Hay, Captain Lord Charles, 116
Hennersdorf, battle of, 149
Hertslet, Colonel van, 83
Hessen-Phillipsthal, Prince Ludwig, von, 108
Hessian troops, 14, 58, 63, 81, 155
Hochkirk, battle of, 173
Hofburg palace, ix
Hohenfreidberg, battle of, 146
Holy Roman Empire, 4, 8
Howard, Lieutenant–Colonel George, 130
Hubertesberg, treaty of, 173
Huy, 80

Ilten, General Thomas Eberhard, von, 96
Infantry squares, 32–3
Ingoldsby, Brigadier General, Sir Richard, 28, 92; attack on Bois de Barri, 101–3; hesitation, 104–7; wounded, 112; 120, 136, 139–40; court martial, 181–4
Inverness, 159–61
Irish Brigade, 93–4, 118, 126, 129–30
Isnard, Captain Hercules, 129

Jacobites, xiii, 59, 77, 146, 154; regarded as rebels, 157; 158, 161; treatment after Culloden, 162–3
James II (VII), King of England, 77, 153
Joseph I, Emperor of Austria, xv, 5

Kauntiz, Count Matthias, 148–9
Kehl, siege of, 50
Kloster Zeven, Convention of, 63–4, 73, 172
Königsegg-Rothenfels, Luther-Joseph-Dominik, Graf von, Field Marshal, 13, 19, 59, 71; early military service, 71;

diplomatic duties, 71; President Imperial War Council, 71–2; at Fontenoy, 72, 78–9, 83–4, 90, 97, 110–11, 114, 122–4, 132–3, 138, 145; death, 72
Konigsmarck, Countess Maria Aurora, 47
Kunersdorf, battle of, 173

Lauffeldt, battle of, xvi, 34, 60, 72–3, 168–70
Lecsinsky, Stanislaus, 50–1
Leopold I, Emperor of Austria, 3
Le Quesnoy, 84, 135
Lessines, 144
Leuthen, battle of, 172
Leuze en Hainault, xiii, 85, 88, 93, 98, 129
Lewis, Colonel Jonathan, 104, 124
Liège, 54, 59, 80, 144, 165
Ligonier, General Sir John, 18, 30, 59; early life, 72; patronage, 72; defence of Hanover, 73; Dettingen, 73; 78, 88; commands infantry at Fontenoy, 73, 81, 106–7, 114, 123–4, 131, 136; defeated at Rocoux, 165–6; skilful handling of cavalry at Lauffeldt, 73, 168–70; made Field Marshal, 73; death, 73; 78, 88
Lille, 18, 43
Louis XIII, King of France, 6
Louis XIV, King of France, 3, 14, 22, 25, 41, 46
Louis XV, King of France, x, 3, 10, 14–16; seeks peace terms, 19, 167; 25, 50, 54, 63, 79; with the field army, 91, 99; 101, 105; refuses to leave the field, 118–19; 124, 134, 147–9, 155, 165, 169; revulsion at sack of Bergen-op-Zoom, 170; 171
Louvain, 148
Löwendahl, Ulrich-Frederik, Waldemar, Count von, 70; Habsburg service, 69; enters French service, 69; capture of Menin, 70; at sack of Bergen-op-Zoom, 70, 170; Marshal of France, 70; 83, 93; commands reserves at Fontenoy, 129; 133; captures Ghent, 145; 147

Maastricht, 55, 60, 80, 93, 165, 168, 170
MacDonald, clan, 160
MacLeod, Sergeant Donald, looting in Fontenoy, 113
Madrid, 3, 7
Malplaquet, battle of (1709), 7, 27, 39, 46, 49, 79, 105, 138, 192, 195
Mantua, 71
Maria-Amalia, Duchess, 5, 6
Maria-Josepha, Duchess, 5–6
Maria-Theresa, Duchess, ix; early life, 4–7, 191; lack of experience, 8; 11; crowned Queen of Hungary, 11–12, 17; 13; British support for, 14; 51, 71, 77–8, 81, 138, 149, 165–7, 170, 172–3
Marlborough, John Churchill, 1st Duke of, 15; devastates Bavaria, 22–4; 25, 27, 32, 42–3, 48, 72, 86, 88, 145, 192
Mauberge, 79, 79, 82, 84, 87, 135
Maubray village, 88, 90
Maximilien-Emmanuel Wittlesbach, Elector of Bavaria, 7
Medical care, 38–40, 135–6
Melle, battle of, 145
Menin, 17, 70
Minden, battle of, 65, 173
Mollwitz, battle of, 10, 191
Mons, 42, 54, 81–3; French threat to, 87; 105, 165
Montesson, Comte de, 130
Moulbaix, 88
Munro, Colonel Robert, 101, 111–12, 194
Murray of Atholl, Lord George, 159–60

Nairn, 158–9
Namur, 54, 81, 165
Nine Years' War (1689–1697), 21
Noailles, Adrien-Maurice, Duc de, Marshal of France, 15, 51, 53, 80, 106, 118
Norris, Admiral Sir John, 58
Nymphenberg, treaty of, 11

Ostend, 146–7
Ottomans (Turkish Empire), ix, 4, 6, 12, 24, 26, 49, 69–71
Oudenarde, 17, 70, 80, 143, 146

Index

Paris, treaty of, 173
Perth, 154, 158
Philip V, King of Spain, 3, 10
Phillipsbourg, siege of, 51
Piedmont-Sardinia (Savoy), 10, 13
Platoon firing, 33–4, 117–18
Polish Succession, War of, 50, 70
Pragmatic army, ix, 14–16
Pragmatic Sanction, the, ix, 3–7, 10, 16
Prague, xv, 11–13, 52, 172
Prestonpans, battle of, 154–5, 160–1

Quadruple Alliance, treaty of, 77
Quiberon Bay, 66

Rainsford, Captain, 113
Ralphson, Mary, 15
Ramcroix village, 85, 107
Ramillies, battle of (1706), 72, 195
Ratstadt, treaty of, 71
Richelieu, Louis Armand, Duc de, 63–4
Roucoux, battle of, xvi, 54, 59, 71–3, 166–7
Rossbach, battle of, 172

Saxe, Arminius-Maurice, Comte de, Marshal of France, ix–xi; ill-health, x, 54–5, 79, 90, 99, 105–6, 139; 17, 46; birth and parentage, 47–8; at Malplaquet, 49; enters French service, 49–50; styles himself Duke-Elect of Courland, 50; riding injury, 52; at siege of Egra, 52; visits Moscow, 53; Marshal of France, 53; French citizen, 54; made Marshal General, 55; death, 55; mishandles battle of Lauffeldt, 60, 168–70; 77; tactical judgement at Fontenoy, 89–91; preparations for battle, 92–4, 97; aim at Fontenoy, 98; 101, 121, 123; orders cavalry attacks, 124; fails to pursue, 133–4, 139; takes Tournai, 144–5; captures Brussels, 148–9; 163; at Rocoux, 166–7
Scheldt river, 60, 80, 82–4, 86, 91, 98, 139, 148
Schlippenbach Regiment, 109
Schmidt, Sluice-master, 83–4
Schomberg-Lippe, Lieutenant General, von, 113
Schulemberg, Count Matthias, 47–8
Seven Years War, 61, 172–3
Silesia, xv, 8–9, 18, 173
Spanish Succession, War of (1701–1714), xv, 21, 28, 47
Stair, John Dalrymple, 2nd Earl of, 14, 59, 78
States-General of Holland, 18
Stirling, 157

Targau, battle of, 173
The Hague, 18–19, 71, 137
Tournai (Doornick), ix–x, 40, 46, 48; strategic importance, 80–4; siege of, 85–8; sabotage of defences, 83–4, 93; chances to lift the siege, 138–9; 143–5, 155
Tulipe, Sergeant, 89
Turin, siege (1706), 71

Utrecht, treaty of (1713), xv, 3, 5, 11, 72

Valenciennes, 79, 84, 135, 165–6
Vanguyon, Marquis de la, 92–3
Vauban, Sébastien le Prestre, Marshal of France, ix, 14–15, 40, 42, 48, 81, 97, 145
Vendôme, Louis-Joseph, duc de, 81
Vezon village, 89, 98, 107, 114, 132, 134
Vienna, ix, xiii; Ottoman siege of, 4; 9; second Treaty of, 11; 16, 52, 60, 77
Villars, Claude-Louis-Hector, Marshal of France, 27, 51, 196

Wade, Field Marshal George, 17–18, 78, 156
Waldeck-Pyrmont, Karl-August-Frederick, Prince, 19, 30; family connections, 70; at battle of Klausen, 70; Fontenoy, 70–1, 108–9; Rocoux and Lauffeldt, 72; 78, 83; capabilities, 85; 97, 99, failed attack, 110; 115, 120, 123, 128, 132–3; strict orders from the Hague, 137–8; 145, 149, 165–6
Watts, Captain, 143

Wendt, General Joseph, 78
Wheelock, Sergeant, 130, 134
White, Daniel, 147
White Eagle, Order of Poland, 49
William IV, Prince of Orange, 167, 171
'Wings' of an army, 29–30
Wittelsbach, House of, ix, 5, 7, 19
Wolfe, Colonel James, 163

Ypres, 17

Zastrow, Major General Ludwig von, 112, 182
Zenta, battle of (1697), 4
Zorndorf, battle of, 172